Ways of Knowing in Science and Mathematics Series

RICHARD DUSCHL, SERIES EDITOR

ADVISORY BOARD: Charles W. Anderson, Raffaella Borasi, Nancy Brickhouse, Marvin Druger, Eleanor Duckworth, Peter Fensham, William Kyle, Roy Pea, Edward Silver, Russell Yeany

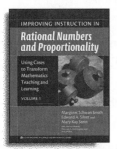

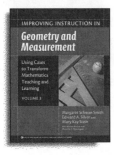

Improving Instruction in Algebra

Using Cases to Transform Mathematics Teaching and Learning, Volume 2

Margaret Schwan Smith,
Edward A. Silver,
Mary Kay Stein

*with Marjorie A. Henningsen,
Melissa Boston,
and Elizabeth K. Hughes*

TEACHERS COLLEGE PRESS

Teachers College, Columbia University
New York and London

The material in this book is based on work supported by
National Science Foundation grant number ESI-9731428 for the
COMET (Cases of Mathematics Instruction to Enhance Teaching)
Project. Any opinions expressed herein are those of the
authors and do not necessarily represent the views of the
National Science Foundation.

Published by Teachers College Press, 1234 Amsterdam Avenue, New York, NY 10027

Library of Congress Cataloging-in-Publication Data

Smith, Margaret Schwan.
     Improving instruction in algebra / Margaret Schwan Smith,
  Edward A. Silver, Mary Kay Stein, with Marjorie A. Henningsen, Melissa Boston, and
  Elizabeth Hughes
       p. cm. — (Using cases to transform mathematics teaching and learning ; v. 2) (Ways of
  knowing in science and mathematics series)
  Includes bibliographical references and index.
  ISBN 0-8077-4530-8 (pbk. : acid-free paper)
  1. Algebra—Study and teaching (Middle school)—United States—Case studies.   I.
Silver, Edward A., 1948– II. Stein, Mary Kay. III. Title IV. Series.
  QA159.S65 2005   2004055361

ISBN 0-8077-4530-8 (paper)

Printed on acid-free paper
Manufactured in the United States of America

12   11   10   09   08   07   06   05   8   7   6   5   4   3   2   1

To the teachers in the QUASAR Project—although nearly a decade has passed since our work together ended, we continue to draw inspiration from your work. You were true pioneers in creating instructional environments that promoted mathematics learning for all students. Thank you for sharing your successes and struggles with us. We continue to learn so much from you.

Contents

Acknowledgments

The ideas expressed in this book grew out of our work on the QUASAR Project and have developed over the past decade through our interactions and collaborations with many teachers, teacher educators, and mathematicians. We would like to thank mathematicians and mathematics teacher educators Hyman Bass, John Beem, Nadine Bezuk, Kathleen Cramer, George Bright, Victoria Kouba, John Moyer, John P. Smith III, Judith Roitman, and Orit Zaslavsky, who provided feedback on early versions of the cases. Your thoughtful comments helped ensure that the cases were both sound and compelling.

We are indebted to Victoria Bill whose varied and frequent use of the cases over the past 5 years has helped us recognize the flexibility and power of the cases to promote learning in a range of situations; and to our colleagues Fran Arbaugh, Cathy Brown, Marta Civil, Gilberto Cuevas, Beatrice D'Ambrosio, Skip Fennell, Linda Foreman, Susan Friel, Judith Jacobs, Jeremy Kahan, Rebecca McGraw, Jack Moyer, Kathy Pfaendler, Elizabeth Phillips, and Judith Zawojewski who piloted early versions of the cases, provided helpful feedback, and expanded our view regarding the possible uses of the cases and related materials.

Finally we would like to acknowledge the contributions of Cristina Heffernan who developed the COMET website, provided feedback on early versions of the cases and facilitation materials and identified tasks in other curricula that corresponded to the cases; Michael Steele who updated the COMET website and created final versions of the figures; Amy Fleeger Hillen who assisted in editing the final manuscript; and Kathy Day who provided valuable assistance in preparing initial versions of the figures, locating data, and copying materials.

Introduction

Teachers of mathematics in the middle grades face a difficult task. For many years, middle school mathematics teachers may have felt overlooked, as attention was paid to the secondary school because of pressure from colleges and employers, or to the primary grades because of interesting research-based initiatives related to young children's learning of mathematical ideas. In recent years, however, the spotlight has shown brightly on middle grades mathematics.

GREAT EXPECTATIONS FOR MIDDLE-GRADES MATHEMATICS

Evidence of mediocre U.S. student performance on national and international assessments of mathematical achievement has sparked public and professional demand for better mathematics education in the middle grades. National organizations and state agencies have published guidelines, frameworks, and lists of expectations calling for more and better mathematics in grades K–12. Many of these give specific attention to raising expectations for mathematics teaching and learning in the middle grades. For example, *Principles and Standards for School Mathematics*, published by the National Council of Teachers of Mathematics (NCTM, 2000), calls for curriculum and teaching in the middle grades to be more ambitious. To accomplish the goals of developing conceptual understanding and helping students become capable, flexible problem-solvers, there are new topics to teach and old topics to teach in new ways.

There is some variation across the many policy documents produced in recent years regarding the teaching and learning of mathematics in the middle grades, but the essential message is the same: The mathematics instructional program in the middle grades needs to be more ambitious, setting higher expectations for middle school students and for their teachers. Compared with the situation at the beginning of the 1990s, guidelines for mathematics instructional programs in virtually every state and many local school districts in the country have been revised to reflect higher expectations for student learning of important mathematical ideas.

New Curricular Materials

Some help in meeting higher expectations for mathematics teaching and learning in the middle grades is likely to come from new mathematics curriculum materials that reflect more ambitious demands. Some new materials have been developed along the lines suggested by the NCTM standards. In general, these curriculum materials provide teachers with carefully sequenced, intellectually challenging instructional tasks that focus on important mathematical ideas and that can be used with students to develop their mathematical proficiency.

New curriculum materials with interesting and challenging tasks are undoubtedly crucial to any effort to upgrade the quality of mathematics education, but ambitious materials will be effective only if they are implemented well in classrooms. And good implementation is a nontrivial matter since a more demanding curriculum requires that middle school teachers become effective in supporting student engagement with complex intellectual activity in the classroom. In short, new curriculum materials are unlikely to have the desired impact on student learning unless classroom instruction shifts from its current focus on routine skills and instead focuses on developing student understanding of important mathematics concepts and proficiency in solving complex problems.

Improving Teacher Preparation and Continuing Support

The success of efforts to enhance mathematics teaching and learning in the middle grades hinges to a great extent on the success of programs and practices that prepare teachers to do this work and on those that continue to support teachers along the way. Unfortunately, the approaches typically used to prepare and support teachers in the middle grades have well-documented limitations. Many who currently teach mathematics in the middle grades received their initial preparation in programs intended for generalists rather than for mathematics specialists. In such programs too little attention is paid to developing the specific proficiencies needed by mathematics teachers in the middle grades, where the mathematical ideas are complex and difficult for students to learn. Moreover, components of the knowledge needed for effective teaching usually are taught and learned in isolation from one another—mathematics in the mathematics department, issues of student learning in a psychology (or educational psychology) department, and pedagogy in a teacher education department. Rarely is the knowledge integrated and tied to settings where it is used by teachers. As a consequence, this fragmented, decontextualized approach often fails to build a solid foundation for effective teaching of mathematics in the middle grades. Compounding the challenge is the fact that most schools and school districts usually are not able to offer the right kinds of assistance to remedy weaknesses in preparation that their teachers may possess.

The current set of challenges facing teachers of mathematics in the middle grades calls for a new approach and new tools to accomplish the work. Just as new curriculum materials can assist teachers of mathematics to meet the challenges they face, new resources can assist teacher educators and professional development specialists in their work. What is needed is an effective way to support teachers to increase their knowledge of mathematics content, mathematical pedagogy, and student learning of mathematics, in a manner likely to affect classroom actions and interactions in support of improved student learning. The materials in this volume have been designed to help teachers of mathematics and those who prepare and support them in their work to meet the challenges that inhere in the higher public and professional expectations.

THE MATERIALS IN THIS VOLUME

This volume is divided into two parts. Part I is written primarily for teachers, prospective teachers, or other readers interested in exploring issues related to mathematics teaching and learning. Part I begins with a chapter that describes the use of cases to promote learning (Chapter 1) and includes four chapters (Chapters 2–5) that feature narrative cases of classroom mathematics lessons along with materials intended to engage readers in thinking deeply about the mathematics teaching and learning that occurred in the cases. Part II is written for teacher educators or other professional development providers who work with teachers. Part II begins with a chapter that provides general suggestions for case facilitation (Chapter 6) and includes four chapters (Chapters 7–10) that feature facilitation materials, including suggestions for using the case materials in Chapters 2 through 5. Following Part II is a set of appendices that contain sample responses for selected activities presented in the case chapters in Part I. The contents of Parts I and II and the appendices are described in more detail in the sections that follow.

Part I: Using Cases to Enhance Learning

The centerpiece of Part I is a set of narrative cases of classroom mathematics lessons developed under the auspices of the NSF-funded COMET (Cases of Mathematics Instruction to Enhance Teaching) Project. The goal of COMET was to produce professional development materials based on data (including more than 500 videotaped lessons) collected on mathematics instruction in urban middle school classrooms with ethnically, racially, and linguistically diverse student populations in six school districts that participated in the QUASAR (Quantitative Understanding: Amplifying Student Achievement and Reasoning) Project (Silver, Smith, & Nelson, 1995; Silver & Stein, 1996). QUASAR was a national project (funded by the Ford Foundation) aimed at improving mathematics instruction for students attending middle schools in economically disadvantaged communities. The teachers in schools that participated in QUASAR were committed to increasing student achievement in mathematics by promoting conceptual understanding and complex problem-solving.

Chapters 2 through 5 each feature a case and related materials for engaging the reader in analyzing the teaching and learning that occur in the classroom episode featured in the case. Each case portrays a teacher and students engaging with a cognitively complex mathematics task in an urban middle school classroom. By examining these instructional episodes, readers can wrestle with key issues of practice, such as what students appear to be learning and how the teaching supports or inhibits students' learning opportunities. The cases are based on real teachers and events, drawing on detailed documentation (videotapes and write-ups) of classroom lessons and interviews with teachers about the documented lessons. At times, cases enhance certain aspects of a lesson in order to make a particular idea salient. However, every attempt has been made to stay true to the predispositions and general teaching habits of the teacher who inspired the case. Although the names of the teachers, their schools, and their students have been changed so as to protect their anonymity, each teacher portrayed in a case agreed to share his or her story so that others might learn from their efforts to improve mathematics teaching and learning.

As an opening to Part I, Chapter 1 describes how the case chapters can be used as a resource for professional learning. In each case chapter, readers are guided through a set of coordinated experiences that encourage reflection on, analysis of, and inquiry into the teaching and learning of mathematics in the middle grades. Readers of the cases are encouraged to use the particular episodes portrayed in the cases as a base from which to generalize across cases, from cases to general principles, and, when applicable, from the cases to their own teaching.

Teachers of mathematics, individuals preparing to become teachers of mathematics, or other readers using this book as learners will want to focus on Part I. A reader might learn from our materials by engaging in them independently, but, if at all possible, we encourage interaction with others around the issues and ideas that surface in the cases. Through careful reading of the cases in this volume, accompanied by thoughtful analysis and active consideration of issues raised by the cases, readers have an opportunity to learn a great deal about mathematics and the teaching of mathematics. Readers also have a chance to learn about student thinking because examples of student thinking about mathematical ideas are embedded in each case.

Part II: Facilitating Learning from Cases

In Part II, teacher educators or other professional development providers who work with teachers will find materials that are intended to support the use of the cases presented in Part I. As an opening to Part II, Chapter 6 provides a rationale for selecting narrative cases as a vehicle for helping mathematics teachers, prospective mathematics teachers, or others interested in exploring issues in mathematics teaching and learning to develop more thoughtful and ambitious notions about the teaching and learning of mathematics. After a short explanation of how participants learn from cases and what we expect participants to learn from our cases in particular, a description of the kinds of support that can be found in each of the facilitation chapters (Chapters 7 through 10) is provided.

Chapters 7 through 10 provide facilitation materials corresponding to each of the cases presented in Part I. The suggestions in these facilitation chapters are based on our own experiences using the cases. They reflect the lessons that we have learned about what works well and what does not with respect to preparing participants to read the case and guiding their discussion of it, and in designing follow-up activities that will help practicing teachers connect the case experience to their own classrooms.

Each facilitation chapter begins with a short synopsis of the case. The heart of the facilitation chapter is the case analysis section that specifies the key mathematical and pedagogical ideas embedded in each case and identifies where in the case those ideas are instantiated. The remaining sections of these chapters provide support to the facilitator for enacting case discussions and case-related activities.

Part II will be of special interest to case facilitators—those who intend to use the materials to assist preservice and/or inservice teachers to learn and improve their practice, or who provide professional development to other individuals interested in improving mathematics teaching and learning. Case facilitators include any professionals who contribute to improving the quality of mathematics teaching and learning through their work in diverse settings: schools (e.g., teacher leaders, coaches, mentors, administrators); school district offices (e.g., curriculum coordinators, staff developers); regional intermediate units and state agencies; or colleges and universities (e.g., instructors of mathematics or methods courses).

Building on Extensive Research and Prior Experience

As noted earlier, the cases in this volume are based on research conducted in middle schools that participated in the QUASAR Project. A major finding of this research was that a teacher's actions and interactions with students were crucial in determining the extent to which students were able to maintain a high level of intellectual engagement with challenging mathematical tasks (see Henningsen & Stein, 1997). More specifically, the quality and quantity of student engagement in intellectually demanding activity sometimes conformed to a teacher's intentions but often did not (see Stein, Grover, & Henningsen, 1996). Our research also showed that there were different consequences for student learning depending on teachers' ability to maintain high intellectual demands (Stein & Lane, 1996). In classrooms where high-demand tasks were used frequently, and where the intellectual demands usually were maintained during lessons, students exhibited strong performance on a test assessing conceptual understanding and problem-solving. In contrast, in classrooms where intellectually demanding tasks were rarely used or where the intellectual demands frequently declined during lessons, student performance was lower.

This research also identified characteristic ways in which cognitively demanding tasks either were maintained at a high level or declined. For example, tasks sometimes declined by becoming proceduralized; in other cases, they declined due to unsystematic and nonproductive student exploration. In our first casebook, entitled *Implementing Standards-Based Mathematics Instruction: A Casebook for Professional Development* (Stein, Smith, Henningsen, & Silver, 2000), we presented six cases that serve as prototypes to illustrate the distinct patterns of maintenance or decline of cognitively challenging tasks.

The materials featured in this book build on that earlier work in important ways. First, the cases make salient key instructional factors and pedagogical moves that affect the extent and nature of intellectual activity in classroom lessons involving cognitively complex mathematics tasks. For example, the cases illustrate how a teacher might uncover student thinking and use it productively to encourage students to explain and justify their thinking or to make connections among ideas. Second, the cases extend the earlier work by sharpening the focus on the specific mathematical ideas at stake in the lesson and by explicitly calling attention to ways in which the instructional actions of the teacher support or inhibit students' opportunities to learn worthwhile mathematics. In particular, the cases in this volume draw attention to key aspects of algebra as the study of patterns and functions. Third, this book contains materials for learners and for case facilitators that the first casebook did not contain. For example, in addition to providing questions that foster analysis of the teaching

and learning in the cases, this book includes activities and resources specifically designed to promote generalizations to ideas and issues in teaching and learning mathematics and, when applicable, connections to teachers' own instructional practices. This book also provides support for facilitating the activities presented in the case chapters.

The Appendices

The appendices following Part II contain sample responses for the opening mathematics activity and for the task posed in the "Analyzing the Case" section in each of the case chapters. These sample responses are often products from our work in using the case materials in professional development settings. In some instances, the sample responses are the work of the participants in the professional development session; sometimes the sample responses were generated by the case facilitator in preparation for using the case. References to the appendices are made in the case and facilitation chapters when appropriate.

Each case chapter in Part I is related to a facilitation chapter in Part II and to a set of sample responses in an appendix. The relationship between case chapters, facilitation chapters, and appendices is as follows:

- The Case of Catherine Evans and David Young: Chapter 2, Chapter 7, and Appendix A
- The Case of Ed Taylor: Chapter 3, Chapter 8, and Appendix B
- The Case of Edith Hart: Chapter 4, Chapter 9, and Appendix C
- The Case of Robert Carter: Chapter 5, Chapter 10, and Appendix D

In the following section we provide a rationale for selecting patterns and functions in algebra as the content focus.

WHY PATTERNS AND FUNCTIONS IN ALGEBRA?

Although algebra historically has been viewed as a 1-year course taken by some students in 8th or 9th grade, it now is seen as a major component of the school mathematics curriculum (pre-K–12) for *all* students. In this view, algebra is seen as a "style of mathematical thinking for formalizing patterns, functions, and generalizations" that cuts across content areas and unifies the curriculum (NCTM, 2000, p. 223). As early as elementary school, students can begin to recognize, compare, and analyze patterns as sequences of sounds, shapes, or numbers. By middle school, students are expected to describe, extend, and make generalizations about geometric and numeric patterns using tables, graphs, words, and, ultimately, symbolic rules.

Despite the increased emphasis on algebra, many middle school teachers have limited experience in teaching algebra, and their experiences as algebra students—generally focused more on learning procedures and manipulating symbols than on thinking and reasoning about relationships—provide a limited resource on which to draw. Hence the centrality of patterns and functions in the middle school algebra curriculum gives urgency to the need to help teachers gain greater proficiency in teaching this cluster of mathematical ideas.

The materials in this volume are intended to do just that. In particular, they help readers to focus on the functional relationship between quantities and to use different representational forms (e.g., language, tables, equations, graphs, context) to make sense of the relationships. They also highlight a set of pedagogical moves that support students as they work to make sense of the mathematics, without removing the challenging aspects of the tasks.

THIS VOLUME AND ITS COMPANIONS

This book is one of three volumes of materials intended to help readers identify and address some key challenges encountered in contemporary mathematics teaching in the middle grades. This volume provides opportunities for readers to delve into and inquire about the teaching and learning of algebra as the study of patterns and functions. Two companion volumes have been developed and formatted in the same way as this volume, but with a focus on other familiar and important mathematical topics in the middle grades. These volumes are entitled, *Improving Instruction in Rational Numbers and Proportionality: Using Cases to Transform Mathematics Teaching and Learning, Volume 1* and *Improving Instruction in Geometry and Measurement: Using Cases to Transform Mathematics Teaching and Learning, Volume 3*. We encourage readers of this volume to use the cases provided in the companion volumes to investigate the teaching and learning of mathematics across a broader spectrum of topics in the middle grades.

The materials in this volume and its companions are designed to be used flexibly. As a complete set, the three volumes provide a base on which to build a coherent and cohesive professional development program to enhance readers' knowledge of mathematics, of mathematics pedagogy, and of students as learners of mathematics. These materials, either as individual cases, separate volumes, or the entire set of volumes, also can be used as components of teacher professional development programs. For example, many users of preliminary versions of these materials have included our cases in their mathematics methods and content courses for preservice teachers, in their professional development efforts for practicing teachers, in their efforts to support implementation of reform-oriented curricula, and in their efforts to communicate reform-oriented ideas of teaching and learning of mathematics to school administrators. Our most sincere hope is that these materials will be used in a wide variety of ways to enhance the quality of mathematics teaching and learning in the middle grades.

Improving Instruction in Algebra

Using Cases to Transform Mathematics Teaching and Learning, Volume 2

Part I

USING CASES TO ENHANCE LEARNING

In the Introduction, we provided a rationale for this volume and an overview of the materials it contains. In Part I of this book (Chapters 1–5), we turn our attention to using cases to enhance learning. Chapter 1 serves as an opening to this part of the book and describes how to use the case materials presented in Chapters 2 through 5. These chapters provide case materials intended to engage teachers, prospective teachers, or other readers in analyzing and reflecting on important ideas and issues in the teaching and learning of mathematics.

1

Using Cases to Learn

In this chapter, we describe the cases and discuss the opportunities for learning they afford. We then provide suggestions for using the cases and related materials for reflection and analysis, and, when applicable, as springboards for investigation into a teacher's own instructional practices.

THE CASES

Each of the four cases in this book portrays the events that unfold in an urban middle school classroom as a teacher engages his or her students in solving a cognitively challenging mathematical task (Stein et al., 2000). For example, in Chapter 5 Robert Carter (the teacher featured in the case in this chapter) and his students interpret and construct qualitative graphs of a bicycle ride and a walk. Since the graphs contain no numeric data and there are no suggestions regarding what to attend to in the graphs, the students in Mr. Carter's class must decide how to interpret the graphs in a way that coordinates speed and time.

Each case begins with a description of the teacher, students, and school so as to provide a context for understanding and interpreting the portrayed episode. The case then presents the teacher's goals for the lesson and describes the unfolding of the actual lesson in a fairly detailed way. To facilitate analysis and discussion of key issues in relation to specific events in a case, the paragraphs in each case are numbered consecutively for easy reference.

Each case depicts a classroom in which a culture has been established over time by the implicit and explicit actions and interactions of a teacher and his or her students. Within this culture, a set of norms have been established regarding the ways in which students are expected to work. The cases illustrate authentic practice—what really happens in a mathematics classroom when teachers endeavor to teach mathematics in ways that challenge students to think, reason, and problem-solve. As such they are not intended as exemplars of best practice to be emulated but rather as examples to be analyzed so as to better understand the relationship between teaching and learning and the ways in which student learning can be supported.

The cases in this volume have been created and organized so as to make salient important mathematical ideas related to patterns and functions and a set of pedagogical ideas that influence how students engage in mathematical activity and what they learn through the process. Each of these is described in the sections that follow.

Important Mathematical Ideas

Exploring patterns and functions is a key focus of algebra in the middle grades (NCTM, 2000). In this view, algebra involves much more than fluency in manipulating symbols. It involves representing, analyzing, and generalizing patterns using tables, graphs, words, and symbolic rules; relating and comparing different representations for a relationship; and solving problems using various representations (NCTM, 2000).

Exploring patterns helps to develop students' ideas about variables and functions. The notion of a variable arises as students analyze situations where quantities change in joint variation (i.e., where a change in one variable determines the change in the other) and find rules to express the functional relationship between variables.

Joint variation of variables can be explored in multiple contexts and in different representational forms.

In fact, translating back and forth among various representations is an essential component of students' understanding of functions. (According to Knuth [2000], the ability to move flexibly between different representations of functions in different directions contributes to the development of a robust understanding of functions.) In general, using different representations of a concept can help students better understand it (Lesh, Post, Behr, 1987). The diagram in Figure 1.1 shows five different representations of a function, each of which is described in the list that follows (Van de Walle, 2004):

- *Context* situates the functional relationship outside of the world of mathematics, such as in the cost of a dinner card.
- *Language* expresses the functional relationship using words.
- *Tables* match up selected elements that are paired by the functional relationship.
- *Graphs* (coordinate graphs) translate the relationship between the paired elements in the functional relationship into a picture.
- *Equations* express the functional relationship using mathematical symbolism.

Each case features students working on a mathematical task in which they explore and analyze the functional relationship between two variables (e.g., number of hexagons in a pattern train and the perimeter of the train, the number of meals purchased and the total cost of a meal plan, the elapsed time and speed of a bicycle ride) and use different representational forms (e.g., language, tables, equations, graphs, context) to make sense of the relationship. As a collection, the tasks highlight both linear and nonlinear functions, make salient different meanings and uses of variables, and explore rate of change in a variety of contexts (e.g., the increase in the perimeter of the hexagon pattern train as additional hexagons are added, the increase in the cost of a meal plan as additional meals are purchased).

The teacher featured in a case usually solicits several different approaches for solving a problem so as to help students develop a flexible set of strategies for recognizing and generalizing patterns. For example, in "The Case of Ed Taylor" (Chapter 3) we see students analyzing a growth pattern involving arrangements of square tiles using both arithmetic-algebraic approaches that use the number of tiles to form the general pattern of growth, and visual-geometric approaches that focus on the shape of each figure in the pattern.

Pedagogical Moves

Each case begins with a challenging mathematical task that has the potential to engage students in high-level thinking about important mathematical ideas related to patterns and functions (e.g., rate of change). Throughout the case the teacher endeavors to support students as they work to make sense of the mathematics, without removing the challenging aspects of the task. This support includes pressing students to explain and justify their thinking and reasoning in both public and private forums, encouraging students to generate and make connections between different ways of representing a function, and using student thinking in productive ways.

As such, each case highlights a set of pedagogical moves that support (and in some cases inhibit) student engagement with important mathematical ideas. For example, in "The Case of Edith Hart" (Chapter 4), students were asked to determine the equations for three sets of data presented in graphical form. Ms. Hart supported her students' engagement in this activity by consistently pressing them to elaborate their observations and explanations regarding the points on the graph, by providing multiple opportunities for students to share their thinking with and question their peers, and by challenging students to make connections between different representations of the data. By orchestrating the lesson as she did, Ms. Hart advanced her students' un-

FIGURE 1.1. Diagram of Five Representations of Functions

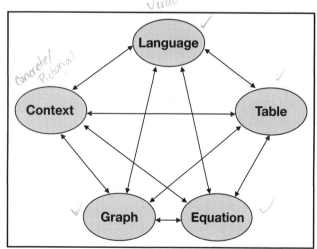

From John A. Van De Walle, *Elementary and Middle School Mathematics: Teaching Developmentally,* 5e. Published by Allyn and Bacon, Boston, MA. Copyright © 2004 by Pearson Education. Adapted by permission of the publisher.

derstanding of the relationship between the behavior of the graph, the story situation, and the formula—the ultimate goal of the lesson.

One case in this collection, "The Case of Catherine Evans and David Young" (Chapter 2), provides an opportunity to see how the presence or absence of key pedagogical moves can influence students' engagement with mathematical ideas. By juxtaposing the instruction of two teachers who are enacting the same set of pattern tasks with their students, the differences in what the teachers did and did not do and the impact of their actions on student learning are made salient. For example, although Mr. Young consistently presses students to explain their thinking, this move seldom occurs in Mrs. Evans's class. As a result, students in Mr. Young's class learn to make sense of their solutions and methods, while Mrs. Evans's students end up following procedures that have little or no meaning.

THE CASES AS LEARNING OPPORTUNITIES

Reading a case is a unique experience. Although it bears some similarities to reading other narratives (e.g., the reader has a story line to follow, may identify with the joys and dilemmas experienced by the protagonist, may end up glad or sad when the story concludes), it differs from other narrative accounts in an important way. Cases are written to highlight specific aspects of an instructional episode in order to stimulate reflection, analysis, and investigation into important issues in teaching and learning. By analyzing the particular ideas and issues that arise in a case, readers can begin to form general principles about effective teaching and learning. Cases can foster reflection on and investigation into one's own teaching and, in so doing, help teachers or prospective teachers continue to develop their knowledge base for teaching. Cases also can help those in administrative roles to gain greater insight into important issues in teaching and learning mathematics.

By reading and discussing a case and solving the related mathematical task, readers can examine their own understanding of the mathematics in the lesson and how the mathematical ideas are encountered by students in the classroom. Through this process, readers can develop new understandings about a particular mathematical idea, make connections that they previously had not considered, and gain confidence in their ability to do mathematics. In addition, readers may begin to develop an appreciation of mathematical tasks that can be solved in multiple ways and allow entry at various

levels. Take, for example, "The Case of Ed Taylor" (Chapter 3). As readers attempt to make sense of the methods Mr. Taylor's students used to find the total number of tiles for any figure in the pattern, they may begin to see for the first time that visual patterns can be viewed in many different ways, each of which can lead to a correct and equivalent symbolic equation. With this insight, readers may see that students can access many problems prior to learning specific rules and procedures for solving them.

Cases also provide the reader with an opportunity to analyze the pedagogical moves made by the teacher in the case. Through this analysis readers are encouraged to investigate what students are learning about mathematics and how the teaching supports that learning. For example, in Chapter 4 Edith Hart's students are beginning to relate their understanding of the y-intercept from the graph (the point on the graph with an x value of zero), to the symbolic formula (the constant value in the equation in slope-intercept form), and to the problem situation (the initial cost of the dinner card). A deeper analysis requires the reader to account for what Edith Hart did to help her students make connections between these different representational forms.

Finally, cases can provide readers with an opportunity to focus on the thinking of students as it unfolds during instruction and to offer explanations regarding what students appear to know and understand about the mathematics they are learning. Through this process, readers expand their views of what students can do when given the opportunity, develop their capacity to make sense of representations and explanations that may differ from their own, and become familiar with misconceptions that are common in a particular domain. For example, in reading "The Case of Robert Carter" (Chapter 5) readers may see that some students misinterpret the qualitative graph of a bicycle ride as a picture of riding a bicycle over hills. As readers analyze the responses given by Tonya and Travis (students who saw the graph as hills) and consider Mr. Carter's ongoing concern about the students' understanding, they come to realize that Tonya's and Travis's confusion is more than a simple incorrect answer. Rather, it represents confusion about the relationship between the quantities represented in the graph (in this case time and speed) and an overgeneralization of real-world knowledge (in this case about bicycle rides) and is at the heart of many of the difficulties students have in interpreting qualitative graphs.

Reading and analyzing a case thus can help a teacher or prospective teacher to develop critical components of the knowledge base for teaching—knowledge of subject matter, of pedagogy, and of students as learners—through the close examination of classroom practice. Although this is a critical step in developing knowledge for improved practice, the payoff of learning from cases is what teachers take from their experiences with cases and apply to their own practice.

USING THE CASE MATERIALS

It is important to note that learning from cases is not self-enacting. Reading a case does not ensure that the reader will automatically engage with all the embedded ideas or spontaneously make connections to his or her own practice. Through our work with cases, we have found that the readers of a case need to engage in specific activities related to the case in order to maximize their opportunities for learning. Specifically, readers appear to benefit from having a lens through which to view the events that unfold during a lesson and that signals where they might profitably direct their attention. For that reason we have created a set of professional learning tasks that provide a focus for reading and analyzing each case.

In the remainder of this chapter we provide suggestions for using the cases and related materials that are found in Chapters 2 through 5. These suggestions are based on our experiences in a range of teacher education settings over several years. For each case, we describe three types of professional learning tasks: solving the mathematical task on which the case is based; analyzing the case; and generalizing beyond the case (i.e., making connections to teachers' classroom practices and to the ideas of others).

Although it is possible to read through the cases and complete the accompanying professional learning tasks independently, we recommend working with a partner or, better yet, a group of peers who are likewise inclined to think about and improve their practice. In this way, readers will not only feel supported, but also develop a shared language for discussing teaching and learning with their colleagues.

Solving the Mathematical Task

Each case begins with an Opening Activity that consists of the same mathematical task that is featured in the case (or a similar task). It is important to spend sufficient time solving the task, ideally working through it in more than one way. This is a place in which working

with colleagues is particularly advantageous. Different people will approach and solve the tasks in different ways; seeing a variety of approaches will help to enrich readers' understanding of the mathematical ideas in the task and expand their repertoire of applicable strategies for solving the task.

We have found that it is important to engage with the mathematical task *before* reading the case. By engaging with the mathematical ideas themselves, whether individually or with the help of colleagues, readers will be "primed for" and able to recognize many of the solution strategies put forth by students in the case, making it easier to understand and follow students' thinking, identify students' misconceptions, and recognize the mathematical possibilities of the task.

For each of the cases in Chapters 2 through 5, there is a corresponding appendix (A through D, respectively) that provides a set of solutions to the Opening Activity. We encourage the reader to review these solutions after she or he has completed the task, and we encourage readers to try to make sense of and relate the different approaches.

Analyzing the Case

We have found it helpful to focus the reading and analysis of the case by providing a professional learning task (PLT). The PLT begins in the "Reading the Case" section of Chapters 2 through 5, with the intention of focusing the reader's attention on some aspect of the teaching and learning that occur in the case. The analysis continues in the "Analyzing the Case" section as the reader, after reading the case, is asked to explore the pedagogy in a deeper way, focusing on specific events that occurred in the classroom and the impact of these events on students' learning. For example, in the PLT in Chapter 5 readers initially are asked to identify, by paragraph numbers, decisions that Robert Carter made during the course of instruction that appeared to influence his students' learning of mathematics. The PLT stimulates a deeper analysis of the case by asking readers, after reading the case, to select three decisions made by Mr. Carter that they feel had the most significant influence on students' learning and to consider reasons why Robert Carter may have made those decisions at that point in the lesson.

For each case, we have identified a specific focus of analysis for the PLT. This focus is intended to highlight what each case can best contribute to the reader's investigation of teaching and learning. For example, in "The Case of Catherine Evans and David Young" (Chapter

2) readers are asked to consider the similarities and differences between Mrs. Evans's and Mr. Young's classes. The dual nature of this case provides a unique opportunity to compare the pedagogy of two teachers who have different views of what it means for students to be successful and to see the impact of these perspectives on classroom instruction and on student learning.

Additional questions are provided in the "Extending Your Analysis of the Case" section. These questions focus the reader's attention on a specific event depicted in the case and invite the reader to critique or explain what occurred. Readers may want to review the questions and identify one that resonates with their experiences or interests. These questions vary greatly from case to case and represent our best effort to bring to the fore a wider set of issues that might be explored within the context of a case.

The true value of the case analysis is realized when readers share their ideas about the PLT with others during a group discussion. It is through these discussions that teachers, future teachers, or other readers of the case will begin to develop a critical stance toward teaching and learning. If there is not an opportunity for a face-to-face group discussion about the case, the reader may want to consult the sample responses to the PLT provided in the appendix that corresponds to the case. Alternatively, new technologies may make it reasonable to conduct a discussion about a case via email or a web-based discussion group.

Generalizing Beyond the Case

Following the analysis of each case, readers are invited to engage in one or more activities in which the mathematical and pedagogical ideas discussed in the case are connected to their own teaching practice (when applicable) or to other related ideas and issues regarding mathematics teaching and learning. In the section entitled "Connecting to Your Own Practice," readers who are currently teaching are provided with opportunities to move beyond the specifics of a case and task and begin to examine their own practice in light of new understandings about mathematics, instruction, and student learning. This process is critical to the transformation of a teacher's practice.

While the specific activities vary from case to case, there are three general types of connections to practice

that we recommend: enacting high-level tasks in a mathematics lesson, analyzing one's own teaching, and working on specific issues that were raised during the case reading and analysis. The activities in this section are intended to build upon the reader's analysis of the case and extend this analysis to his or her own classroom. For example, following the analysis of Robert Carter's decision-making in Chapter 5, readers are asked to record a lesson in their own classroom and to reflect on their decision-making during the lesson and on the extent to which their decisions were based on an assessment of students' understanding. In doing so, teachers can become more aware of the extent to which what their students are thinking and doing informs the instructional decisions they make.

In the "Exploring Curricular Materials" section, readers are invited to investigate mathematics curricula to determine the ways in which mathematical ideas related to patterns and functions are developed and the opportunities that are provided for students to think and reason about mathematics. In this section, readers also are encouraged to explore mathematical tasks from other curricula that make salient the mathematical ideas featured in the case.

In the last section of Chapters 2 through 5, "Connecting to Other Ideas and Issues," we identify a set of readings from teacher-oriented publications (e.g., *Mathematics Teaching in the Middle School*) and other sources that elaborate, extend, or complement the mathematical and pedagogical content in the case in some way. The readings report findings from research on student learning (e.g., the Leinhardt, Zaslavsky, & Stein article referenced in Chapter 4); present actual activities that could be used in the classroom in a unit on patterns and functions (e.g., the Phillips book referenced in Chapter 3), and provide additional lenses through which to analyze a case (e.g., the English & Warren article referenced in Chapter 2). In each case chapter, a specific set of suggestions are given regarding how to use the cited material to support the reader's understanding of the case or the ideas and issues that arise from it.

We feel that the suggestions for using the case materials presented in this chapter will allow readers to gain the most from our cases and case materials. We hope that readers find the experience of engaging in the case-based activities rewarding, challenging, and insightful.

2 Examining Linear Growth Patterns

The Case of Catherine Evans and David Young

Chapter 2 has been designed to engage readers in considering important issues in mathematics teaching and learning related to linear growth. Prior to reading "The Case of Catherine Evans and David Young"—the centerpiece of this chapter—we suggest that all readers begin by completing the Opening Activity. The primary purpose of the Opening Activity is to engage readers with the mathematical ideas that will be encountered when reading the case.

OPENING ACTIVITY

The Hexagon-Pattern Task shown in Figure 2.1 is one of a set of pattern tasks explored by students in both lessons featured in "The Case of Catherine Evans and David Young." After finding one way to express the perimeter, you are encouraged to engage in the "Consider" portion of the activity in which you are challenged to find different strategies for determining the perimeter and to justify your strategies.

Once you have completed the activity, you may want to refer to Appendix A, which contains a set of solutions based on strategies generated by teachers who completed the Opening Activity as part of a professional development experience featuring "The Case of Catherine Evans and David Young." We encourage you to make sense of the different solutions provided and to consider the relationship between your solution and those produced by others.

READING THE CASE

As you read the case, we encourage you to consider what you think students in each class were learning. For example, you might identify specific mathematical ideas (e.g., perimeter), processes (e.g., problem-solving, reasoning, communication), or norms for participating in a lesson (e.g., providing alternative approaches is valued) that students appeared to be learning during the instructional episode portrayed in the case.

We encourage you to record paragraph numbers from the case that support your claims regarding what students in each class were learning. You can then compare and contrast your list with one created by a colleague who also has read the case and engage in a spirited discussion about points of disagreement. You also might continue to investigate student learning as you read additional cases.

If you currently are teaching mathematics, issues that surface in reading "The Case of Catherine Evans and David Young" might serve as a starting point for exploration of student learning in your own classroom. For example, you may identify with Catherine Evans's need to parse difficult tasks into smaller, more manageable parts and now begin to consider how this might impact student learning in your classroom. We will discuss additional connections to your own practice at the end of the chapter.

FIGURE 2.1. The Hexagon-Pattern Task for the Opening Activity in "The Case of Catherine Evans and David Young"

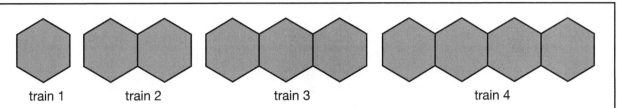

train 1   train 2   train 3   train 4

Solve

Trains 1, 2, 3, and 4 are the first 4 trains in the hexagon pattern. The first train in this pattern consists of one regular hexagon. For each subsequent train, one additional hexagon is added.

For the hexagon pattern:

- compute the perimeter for the first 4 trains;
- determine the perimeter for the tenth train without constructing it; and
- write a description that could be used to compute the perimeter of any train in the pattern. (Use the edge length of any pattern block as your unit of measure. If pattern blocks are not available, use the side of a hexagon as the unit of measure.)

Consider

Find as many different ways as you can to compute (and justify) the perimeter.

Illustration from *Visual Mathematics Course I, Lessons 16–30* published by The Math Learning Center. Copyright ©1995 by The Math Learning Center, Salem, Oregon. Reprinted by permission.

THE CASE OF CATHERINE EVANS

1.   Catherine Evans had spent most of her 20-year career teaching in self-contained classrooms (ranging from grades 1–6) where she taught all subjects. Although she taught mathematics nearly every year, she preferred to teach literature, writing, and social studies because, in her view, instruction in these areas allowed for discussions with students and opportunities for creative expression rather than focusing on memorization and procedures.

2.   Catherine viewed teaching mathematics very differently than teaching other subjects. She described her mathematics instruction as following a regular pattern: correcting homework assigned during the previous class by reading answers and having students mark problems as correct or incorrect; presenting new material (either to the whole class or to small groups) by explaining the procedure to be learned and demonstrating a small number of sample problems; monitoring student completion of a few problems; and having students work individually on a larger set of similar problems using the preferred strategy. She saw math as the easiest period of the day, since it did not require much preparation. In addition, Catherine admitted, "probably during most of my teaching, I never thought of math as being as important as reading and writing."

3.   Catherine Evans had been teaching at Quigley Middle School for 3 years when the opportunity arose to participate in a new math project. She was intrigued with the approach to mathematics teaching that was being proposed—one that emphasized thinking, reasoning, and communicating ideas—since these were the processes and skills that were central to her teaching in other content areas. Although she did not have any idea what this would mean in mathematics, she was ready for a new challenge and made the commitment to her colleagues to change the way mathematics was taught and learned in her classroom.

4.   Catherine knew this would be hard, but she was confident about her abilities as a teacher. She had always been successful—her students did well on the district standardized tests, teachers in subsequent grades who had her students always remarked about how well prepared they were, and parents often requested that their children be placed in her classroom. In addition, she had a deep commitment to her students and an enthusiasm for teaching. She saw herself as someone who related well to students and was able to motivate them to learn. She felt that her humor—the ability to laugh at herself and situations—was a valuable asset in the classroom no matter what she was teaching.

Catherine Evans Talks About Her Class

5.   I have been teaching the new curriculum for about 6 weeks now and I have found that my 6th-graders are not always prepared for the challenges presented. The tasks in the curriculum generally can't be solved by just using an algorithm, the solution path is not immediately evident and usually involves exploring and reasoning through alternatives, and most tasks involve providing a written explanation. If my students can't

solve a problem immediately, they say, "I don't know," and give up. They have had limited experience in elementary school actually engaging actively with mathematics and expressing their thinking, and have found this to be very difficult.

6.   Seeing students give up has caused me great concern. I can't buy the idea that kids don't feel bad starting off with what they perceive to be failure. When they have work they can't do or don't have the confidence to do, then I have to intervene. I decided to help kids do more verbalization in class and to get to the kids who didn't volunteer and guarantee them success by asking them to do things they couldn't fail to do right. I can't ignore the fact that success breeds success. Too many are starting out with what I'm sure they perceive to be failure.

7.   In order to ensure student success, I have started to make some modifications in the curriculum, at times putting in an extra step or taking out something that seems too hard; rewriting problem instructions so that they are clearer and at an easier reading level; and creating easier problems for homework. In addition, during classroom instruction I try to break a task into small subtasks so that students can tackle one part of the task at a time.

8.   We have been talking about patterns for a few weeks. The new unit that we started last week uses trains of pattern blocks arranged in a geometric sequence. The unit is supposed to help students visualize and describe geometric patterns, make conjectures about the patterns, determine the perimeters of trains they build, and, ultimately, develop a generalization for the perimeter of any train in a pattern. This unit really lays the groundwork for developing the algebraic ideas of generalization, variable, and function that students will explore in grades 6 through 8. Experiences like these lay the foundation for more formal work in algebra in 8th grade.

9.   We spent some time in the beginning of this unit just making observations about the trains—the number of pattern blocks in a train, the geometric shapes that constitute a train, and the properties of a train (e.g., each train has four sides, opposite sides of the train are parallel). Students got pretty good at making observations about specific trains once we had done a few, but I had to keep reminding them that the observations needed to be mathematical. For some patterns I got some really weird responses like, "It looks like a squished pop can," or "It looks like a belt buckle." But once I reminded students that one reason for making observations was to be able to predict what larger trains were going to look like, they were able to move beyond these fanciful responses.

The Class

10.   Yesterday for the first time we started determining the perimeters of the trains using the side of the square as the unit of measure. Last night's homework had been to find the perimeters of the first three trains in the pattern shown in Figure 2.2. I also asked students to find the perimeter of the tenth, twentieth, and one-hundredth trains in this pattern. My plan for class was to begin by discussing the pattern task (Figure 2.2) that had been assigned for homework and then have students explore another pattern.

FIGURE 2.2. The Square-Pattern Train

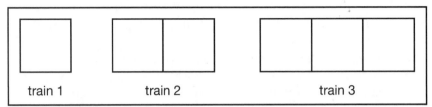

From *Visual Mathematics Course I, Lessons 16–30* published by The Math Learning Center. Copyright ©1995 by The Math Learning Center, Salem, Oregon. Reprinted by permission.

11.   As students entered the classroom and got their papers out, I made a quick trip to the back of the room to check on the video camera. My colleagues and I decided to videotape some of our classes this year so that we could use the tapes to reflect on how things were going with the new curriculum and to talk about various issues that arose in using the materials. This was my first day of taping, and I was a little nervous about being on film. Students asked about the camera as they entered the classroom, but seemed unfazed by the idea of being taped. I just hoped I could forget that it was there.

12.   *Discussing the square-pattern trains.* In order to get things started, I asked students to make observations about the pattern. Shandra said that she had noticed that all of the trains were rectangles. Jake said that he noticed that the perimeter of the first train was 4. I asked him to come up and show us. When he got to the overhead he took a square tile (black) and laid an edge of the square next to each side of the train as he counted the sides. This was the procedure that we had established yesterday, illustrated in Figure 2.3, and I was pleased to see him use it. I thanked him and he returned to his seat.

13.   Since Jake had started talking about perimeters, I decided that we might as well continue in this direction. I asked Zeke what he found for

FIGURE 2.3. Jake's Method of Finding the Perimeter of the First Train in the Square Pattern

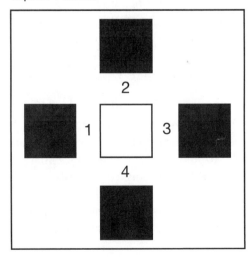

the perimeter of the second train. Zeke said he thought it was 4. I asked him if he would go to the overhead and show us how he got 4. Using the diagram shown in Figure 2.4, he explained, "The train has four sides—I just counted them 1, 2, 3, and 4."

14.   I saw what Zeke was doing. He was counting the number of sides, not the number of units in the perimeter. The number of sides and number of units were the same in the first figure, but not in the second figure. I asked Zeke to stay at the overhead and I asked the class if someone could review what perimeter is. Danny said that it was the sides all the way around. I asked if anyone had another way to say it. Danny's definition really supported what Zeke had done, and I was looking for a definition that would cause students to question Zeke's solution. Finally Nick said that the perimeter would be 6. Nick explained, "I used Jake's way and measured all the way around the outside of the train with the square tile. It's not four because the top and bottom each have two units." Although this was not the definition I was looking for, I figured that this explanation would help students see why the perimeter was 6 and not 4.

15.   At this point I decided to ask Desmond to come up and measure the perimeter of the third train for us using the procedure that Nick had just described. I have been trying all year to get him involved. Lately I have been asking him questions that I was sure he could answer. They were not meant to challenge him in any way, just help him feel successful. These experiences had an immediate positive effect on Desmond—he would actively participate in class following these episodes. So Desmond came up to the overhead and I gave him the black square and asked him to measure the third train. I really thought that this would be a simple task, but Desmond did not seem to know what to do. Since this experience was supposed to be about experiencing success, I took his hand and helped him move the square along the outside of the train, counting as we proceeded, as shown in Figure 2.5.

16.   I thanked Desmond for his help. I was sure that this would clear up the confusion. I told Zeke that a lot of people make the same mistake that he did the first time they do perimeter. Just to be sure that Zeke understood the way to find perimeter, I asked him if he could build the fourth train in the pattern. He quickly laid four squares side to side. I then asked him if he could find the perimeter by measuring. He proceeded to count the sides while moving the side of the square along the

FIGURE 2.4. Zeke's Method of Finding the Perimeter of the Second Train in the Square Pattern

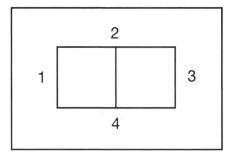

FIGURE 2.5. Mrs. Evans Uses the Square Tile to Help
Desmond Find the Perimeter of the Third Train

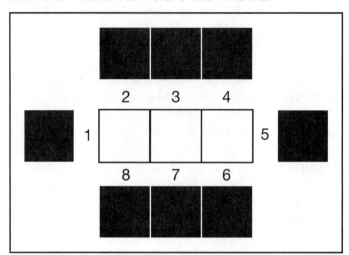

perimeter of the train—1, 2, 3, 4, 5, 6, 7, 8, 9, 10. He looked up when he finished and announced, "It will be ten!" I thanked him for hanging in there with us, and he returned to his seat.

17.　　Before moving on to the next part of the assignment I asked if anybody had noticed anything else about perimeter when they did just the first three. Angela had her hand up, and I asked her what she had noticed. She explained, "On the third train there are three on the top and three on the bottom, which makes six, and one on each end." I asked her if she would go to the overhead and show us what she meant. Using the diagram shown in Figure 2.6 she restated, "See, there are three up here (pointing to the top of the train) and three down here (pointing to the bottom of the train) and then one on each end.

18.　　I was surprised by this observation so early on, but knowing that it would be helpful in determining the perimeters of larger trains, I asked Angela if she could use her system to find the perimeter of the fourth train. She quickly said, "Ten." I asked her to explain. She proceeded, "Four on the bottom and four on the top and one on each end."

FIGURE 2.6. Angela's Strategy for Finding the
Perimeter of the Third Train in the Square Pattern

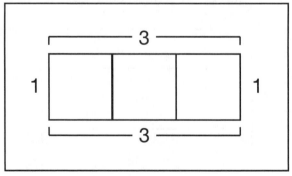

19.　　　Class can be pretty fast paced sometimes, with individual students, the whole class, and me going back and forth in a rapid exchange. A good example of this happened at this point as I tried to put Angela's observation to the test and see if I could get the whole class involved in using her observation to predict future trains. Once Angela's pattern became obvious to *her*, I wanted to make sure that everyone in the class saw it too. So I proceeded with the following question and answer exchange:

> ME:　Using your system, do you think you could do any number I say? What would you do for 10? How many on the top and the bottom?
>
> ANGELA:　10.
>
> ME:　How many on the ends?
>
> ANGELA:　2.
>
> ME:　How many all together?
>
> ANGELA:　22.
>
> ME:　Let's do another one. Listen to what she's saying and see if you can do it also. Angela, in train 12, how many will there be on the top and bottom?
>
> ANGELA:　12.
>
> ME:　And then how many will there be on the ends?
>
> ANGELA:　2.
>
> ME:　How many will there be all together?
>
> ANGELA:　26.
>
> ME:　Tamika, what's she doing?
>
> TAMIKA:　She's taking the train number on the top and bottom and adding two.
>
> ME:　OK, let's everybody try a few. I can pick any number. Train 50. How many will there be on the top and bottom? Everybody!
>
> CLASS:　50. (*With enthusiasm*)
>
> ME:　How many on the ends?
>
> CLASS:　2.
>
> ME:　How much all together?
>
> CLASS:　102.
>
> ME:　Train 100, how many on the top and bottom?
>
> CLASS:　100. (*Louder and with even more enthusiasm*)
>
> ME:　How many on the ends?
>
> CLASS:　2.
>
> ME:　How much all together?
>
> CLASS:　202.
>
> ME:　Train 1,000, how many on the top and bottom?
>
> CLASS:　1,000. (*Loudest of all*)
>
> ME:　How many on the ends?
>
> CLASS:　2.
>
> ME:　How much all together?
>
> CLASS:　2,002.

20.　　　At this point I asked if they could describe anything I gave them. Another resounding "YES" answered my question. One of the things that I have found is that responding in unison really engages students and helps their confidence. When they respond in unison they feel that they are part of the group. Everyone can participate and feel good about themselves.

21.   Angela's observation had really led us to finding the perimeters for any train so I decided to continue on this pathway. I asked if anyone had figured out the perimeters using a different way. I looked around the room—no hands were in the air. I wanted them to have at least one other way to think about the pattern so I shared with them a method suggested by one of the students in another class. I explained that she had noticed that the squares on the ends always have three sides—they each lose one on the inside—and that the ones in the middle always have two sides. I used train three, shown in Figure 2.7, as an example and pointed out the three sides on each end and the two sides on the middle square.

22.   I wanted to see if students understood this so I asked how many squares would be in the middle of train 50 with this system. Nick said that there would be 48. I then added that there would be 48 twos, referring to the number of sides that would be counted in the perimeter, and three on each end. I asked what 48 twos would be. Carrie said it would be 96. I then asked what the perimeter would be. Shawntay said that it would 102. She went on to say that that was the same as what we got from train 50 when we did it Angela's way! I told the class that was right; there isn't just one way to look at it.

23.   *Considering a new pattern.* We had spent nearly 20 minutes on the square pattern, and it was time to move on to another pattern. I quickly got out my pattern blocks and built the hexagon-pattern train (shown in Figure 2.1) on the overhead. I told students that I wanted them to work with their partners and build the first three trains in the pattern, find the perimeters for these three trains, and then find the perimeters for the tenth, twentieth, and one-hundredth trains. I put the pattern of square trains (Figure 2.2) that we had just finished back up on the overhead underneath the hexagon pattern and suggested that they might want to see if they could find anything that was the same for the hexagon pattern and the square pattern that would help them. Since the generalizations for the perimeters of these two trains had some similarities, I thought this would help them find the perimeters for the larger trains in the hexagon pattern.

FIGURE 2.7. An Alternative Solution for Finding the Perimeter of the Square-Pattern Train Demonstrated by Mrs. Evans

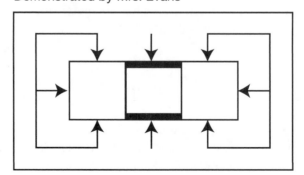

24.   After about 5 minutes students seemed to be getting restless. Since most seemed to have made progress on the task, I decided to call the class together and see what they observed about the pattern. Although this is not exactly what I asked them to do—make observations—I felt that it provided a more open opportunity for all students to have something to say. I asked Tracy what she had noticed. She said that every time you add one. "Add one what?" I asked. "A hexagon," she responded. I then asked about the perimeter. Devon said that he discovered that it was 6. "What was six?" I asked. Devon clarified that 6 was the amount around the hexagon—around the edges on the first train. I asked Devon about the second train. He explained, "The hexagon has six around it and then you take away one for each side in the middle so it is 5 + 5 or 10. Then on the third one you still have 5 + 5 for the end ones and you add four more sides for the new hexagon you added."

25.   I wanted to see if Devon realized that his observation would lead to a generalization. I asked him if what he had discovered would tell him anything about building another train. Devon said, "Yeah. On train four there would be four hexagons. The end ones would each have five and the two middle ones would each have four." "If you were to build train 10," I asked, "could you tell me how many would have four sides and how many would have five sides?" Devon appeared to think about it for a few seconds and then responded that eight hexagons would have four sides and two hexagons would have five sides. I wanted to make sure that students understood what Devon was saying so I asked him where the two with the five sides would be. He looked at me as though I were crazy and said, "Mrs. Evans, they would have to be on the ends!"

26.   Again, I wanted to see if students could use Devon's method on any train. I asked Tommy if he could describe the twentieth train. Tommy explained, "For train 20 you'd count the sides and count the ends. You subtract 2 from 20 and that would be 18 and then you multiply 18 by 4, because all the hexagons in the middle have four and then you would add 10 from the ends." I was impressed with his explanation, and he seemed to be pretty proud of himself too. I wanted to make sure that everyone had all the steps that Tommy had so nicely explained.

27.   I then asked Jeremy if he could do the thirtieth train. He said that he didn't know. I felt that he probably could do this if I provided a little structure for him. I asked him how many hexagons would have five sides. He said in a questioning tone, "Two?" I nodded and said that this was correct. I then asked how many hexagons would be in the middle. He wrote something down on paper that I could not see and indicated that there would be 28. I then asked him how many sides each of the 28 hexagons would have on the perimeter. He responded more confidently this time with, "Four."

28.   I then asked the class how we could write 2 fives and 28 fours. No hands shot up immediately and I glanced at the clock. Where had the time gone—the bell was going to ring any minute. I told the students that for homework I wanted them to come up with a way to calculate the perimeter of the thirtieth train and any other train we could come up with. I thought that this would push us toward more formal ways of recording calculations and, ultimately, generalizations.

Reflecting on Class Later That Day

29.　　　The lesson was all I could have asked from the kids! They found the perimeters of the trains and were even making progress on finding generalizations. I have had this kind of a lesson about five times this year and it is very exciting. I want to see the tape as soon as possible to find other things I could have done. The kids were very proud of themselves, I think, and so was I!

Reflecting on Class Several Weeks Later

30.　　　A few weeks after this class I had the opportunity to share a 10-minute segment of a videotaped lesson with my colleagues at one of our staff development sessions. I decided to show a segment from the pattern block lesson since I thought it had gone so well. Although they didn't say so directly, I think they felt that I was too leading. Maybe they were right. It is easy to be too leading and feel OK about it because the kids seem happy. After all, many kids are happy with drill and practice.

31.　　　I decided to go back and watch the entire tape again and see if I could look at it objectively. The lesson contained too much whole-group teacher questioning and students explaining and not enough time for students to stretch and discover independently and collaboratively. I wondered, in particular, what most students really understood about Angela's method. Sure many of them answered my questions, but were they just mindlessly applying a procedure that they had rehearsed? Did it mean anything to them? Although choral response might make kids feel good, it really masks what individual students are really thinking and what it is they understand. Just because they could come up with answers to my questions doesn't mean that they really understand or that they have any idea how to apply it. I am now left wondering what they really learned from this experience.

Reflecting at the End of the School Year

32.　　　In early June, at the end-of-the-year retreat, my colleagues and I were asked to make a 10-minute presentation regarding the aspects of our teaching that we thought had changed most over the year. I began by showing a clip of one of my fall lessons—the one in which Desmond went to the overhead to measure the perimeter of the pattern train and in which I assumed control, even moving his hands. I told my colleagues, "I'd like to start with the first clip because I feel it pretty much sums up how I taught at the beginning of the year, and I'd like to show you that I really have become less directive than this tape." I showed the clip without sound. Attention was drawn to two pairs of hands on the overhead, the large pair (mine) that seemed to be moving the smaller pair (Desmond's). I explained, "You'll see Desmond comes up and I am very helpful—very directive—and move the lesson along. That was a big thing with me—to move these lessons—and if they didn't get it, I'd kinda help them do so." I added that I asked many yes or no questions very quickly and did not provide time for students to think. In contrast, I then showed video clips from the spring, in which I walked around the room, asking groups of students questions that would help them focus their efforts rather than telling or showing them what to do. For me, the differences in my actions and interactions with students on these two occasions provided evidence that I had changed.

TRANSITION

33.   Catherine Evans and her colleagues continued their efforts to improve the mathematics teaching and learning at Quigley Middle School. They met frequently to talk about their work and attended professional development sessions once a month and during the summers to support their growth and development. And their efforts were paying off—students were showing growth not only in basic skills but also in their ability to think, reason, and communicate mathematically.

34.   At the beginning of the third year of the math project a new teacher joined the faculty at Quigley—David Young. Catherine and her colleagues welcomed David into their community. From their own experiences they knew how hard it was to teach math in this way. But David had something that Catherine and her colleagues did not have initially—the opportunity to work beside teachers who had experience with the curriculum.

35.   The Case of David Young picks up at the beginning of David's second year at Quigley. He has been working with Catherine and others and has had 1 year's experience teaching this new way. Catherine is now beginning her fourth year of the math project.

THE CASE OF DAVID YOUNG

36.   David Young has just started his second year at Quigley Middle School. The job at Quigley was at first overwhelming for David. His mathematics teacher colleagues were implementing an instructional program based on a constructivist view of learning. Although such approaches had been foundational to his teacher preparation program, his teaching up to this point had been fairly traditional. The schools he had been in for student teaching and his first year teaching did not support innovation; therefore, he had no experience putting into practice things that he had learned in his preservice training. But at Quigley the students were not passive recipients of what the teacher dished out, and drill-and-practice seemed to have a fairly limited role in instruction. Students were actually doing mathematics—exploring, making conjectures, arguing, and justifying their conclusions.

37.   The enthusiasm and energy he saw in his colleagues was invigorating but also scary. His colleagues all had lots of experience, but he had almost none. He worried about his ability to be a contributing member of the community and whether he would be able to teach in a new way. David's fears were put to rest early in his first year. His colleagues were very supportive and understanding. In their monthly meetings they told him war stories about their initial experiences in teaching this new way

and how they had helped one another through the tough times. They would see him at lunch, in the morning before school, or in the hallway and ask, "What are you doing today?" and "How is it going?" They would give him some suggestions based on what had worked well for them, but they never told him what to do or harshly judged the decisions he made. Mostly they listened and asked a lot of questions. Over time David felt that he could ask or tell them anything. It was, he decided, the perfect place to teach.

38.   During his tenure at Quigley, David had been working hard to help students develop confidence in their ability to do mathematics, which he felt in turn would influence their interest and performance in the subject. Far too many students, he thought, came to Quigley hating math in large measure because they had not been successful in it. He had talked a lot with Catherine Evans about his concerns. Catherine had been quite open about her early experiences in teaching math the new way (just 3 years ago) and her misstarts in trying to help students feel successful. David came to believe that developing confidence as a mathematics doer resulted from facing challenges and persevering in the face of them. The key, Catherine often had said, was trying to find a way to support students in solving a challenging task—not creating less challenging tasks for students to solve.

David Young Talks About His Class

39.   This is the beginning of my second year teaching 6th grade with this new curriculum. The first year was rough for me and the kids as we tried to settle into our new roles in the classroom: me as the facilitator and my students as constructors of knowledge. When things did not go well my colleague Catherine was always there with a sympathetic ear and a word of encouragement. She is such a wonderful teacher—everything in her classroom seems to always go so well. (She is right next door and we have a connecting door between our rooms. Sometimes during my free period I leave the door open and listen in on what is happening over there.) Although she has repeatedly said that it was a long and painful trip from where she started to where she is today, it is hard to believe. I guess it is comforting, though, to know that if she made it, I can too.

40.   Catherine and I are both teaching 6th grade this year, so we touch base nearly every day about what we are doing. We are only one month into the school year, and so far we have been working with patterns. Up to this point we have focused primarily on numeric patterns. The new unit that we started yesterday uses trains of pattern blocks arranged in some geometric sequence. The unit is supposed to help students visualize and describe geometric patterns, make conjectures about the patterns, determine the perimeters of trains they build, and, ultimately, develop a generalization for the perimeter of any train in a pattern.

41.   Last year this unit did not go well. There was too much teacher talk and too little time for students to think. I moved them through the entire set of exercises in one period. I felt great because I had really covered the material, but a week later it was clear that the students hadn't gained much from the experience. When I talked with Catherine about it she told me about her first time teaching this unit 3 years ago.

She said that one thing she learned is that kids need time to think, to struggle, and to make sense of things for themselves. If you make it too easy for them they will never learn to figure things out for themselves. This made sense to me, but it was hard not to step in and tell them what to do. I was determined, however, to do a better job this time around.

The Class

42.　　Yesterday, my 6th-grade class spent some time getting familiar with the pattern blocks—identifying the shapes and determining the perimeters of the blocks. Today, they are going to make observations about trains of pattern blocks and determine the perimeters for the trains. Basically, I am just going to follow the curriculum here. It suggests giving students a pattern sequence and having them compute the perimeter for the first three or four trains and then determine the perimeter of a larger train like 10 or 20. Ultimately, the curriculum suggests asking students to imagine that they are constructing the one-hundredth train and to look for ways to find the perimeter. I will see how things go, but I hope to be able to follow this suggestion and use large numbers like 1,000 so there is no way they can build or draw the trains and count the number of sides.

43.　　*Getting started: The square tile pattern.* I started by building the pattern of squares (shown in Figure 2.2) on the overhead and asking students to work with their partners to find the perimeters of the first 4 trains in the sequence. Emily immediately asked for pattern blocks so she could actually build the trains. This of course started a series of requests to use the blocks. I hadn't anticipated this, but I had no problem with it, either. I grabbed a few bags of blocks and dropped them off at the tables of students who had requested them.

44.　　Students started building the trains and quickly seemed to realize that the fourth train would have four squares. They then began to determine the perimeter and record their findings. This initial activity seemed to be pretty easy for students. After about 5 minutes I asked Derek to go to the overhead and show us how he found the perimeter for the first 3 trains. Using a technique that several students had come up with yesterday when we began exploring the perimeter of the blocks, Derek drew line segments parallel to the side of the square as he counted, as shown in Figure 2.8, in order to show that he had counted a particular segment. Once he had completed the count he

FIGURE 2.8. Derek's Strategy for Counting the Sides of the Pattern Train

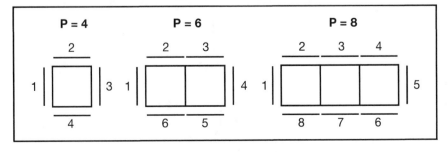

recorded the perimeter on top of the train. I asked Derek what the numbers "4," "6," and "8" represented. He responded that "these are the distance around the outside of the train in units." I asked what a unit was and he explained that he had used the side of the square as the unit. (The previous day we had discussed the fact that we were going to be measuring using the side of the square as our unit. That way we could talk about the number of units without worrying about actual measurement.)

45.   I then asked the class what they thought the perimeter of the fourth train would be. Crystal said that she thought it would be 10. I asked her how she found it. She explained, "I just built the fourth one and counted the way Derek did." Jamal said that he got 10, too, but that he just added two more to the third train. I asked him to explain. He said, "When you add on one more block to the train the perimeter only gets bigger by two more units 'cause only the new piece on the top and bottom add to the perimeter." I asked the class if they had any questions for Jamal. Kirsten said that there were four sides in every square, so how could the perimeter only increase by two? Jamal went to the overhead and explained, "See, if you look at the second train there are two units on the top and bottom, and one on each side. When you go to train three and add one more square (as shown in Figure 2.9) you still only have one unit on each end 'cause two sides of the new square are on the inside not on the perimeter."

46.   I then asked students to take a few minutes and think about what the tenth train would look like. I wanted to be sure that all students had time to consider this larger train. I know that sometimes I move too quickly and don't allow enough wait time for students to think about things. This tends to work against the students who have good ideas but work at a slower pace. Since I have been waiting longer, more students have been involved.

47.   I started by asking Michele what she thought the perimeter would be. She said she got 22. I asked her if she could explain to us how she got this answer. She indicated that she had built the tenth train and then counted. Although this was a perfectly good approach for the tenth figure, it was going to be less helpful when we started considering larger trains. I asked if anyone did it another way. Travis said that he got 22, too, but that he just took 10 + 10 + 2. Although his answer was correct, it was not immediately obvious why he added this set of numbers. I asked

FIGURE 2.9. Jamal's Explanation of Why the Perimeter Increases Only by Two for Each Square That Is Added

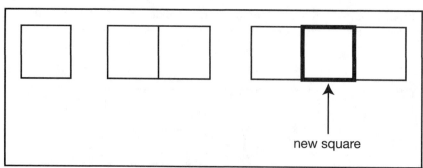

new square

him why he did this. He explained, "See, when I looked at the first four trains I saw that the number of units on the top and bottom were the same as the number of the train. So in train one there was one unit on the top and one on the bottom. In train two there were two units on the top and on the bottom. In train three there were three units on the top and the bottom. So I figured that this would keep going, so the tenth train would have 10 units on the top and the bottom. Then for all the trains you have to add on the two sides because they never change."

48.   I thanked Travis for sharing his strategy and asked if anyone had thought about it another way. Joseph said that he multiplied the number of squares in the train by 4, then subtracted the sides that were in the inside. I indicated that this was an interesting way to think about it and asked him if he would explain. He began, "Well, each square has four sides, so in the tenth train there would be 4 times 10 or 40 sides. But some of these are in the inside, so you have to subtract." "How did you know how many would be on the inside?" I asked. He explained, "Well, there are eight squares in the inside of the train, and each of those squares had two sides that didn't count and that gives you 16. Then there are two squares on the outside of the train and each of those had one side that didn't count, so that gave you 18. So 40 minus 18 gives you 22, and that's the answer."

49.   As he finished his explanation a few hands shot up around the room. I asked the class if they had any questions for Joseph. Kendra asked how he knew that there were eight squares on the inside of the train. Joseph said that he had looked at the first four trains and noticed that the number of squares on the inside was two less than the train number—the second train had zero squares on the inside, the third train had one on the inside, and the fourth had two on the inside. I thanked Joseph for sharing his thinking about the problem with the class. I was really pleased with the two different generalizations that had been offered and decided to ask one more question before moving on to a new pattern to see if the class could apply these noncounting approaches to a larger train.

50.   I asked the class if they could tell me the perimeter of the one-hundredth train. After waiting about 2 minutes for students to consider the question, I asked if anyone had a solution. Alicia said that she thought it would be 202. I asked her how she figured it out. She said she needed to draw and came up to the overhead. She drew a rectangle on the overhead (shown in Figure 2.10) and asked us to pretend that it was 100 squares. She then continued, "Like Travis said, the number of units on the top and bottom is the train number, and then there are the two

FIGURE 2.10. Alicia's Strategy for Determining the Perimeter of a Train

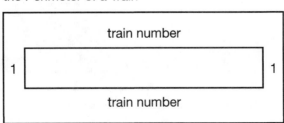

on the sides. So for the one-hundredth train, it would be 100 plus 100 plus 1 plus 1."

51.   I commented that this seemed like a really fast way to do the problem. At this point I decided to pass out a sheet of four additional patterns (shown in Figure 2.11) and see if the discussion that we had about the square-pattern train would give students additional ways to think about the new patterns. Beginning with Pattern 1, I asked students to work with a partner and to sketch the fourth train in the pattern, find the perimeter of each of the four trains, and then see if they could find the perimeter of the tenth train without building the train. I knew the last condition would be a challenge for some, but I wanted them to think harder to find another way.

52.   *Continuing work: The triangle pattern.* I walked around visiting the pairs as they worked on the triangle train (Pattern 1). Again students seem to quickly see the pattern—add one more triangle—and count the sides to find the perimeter. I observed several pairs starting to build the tenth train and asked them to try to find another way. I suggested that

FIGURE 2.11. The Pattern-Train Worksheet That Mr. Young Distributed to His Students

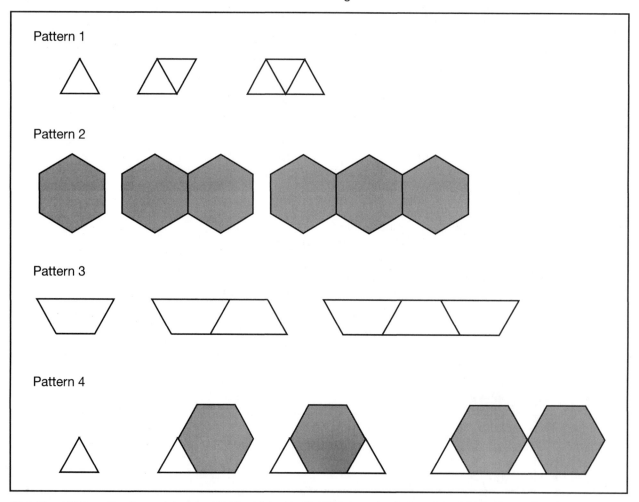

they look at the four trains they had built and see if they could find any patterns that would help them predict the tenth train. In a few cases where the students were really stuck I suggested that they try to see if they could find a connection between the train number and the perimeter as a few students had done in the last pattern.

53.   Once it appeared that most pairs had made progress on this task, I asked James to come up and build the fourth train and describe the pattern. James quickly assembled the triangles, changing the orientation each time he added one. He explained, "You just add one more triangle each time and every new one is turned the opposite way of the last one." I then asked Katie what she found for the perimeter of each train. She said that the first one was 3, the second one was 4, the third one was 5, and the fourth one was 6. I asked her what the fifth one would be. She quickly said, "Seven." I asked her how she did it so fast, and she responded, "After the first one you just add one every time. The fourth train is 6 so the fifth train would be one more."

54.   I then asked if anyone could tell me what the perimeter of the tenth train would be. Janelle said she thought it would be 12. I asked her how she found it. She said she made a table and looked for a pattern. Since this was the first time anyone had mentioned making a table, I thought it would be worth having her explain this strategy to the class. She came up and constructed the table shown in Figure 2.12. She explained, "I looked in the table and I saw that the perimeter kept going up by one, but that the perimeter was always two more than the train number. So that for train number 10 the perimeter would be two more, or 12."

55.   Before I could even ask if anyone had done it another way, Joseph was waving his hand. He announced that he got 12 too, but that he did it another way. He said that the train number was the same as the number of triangles, just like the squares. He went on, "Since each triangle has three sides, I multiplied the number of triangles by 3. So 3 times 10 equals 30. But then, you have to subtract the sides that are in the inside. It's like the square. You take the number of triangles on the inside. For the tenth train, that would be 8. Each of those triangles has two sides that don't count and that gives you 16. Then there are two triangles on the outside of the train and each of those had one side that didn't count, so that makes 18. 30 minus 18 equals 12."

56.   "Wow," I said, "there are lots of different ways to look at these trains, aren't there?" I was ready to move on, but Darrell was trying to get my

FIGURE 2.12. Janelle's Table for the Triangle Train

Train #	Perimeter
1	3
2	4
3	5
4	6

attention. He said, "Aren't you gonna ask us to find the one-hundredth?" That hadn't been my plan, but if he wanted to find the one-hundredth train I was happy to oblige. I asked Darrell if he wanted to tell us what the perimeter of the one-hundredth train would be. He said, "It'll be 102. 'Cause like Janelle said it will always be two more." I asked the class if they agreed with Darrell. I saw lots of nodding heads that convinced me that we were indeed making progress.

57.   *Exploring three new patterns.* I told the class that they would have 15 minutes to work with their partners on Patterns 2, 3, and 4 (see Figure 2.11). For each pattern, they needed to sketch the fourth train, find the perimeter for the first four trains, and determine the perimeter for the tenth train without building the train. I wanted students to have a longer period of time for exploring the patterns without interruption. I figured that in 15 minutes everyone would at least get Pattern 2 done, and Pattern 4 would be a challenge for those who got that far since it was less straightforward than the previous patterns because the odd and even trains would be described differently.

58.   As students worked on the patterns, I again walked around the room observing what they were doing, listening in on their conversations, occasionally asking a question, and reminding them that they would need to be able to justify their methods to the rest of the class. The most challenging aspect of the task for most students was finding the perimeter of the tenth train without drawing it. For Pattern 2, I encouraged them to try to find a way to talk about the perimeter of a figure in terms of the train number. "How are those two numbers related?" I asked as I moved from group to group.

59.   *Discussing the hexagon pattern.* After 15 minutes all students had completed Patterns 2 and 3. Since there were only 10 minutes left in class, I thought I would have them talk about Pattern 2 before the bell rang. I started by asking Jungsen to describe the pattern and give the perimeter for the first four. She explained that each train had the same number of hexagons as the train number and that the perimeters were 6, 10, 14, and 18. "What would the perimeter of the next one be?" I asked. James said he thought it would be 24 because the hexagon had six sides and it would be six more. Michele said that she thought it would be 23, because it would be only five more because all of the sides didn't count. I asked if anyone had a different guess. Derek said that he thought it would be 22. A number of students chimed in with, "I agree!" I asked Derek to tell us how he got 22. He said that every time you added a new hexagon, you only added on four more sides. "The perimeters were 6, 10, 14, and 18. You just keep adding four."

60.   I asked if anyone could explain it another way. Kirsten said that she thought she could. "Every time you add another hex," she explained, "you just add two sides on the top and two on the bottom." She pointed to the trains on the overhead (see Figure 2.13) and continued, "If you look at train two, you have four sides on the top, four on the bottom, and the two on the ends. If you look at train three, you added one more hex, which gives you two more sides on the top and two more sides on the bottom. That gives you just four more sides."

FIGURE 2.13. Kirsten's Strategy for Finding the Perimeter of Pattern 2

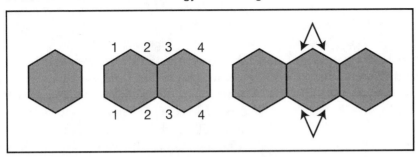

61.   I asked if anyone had found the perimeter of the tenth train. Carmen said that she thought it would be 42. I asked how she got this. She said that the tenth train would have 20 sides on the top, 20 sides on the bottom, and one on each end. I asked how she knew it would be 20. She went on to explain, "The number on top is double the train number. See, the second train has four, the third train has six, so the tenth train would have twenty."

62.   I thanked Carmen for sharing her solution and asked if anyone had another way. Joseph was again waving his hand. I asked Joseph if he used his method on this problem too. He said he did and explained that since each hexagon had six sides, you needed to multiply the train number by 6 to get 60. Then you needed to subtract the inside sides—that would be 18. So it would be 60 minus 18 which was 42. Kirsten asked Joseph if you always subtracted 18 for the tenth train. Joseph said that so far that seemed to work for the squares and the hexagons, but he wasn't sure if it always worked. Kirsten's question was a good one. I made a note to be sure to include a pattern for which it would not work, just to push Joseph to consider what was generalizable about his approach and what wasn't.

63.   I finally asked about the perimeter of the one-hundredth train. It seemed as though everyone thought they had it this time. I took a quick look at the clock. The bell was going to ring any minute. I told students that for homework I wanted them to write down what they thought the perimeter of the one-hundredth one would be and to explain how they figured it out. We would start there the next day and then jump right in and try Pattern 4.

ANALYZING THE CASE

Now that you have had the opportunity to read the case and to consider what students in each classroom were learning, we invite you to consider more broadly the ways in which Mrs. Evans's and Mr. Young's classes are the same and/or different. Here are a few suggestions about how to proceed.

- Review your list of what students in each class appeared to be learning and determine how the two classes were the same and how they were different in terms of what was learned. Identify additional similarities and differences that emerge from a comparison of the two classes. Be sure to cite specific evidence from the case (using paragraph numbers) to support your claims.
- Consider whether the differences between the two classes matter or whether they simply represent two different ways of accomplishing the same goals.
- If you have colleagues who also are reading this case, compare and contrast the similarities and differences you have identified. Note points of disagreement since these are likely to be fruitful topics for ongoing discussion and debate. If you are working on this activity alone, we encourage you to refer to Appendix A, which includes a chart of similarities and differences that were produced by teachers participating in a whole-group discussion of "The Case of Catherine Evans and David Young." You may want to determine whether or not you agree with aspects of this list and examine the rationale for your decision.

You may wish to continue your analysis of the case by considering the questions in the next section. If you currently are teaching mathematics, you might want to proceed to the "Connecting to Your Own Practice" section in which you are encouraged to relate the analysis of the ideas and issues raised in "The Case of Catherine Evans and David Young" to your own teaching practice.

EXTENDING YOUR ANALYSIS OF THE CASE

The questions listed in this section are intended to help you focus on particular aspects of the case related to teacher decision-making and student thinking. If you are working in collaboration with one or more colleagues, the questions can serve as a stimulus for further discussion.

1. Comment on and give examples of whether each teacher's views of mathematics teaching, goals for the lesson, classroom practices, and choice of homework assignment appear to be consistent. What does the homework assignment in each teacher's classroom (Mrs. Evans, para. 28; Mr. Young, para. 63) indicate about that teacher's expectations of students, goals for today's lesson, and goals for the lesson to follow?

2. After a good definition of perimeter does not surface in response to Zeke's misconception (para. 14), Mrs. Evans is convinced that helping Desmond use the class procedure to find the perimeter "would clear up the confusion" (para. 16). Was Mrs. Evans indeed successful in clearing up the confusion (after all, Zeke correctly counts out the perimeter of the next train, in para. 16)? What can you conclude that Desmond and/or Zeke truly knows and understands about perimeter after this episode? What might Desmond and/or Zeke know and understand about perimeter in a context different from the pattern blocks?

3. In Mr. Young's class, Joseph generalizes his method from the square pattern (para. 49) to the triangle pattern (para. 55) and then to the hexagon pattern (para. 62). Another student, Kirsten, questions whether "you always subtracted 18 for the tenth train" (para. 62). Joseph replies that although it has worked so far, he is not sure if it will always work. This suggests to David Young that he needs to "include a pattern for which it would not work, just to push Joseph to consider what was generalizable about his approach and what wasn't" (para. 62). Explain why subtracting 18 for the tenth train has worked for the square, triangle, and hexagon patterns, and create a pattern for which subtracting 18 for the tenth train would not work. Alternatively, consider more broadly what is generalizable about Joseph's approach.

4. Examine the solution methods offered by specific students in "The Case of Catherine Evans and David Young" and discuss whether the students who offered these solutions were ready to move to formal notation. What could Mrs. Evans or Mr. Young have done to facilitate this transition? What might have been gained with respect to student learning by leading students to "invent" symbolic notation? What might have been lost?

5. Neither Catherine Evans nor David Young pushes students to provide written descriptions of their

solution methods. What might Mrs. Evans's students have gained by having a written record of their calculations and procedures? What might Mr. Young's students have gained if they were required to provide written descriptions of their procedures and generalizations, especially those that relate the train number to the perimeter? Would there have been any drawbacks in requiring students to produce written descriptions in either classroom?

6. What might be some ramifications of Catherine Evans removing problematic aspects of the task (para. 7)?

CONNECTING TO YOUR OWN PRACTICE

This section is intended specifically for readers who currently are teaching mathematics. In it, we offer suggestions on ways to connect the specific ideas investigated in "The Case of Catherine Evans and David Young" to a set of larger issues that can be explored in your own classroom. Building on your analysis of "The Case of Catherine Evans and David Young," the activities presented in this section provide opportunities for focused reflection on issues that might be important to your own teaching of mathematics.

- In the "Analyzing the Case" section, you identified similarities and differences between Catherine Evans's and David Young's classrooms. Teach a lesson using the Hexagon-Pattern Task and compare the enactment of the task in your classroom with what occurred in the lessons featured in "The Case of Catherine Evans and David Young." Record the lesson on videotape or audiotape, or have a colleague observe and take notes. As you reflect on the lesson, consider the following questions: In what ways was the pedagogy in your lesson similar to or different from that of Catherine Evans? From that of David Young? In what ways do these similarities or differences influence your students' opportunities to learn mathematics?
- On a notecard, write down one or more pedagogical move(s) from your lesson that you felt were particularly effective in supporting students' learning. Likewise, write down one or more pedagogical move(s) from your lesson that you might need to work on in order to more fully support students' learning. Display the notecards in a place where they will be visible as you plan

future lessons. Reflect on these moves over the next month.
- Catherine Evans and David Young had different ideas about what it meant to experience success as a student of mathematics. Consider your own definition of success. How does it compare with Mrs. Evans's or Mr. Young's definitions? Record a lesson on videotape or audiotape, or have a colleague observe and take notes. As you reflect on the lesson, consider the following questions: In what ways do your notions of success influence your goals for students' learning? What does your notion of success communicate to students about what it means to think and learn mathematically?

EXPLORING CURRICULAR MATERIALS

You may want to explore your mathematics curriculum for ideas related to linear growth by considering the following questions: Are visual pattern tasks used in your curriculum to develop students' understanding of ideas such as variable, covariation, and rate of change? If not, could the curriculum be modified (i.e., by adapting existing tasks or inserting new tasks) so as to provide students with such experiences? How might such experiences contribute to students' understanding of functions?

You also may want to solve additional tasks to continue to explore the mathematical ideas made salient in the case. The following list identifies resources that contain problems that are considered to be "mathematically similar" to the task used in Catherine Evans's and David Young's classes.

Billstein, R., & Williamson, J. (1999a). *Middle grades math thematics: Book 1*. Evanston, IL: McDougal Littell.

Of particular interest is an exploration (pp. 6–7) in which students determine the generalization for two visual patterns made from square tiles.

Education Development Center, Inc. (1998c). *MathScape: Patterns in numbers and shapes: Using algebraic thinking* (Student guide). Mountain View, CA: Creative Publications.

Of particular interest is Lesson 5 (Tiling Garden Beds, pp. 16–17), in which students examine a visual pattern of garden beds framed with a single row of square tiles and determine a generalization that will describe the number of tiles needed to frame any size garden. In addition, students are asked to relate their generalization to the visual pattern.

Foreman, L. C., & Bennett, A. B. Jr. (1995). *Visual mathematics: Course I, Lessons 16–30*. Salem, OR: The Math Learning Center.

Of particular interest in Lesson 18 (Pattern Block Perimeters) are Actions 4–8 and Focus Master A (pp. 204–205). Students are asked to determine the perimeter of a pattern train and to form a generalization about the perimeter of any pattern train in the sequence. A subset of the problems found in this lesson is identical to the problems that appear in "The Case of Catherine Evans and David Young."

Lappan, G., Fey, J., Fitzgerald, W., Friel, S., & Phillips, E. (2002b). *Say it with symbols: Algebraic reasoning. Connected mathematics.*

Of particular interest is Problem 2.1 (pp. 20–21), in which students are asked to generalize the number of tiles needed to form the border of a square swimming pool.

The Mathematics in Context Development Team. (1997a). *Mathematics in context: Building formulas (Student guide).* In National Center for Research in Mathematical Sciences Education & Freudenthal Institute (Eds.), *Mathematics in context.* Chicago: Encyclopaedia Britannica.

Of particular interest are problems 1–5 (pp. 2–4), which present students with patterns of sidewalk tiles that generalize into linear relationships.

CONNECTING TO OTHER IDEAS AND ISSUES

If you have additional time, you may want to explore some aspect of the case in more depth. The resources identified in this section provide some possibilities for exploring the mathematical and pedagogical issues raised by the case. For example, you might: (1) analyze "The Case of Catherine Evans and David Young" with respect to the recommendations made by English and Warren (1998) and consider whether Mrs. Evans or Mr. Young appears to have followed these recommendations; (2) compare the strategies used by the students in "The Case of Catherine Evans and David Young" with those used on a similar task described in Bishop, Otto, & Lubinski (2001), in Scanlon (1996), or in Chapter 1 of *Navigating Through Algebra in Grades 6–8* (Friel et al., 2001); (3) identify places in Catherine Evans's and David Young's lessons where students were beginning to grapple with the notion of function and consider how the metaphor of a function as a mail carrier as described in Sand (1996) could be used to deepen students' understanding of function; (4) using the key elements of successful mathematics teaching described in Smith (2000), analyze Mrs. Evans's and Mr. Young's lessons for evidence of success and consider your own struggles with redefining success in a "reform classroom"; or (5) using Van de Walle (2004) as an example, consider how students in "The Case of Catherine Evans and David Young" explored and ex-

pressed perimeter patterns using different representations and how Catherine Evans and David Young could have encouraged students to use and make connections between different representations.

Bishop, J. W., Otto, A. D., & Lubinski, C. A. (2001). Promoting algebraic reasoning using students' thinking. *Mathematics Teaching in the Middle School, 6,* 508–514.

This article describes a classroom lesson that features a task similar to the one used by Catherine Evans and David Young. A discussion of the teacher's and students' roles in the lesson emphasizes the importance of having students share and explain their algebraic thinking process. The strategies used by the students also are discussed, along with the development of these strategies into algebraic thinking (strategies include recursion, direct-modeling, counting, and determining relationships based on the geometric pattern in the figure).

English, L. D., & Warren, E. A. (1998). Introducing the variable through pattern exploration. *Mathematics Teacher, 91,* 166–170.

This article provides some insight into the potential of pattern exploration to introduce and develop the concept of variable. The article examines students' thinking when grappling with patterning tasks and provides recommendations for enhancing student learning from such tasks.

Friel, S., Rachlin, S., Doyle, D., with Nygard, C., Pugalee, D., & Ellis, M. (2001). *Principles and standards for school mathematics navigations series: Navigating through algebra in grades 6–8.* Reston, VA: National Council of Teachers of Mathematics.

This book is part of the Navigation Series intended to support teachers' implementation of the Principles and Standards (NCTM, 2000). The book focuses on algebraic concepts in grades 6–8. Chapter 1, "Understanding Patterns, Relations, and Functions," offers activities in which students can explore, represent, analyze, and generalize a variety of patterns using tables, graphs, words, and symbolic rules. The chapter also looks at student work to analyze students' mathematical understanding of variable and relationships, as well as the strategies students use in generalizing patterns.

Sand, M. (1996). A function as a mail carrier. *Mathematics Teacher, 89,* 468–469.

This article discusses some of the difficulties secondary students have understanding the concept of function. In particular, the article addresses the ideas that a function is an object rather than a process and that a function does not always have to be defined by a symbolic rule. The author then suggests the metaphor of a function as a mail carrier, as a way to help students understand the concept of function.

Scanlon, D. S. (1996). Algebra is cool: Reflections on a changing pedagogy in an urban setting. In D. Schifter (Ed.), *What's happening in math class? Envisioning new practices through teacher narratives* (pp. 65–77). New York: Teachers College Press.

This chapter describes two algebra lessons involving pattern tasks that were taught in an urban high school classroom. The first is similar to the activity used by Catherine Evans and David Young. The second employs a nonlinear pattern involving staircases and the number of cubes used to build them. The role of the teacher and students is discussed as students explore the patterns, develop their understanding of variable, explain their mathematical reasoning, and create strategies (including recursion, direct-modeling, and relating the formula to the figure) for finding the general rule.

Smith, M. S. (2000). Reflections on practice: Redefining success in mathematics teaching and learning. *Mathematics Teaching in the Middle School*, *5*, 378–382, 386.

This article describes the struggles of one middle school teacher as she begins to redefine what it means to successfully teach mathematics. Her growth over the course of the year is described in detail. Key elements of the definition of success are provided for the teacher and the students; these include examples of new expectations for students, teacher actions that are consistent with the new expectations, and classroom-based indicators of success. The example lesson discussed is very similar to the lesson found in "The Case of Catherine Evans and David Young."

Van de Walle, J. (2004). *Elementary and middle school mathematics: Teaching developmentally*. Boston: Pearson Education/ Allyn & Bacon.

Chapter 23, "Exploring Functions," discusses the big ideas related to the concept of function and the importance of exploring functions through five different representations: context, table, language, graph, and equation. In particular, the section "Functions from Patterns" discusses how perimeter patterns, like the ones used by Catherine Evans and David Young, can be explored and expressed using each of the five representations.

Examining Nonlinear Growth Patterns

The Case of Ed Taylor

Chapter 3 has been designed to engage readers in considering important issues in mathematics teaching and learning related to nonlinear growth.

Prior to reading "The Case of Ed Taylor"—the centerpiece of this chapter—we suggest that all readers begin by completing the Opening Activity. The primary purpose of the Opening Activity is to engage readers with the mathematical ideas that will be encountered when reading the case.

OPENING ACTIVITY

The square-pattern and S-pattern tasks shown in Figure 3.1 feature the same patterns used in "The Case of Ed Taylor." We encourage you to find more than one way to describe any figure in the pattern and to look for ways in which these descriptions might be connected to the geometric structure of the pattern.

Once you have completed the activity, you may want to refer to Appendix B, which contains a set of solutions based on strategies generated by teachers who completed the Opening Activity as part of a professional development experience featuring "The Case of Ed Taylor." You are encouraged to make sense of the different solutions provided and to consider the relationship between your solution and those produced by others.

READING THE CASE

As you read the case, we encourage you to pick one student in Ed Taylor's class and think about what the student understands, what you are not sure the student understands, and what questions you would like to ask the student. For example, you might think that Michael demonstrated an understanding of how the S-pattern grows by indicating that you always add a column and a row to the previous figure in order to get the new one, yet you may not be sure that he understands how to find the number of tiles for any step in the pattern without first knowing the number of tiles for the previous step. Perhaps you would like to ask him if he can find a relationship between the number of columns and rows in a figure and the step number of the figure in order to help him generalize the shape of and number of tiles in any step in the pattern.

We encourage you to write down your thoughts about the student's understanding and cite evidence from the case (i.e., paragraph numbers) to support your claims. This activity will help you to think deeply about the student learning that is occurring in "The Case of Ed Taylor" and prepare you for further analysis of the case. This also can serve as a topic for discussion with a colleague who also has read the case or as an issue to investigate as you read additional cases.

If you currently are teaching mathematics, issues that surface in reading "The Case of Ed Taylor" might serve as a starting point for exploration in your own classroom. For example, you might wonder if your students will be able to find the number of tiles for any step without knowing the number of tiles in the previous step, and how you might help students who use this recursive approach develop an approach that expresses the relationship in two variables. We will discuss additional connections to your own practice at the end of the chapter.

FIGURE 3.1. The Square Pattern and S-Pattern for the Opening Activity in "The Case of Ed Taylor"

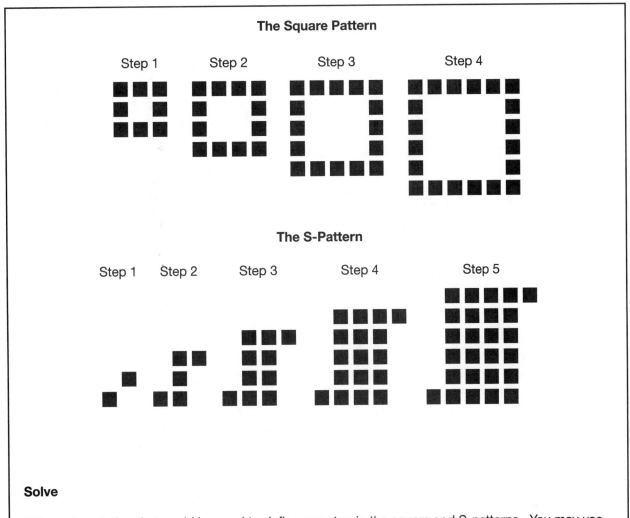

Solve

Write a description that could be used to define any step in the square and S-patterns. You may use drawings, words, and numbers in your explanation. Your answer should be clear enough so that another person could read it and understand your thinking.

Consider

How are the patterns the same and how are they different?

THE CASE OF ED TAYLOR

1. Since Ed Taylor arrived at Richland Middle School he has been impressed with his mathematics teacher colleagues. They seemed to have energy and excitement about their work and they seemed to be making a difference in children's lives—students show growth in their ability to think, reason, and solve problems; their basic skills have improved; and greater numbers of students are eligible to take algebra in 9th grade than historically was the case.

2. The mathematics curriculum they were using at Richland was different—students were actively engaged in constructing and explaining mathematics through the use of models, manipulatives, sketches, and diagrams, and not just sitting quietly listening to lectures. Ed thought this new approach to mathematics learning made sense. Although he had spent his first 2 years at Richland teaching reading, language arts, and social studies, when a math opening became available at the end of his second year, he jumped at the chance to be a member of the community the math teachers had established and to teach what he saw as an exciting and challenging curriculum.

3. Ed is now completing his first year as a mathematics teacher at Richland. Although it has not been an easy year, he feels that he has learned a tremendous amount and has done a pretty good job with his students. He attributes any success he has experienced to Ron Trenton, his colleague who also teaches 7th-grade math. Ron and Ed have a shared period twice a week during which time they discuss the concepts they are going to be teaching, jointly plan lessons, and reflect on how things are going. According to Ed, "Nearly everything we talk about has to do with creating models so that the students will get a better understanding of the concepts."

4. Although it is clear that Ron's support has been extremely helpful, Ed, too, deserves a lot of the credit. Recognizing that he did not have a strong preparation in mathematics, he decided to enroll in a series of three courses that focused on learning mathematics—specifically the mathematics that was in the curriculum he was teaching. Ed is currently enrolled in a course that features a visual approach to teaching and learning algebra. He decided to take this class, along with a few of his colleagues, because algebra was a strand that cut across all grade levels of the middle school curriculum. In fact, it was the last unit he would be working on in his 7th-grade classes, and he was determined to be at least one step ahead of his students.

Ed Taylor Talks About His Class

5. My 7th-grade students were introduced to patterns in the second lesson of the curriculum back in 6th grade. They continued to revisit numeric and geometric patterns as they explored different topics (e.g., odd and even numbers, perimeter, ratios) throughout the year. The focus in 6th grade had been on identifying patterns, describing what larger arrangements in a pattern (like the tenth or twentieth step) would look like, and describing a method for finding the total number of

objects in a pattern for a specific number (e.g., how many objects would be in the twentieth arrangement in the pattern).

6. I thought patterns were useful because they got kids thinking, reasoning, and making conjectures. But as a result of the work I have been doing in the algebra class I am taking, I now realize that early experiences with patterns can lay the groundwork for exploring ideas like variables and functions. This year my 7th-graders began work with patterns by writing directions for finding the total number of objects for any step in the pattern sequence, and moved to using symbols instead of words for these descriptions. I am now in the second day of a unit on patterns, formulas, and graphing. Yesterday my students worked on the Square-Pattern Task (shown in Figure 3.2), first in small groups and then in a whole-class discussion.

7. Today we are going to engage in the same types of activities for another pattern. Tomorrow students will create data tables and graph both patterns and make observations about the graphs. Ron and I still need to plan out exactly what we are going to do beyond that point, but we both agree that we will begin to move away from using physical arrangements of tile patterns so that we can have students begin to consider a larger set of values for their graphs.

FIGURE 3.2. The Square-Pattern Task from Mr. Taylor's Previous Lesson

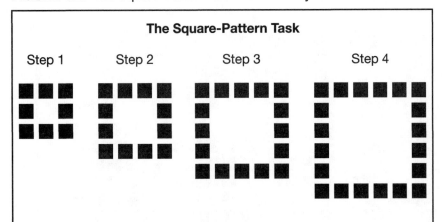

The Square-Pattern Task

Step 1   Step 2   Step 3   Step 4

a. Sketch the next two steps in the pattern.

b. Make observations about the pattern that help describe larger steps in the pattern.

c. Sketch and describe two steps in the pattern that are larger than the twentieth step.

d. Describe a method for finding the total number of tiles in the larger steps.

e. Write a generalized description/formula to find the total number of tiles in any step in the pattern.

The Class

8.   I distributed the S-Pattern Task (shown in Figure 3.3) to students and
asked that they spend 5 minutes working on the task independently. Once
students had time to consider the task individually, I gave them another 15
minutes to discuss the task in their small groups. I realized that this might
not be enough time to complete all aspects of the task, but it would be
sufficient for students to have ideas to add to the whole-class discussion,
which was where I planned to spend most of the math hour today.

9.   *Creating the next two steps.* After the groups had worked for about
15 minutes, I called the class together and asked who wanted to go to the
overhead and show the next two steps in the S-pattern (Part a). Many
hands shot up, including Michael's. He doesn't volunteer very often so I
like to call on him when he does. He drew the sixth and seventh steps in
the pattern, as shown in Figure 3.4, while the other students continued
to talk quietly in their groups. When he was finished with the drawing he
simply stated, "These would be the next ones in the pattern." The other
students in the class were nodding in agreement.

10.   I asked Michael if he could explain how he knew what the sixth and
seventh steps would look like. Michael explained, "You add another
column, then another row, but keep the tiles sticking out on the top and
bottom rows." I asked him if he could show us. Starting with the tile
arrangement shown in Step 5 (see Figure 3.5.a), Michael drew in a new

FIGURE 3.3. The S-Pattern Task

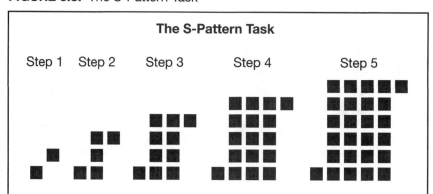

a. Sketch the next two steps in the pattern.

b. Make observations about the pattern that help describe larger
   steps in the pattern.

c. Sketch and describe two steps in the pattern that are larger than
   the twentieth step.

d. Describe a method for finding the total number of tiles in the
   larger steps.

e. Write a generalized description/formula to find the total number
   of tiles in any step in the pattern.

Illustration from *Visual Mathematics Course II, Lessons 1–10* published by The Math Learning
Center. Copyright ©1996 by The Math Learning Center, Salem, Oregon. Reprinted by permission.

FIGURE 3.4. Michael's Drawings of the Sixth and Seventh Steps in the S-Pattern

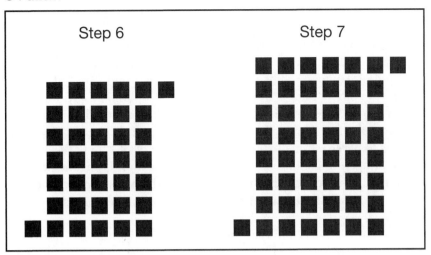

column of squares and shaded them while repeating, "You start with the one that came before and you add another column." He then drew in a new row of squares and shaded them as he continued, "You then add a new row of squares." Once he had shown how he got from the fifth step to the sixth step (as shown in Figure 3.5.b), he repeated the process showing how you could get to the seventh step by again adding a new column and a new row to Step 6 (Figure 3.5.c). I asked Michael if he could build any step in the pattern. Michael replied that you could always get the next one if you knew what the last one was—by adding a column then a row.

11.   *Making observations about the pattern arrangements.* I then asked students to share the observations they had about the arrangements in the pattern while Jason numbered and recorded the class observations on a sheet of newsprint on the easel in the front of the room. I wanted to be able

FIGURE 3.5. (a) The Initial Tile Arrangement in Michael's Solution; (b) Michael Adds a New Column and a New Row of Squares to the Fifth Step in the Pattern to Produce the Sixth Step; (c) Michael Repeats the Process of "Adding a Column and Then a Row" to Produce the Seventh Step

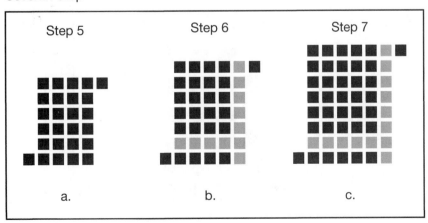

to keep a record of the observations students came up with as a group, so that we could refer to the observations during the rest of the discussion.

12.   Sorrell started us off with the observation that "the top and bottom rows always have one extra tile sticking out on the side." I repeated what he said, both to help Jason as he tried to record the comment and perhaps, more important, because repeating something out loud gives me (and my students) a chance to think about it. I said, "OK," deciding there was nothing else I wanted to pursue at this point. I asked for other observations. Angela claimed that "whatever the step number is, there is one less column." Although I thought I knew what she meant, I have learned to never assume that my students mean what I think they mean. I asked Angela to go up to the overhead and show us. Using the fifth pattern in the sequence, shown in Figure 3.6, she pointed out that there were only four full columns of tiles. The number of columns, she explained, was one less than the step number, or 5.

13.   The observations continued with Sharla pointing out that "the top row is always the step number." I repeated what she said while framing my next question. I asked, "What about the bottom row?" She indicated that the top row was the same as the bottom row and that they were both equal to the step number. I asked if there were any more observations. No one was volunteering but I remembered that Maria's group had been discussing one point that had not yet been made. I asked Maria if she would like to share her group's observation. Maria stated that "the number of rows is always one more than the step number." I quickly looked at Step 5 (Figure 3.7) and tested this, counting out loud 1-2-3-4-5-6 and repeating what she had said. I said, "Nice observation," when I confirmed that this was in fact true.

14.   I asked if anyone had any observations about the entire arrangement. Dwayne said that "if you square the step number and add one you get the total number of tiles." I asked Dwayne if he would come up and explain his observation. He said that he made a table for the first 5 steps, as shown in Table 3.1, and then he looked for a pattern. ("Looking for a pattern" is a strategy that my students often use when trying to make

FIGURE 3.6. Angela's Drawing of the Fifth Step in the S-Pattern That Shows "Whatever the Step Number Is, There Is One Less Column"

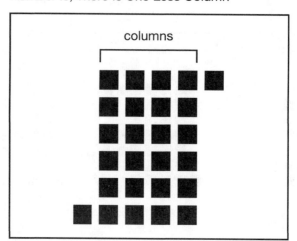

FIGURE 3.7. Mr. Taylor Tests Maria's Observation That "the Number of Rows Is Always One More than the Step Number"

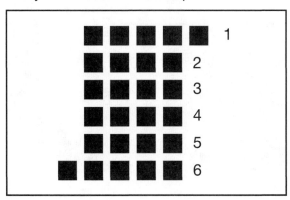

sense of a new situation.) He said that he noticed that if he squared a step number—the number in the first column—and then added one to it, he got the number of tiles (the number in the second column). He explained, "See, if you take Step 2 that would be 2 times 2 which is 4, plus 1 which is 5—and that is the number of tiles." I asked the entire class to check this out for Steps 6 and 7 to see if it worked. Joey yelled out, "If you do Step 6, it should be 37 and I just counted them up and it works!" Marsha added that it also worked for Step 7, since there were 50 tiles in the step, which was 7 times 7 plus 1.

15. I thanked Dwayne for his contribution to our list of observations, then asked for additional observations about the pattern arrangements. Renee said that each arrangement has a square in the middle and two skinny rectangles on the top and bottom. She went up to the overhead and, referring to the fifth step, she drew a box around the square in the middle and ovals around the rectangles at the top and the bottom, as shown in Figure 3.8.a. Renee explained that "they all have a square and two rectangles like this." I thanked Renee for her contribution and asked if there were any others. Kevin said he thought the arrangement was a rectangle with an extra square on the top right and bottom left corners, as shown in Figure 3.8.b.

16. At this point I felt that we probably had exhausted the observations students were going to make. I decided before we moved on that I wanted students to look at the list of observations we had compiled. They seemed

TABLE 3.1. Dwayne's Table for the S-Pattern

Step Number	Number of Tiles
1	2
2	5
3	10
4	17
5	26

FIGURE 3.8. (a) Renee's Drawing to Illustrate "a Square and Two Rectangles"; (b) Kevin's Drawing to Illustrate "a Rectangle with an Extra Square on the Top Right and Bottom Left Corners"

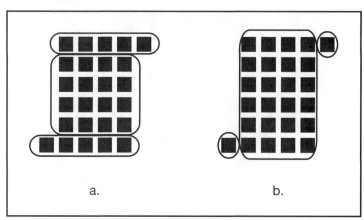

a.   b.

very different to me and I was interested in seeing if my students would see some of the differences. I directed students' attention to the list that Jason had been compiling at the front of the room (see Figure 3.9) and asked them if they wanted to make any comments about the observations and how they were similar to or different from one another.

17.   Jamie said that Dwayne's observation—Number 5 on the list—was different from the others because it was about the number of tiles. She explained that it would give you the number of tiles in any step, but it wouldn't tell you what the step would look like. I asked if that mattered. Jamie went on to say that it would matter if you were trying to build the next one because all you would know was the number of tiles not the shape they would be in, but if you just wanted to make a graph, it would be an easy way.

18.   I asked the class what they thought about Jamie's comment that Dwayne's observation would give you the number of tiles but not tell you what the step would look like. Denise said that she agreed with

FIGURE 3.9. Mr. Taylor's Students' Observations About the S-Pattern

---

Observations About the S-Pattern

1. The top and bottom rows always have one extra tile sticking out on the side. (Sorrell)
2. Whatever the step number is, there is one less column. (Angela)
3. The top row (and the bottom row) is always the step number. (Sharla)
4. The number of rows is always one more than the step number. (Maria)
5. If you square the step number and add one you get the total number of tiles. (Dwayne)
6. Each step has a square in the middle and two skinny rectangles on the top and bottom. (Renee)
7. The arrangement is a rectangle with an extra square on the top right and bottom left corners. (Kevin)

Jamie, but that none of the observations gave you enough information to actually build one. However, if you took a bunch of them together you probably could do it. I commented that I thought Denise had a good point and that as we continued with the problem, I wanted them to think about what observations they were drawing on in their descriptions.

19.   *Describing larger steps.* We now moved on to Parts c and d, which involved providing a description of a larger step number and describing a method for finding the number of tiles in the step. Lamont went to the overhead to describe and sketch the twenty-fifth step. He said that there would be 26 rows and 24 columns with an extra one on the first and last rows. I asked, "Are you sure?" I suggested that we go back to the observations and see if we could check this out. Referring to the list of observations, Lamont said that he was using Observations 1, 2, and 4. I went over these quickly in my head and replied "You're absolutely right, Lamont. That was an excellent observation and an excellent way of describing what the twenty-fifth step number would look like. Good job!" I like to praise students for the kind of thinking they exhibit—then praise is connected to something you want to encourage.

20.   Lamont started to draw each tile in the arrangement. I suggested that he use bars to represent the collection of tiles rather than draw them out individually, since we just needed a sketch that would help us figure out what we needed to do next. Lamont then drew the diagram shown in Figure 3.10. I had learned the hard way that drawing larger arrangements was really time-consuming and a great opportunity for the rest of the class to completely lose interest in what we were doing.

21.   I then asked, "How can we figure out the total number of tiles?" Dwayne immediately said that you need to square the step number and add one. Although I was expecting a description that might be more closely tied to the picture Lamont had just drawn, I was happy to see that

FIGURE 3.10. Lamont's Diagram of the Twenty-Fifth Step

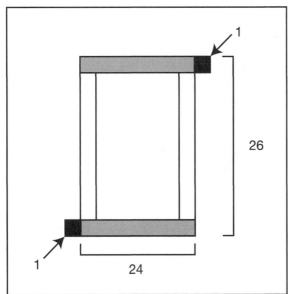

Dwayne was applying the observation he had made. "What is the step number?" I asked. The entire class responded, "25." I asked if anyone knew what 25 times 25 was off the top of their head. No one answered. I told Lamont to grab the overhead calculator, which was on the cart, and reminded students that if they needed a calculator to get one. I don't believe students need to master basic skills and facts before studying more advanced topics, but they need to be able to get correct answers for computations without getting too bogged down. I decided to model a mental math approach to the computation that involved decomposing 25 into (10 + 10 + 5) and then multiplying each number by 25. I asked what 10 times 25 was. I got a choral response of 250. So, I reasoned out loud, "Two of those would be 500. So then there would be 5 left to multiply, and 5 times 25 was 125. So 500 + 125 was 625. Plus one was 626."

22.   I then asked Myesha which step number she would like to describe. She suggested 300! I asked what it would look like based on the observations that we had made. Myesha said that there would be a total of 300 in the first and last rows and then 299 rows of 299. I wasn't exactly sure where this was coming from so I asked her to go to the overhead and show us. Myesha said that she used Observation 6—the one Renee had described—and she drew the sketch shown in Figure 3.11. She explained that the two shaded bars represented the 299 rows and that each row would have 299 in it. This would be the "square in the middle" Renee had talked about. Then, she continued, there would be two rows of 300—the top and bottom rows. These would be the "skinny rectangles." She went on to say that she found the number of tiles by multiplying 299 × 299 and then adding on 600 (2 × 300). We again worked through the multiplication, this time using the calculator, and came up with 90,001.

23.   *Constructing a formula.* We then moved on to the last question—Part e—finding a general description or formula. Ning was the first to

FIGURE 3.11. Myesha's Diagram of the Three-Hundredth Step

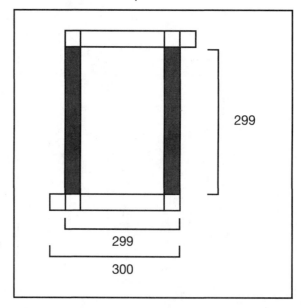

volunteer to share her formula. She went to the overhead and wrote
T = (N + 1) (N − 1 + 2). She explained that N + 1 was the number of
rows (Observation 4)—so in Step 5 there were 5 + 1, or 6, rows—and
that N − 1 was the number of columns (Observation 2)—so in Step 5
there were 5 − 1, or 4, columns, as shown in Figure 3.12. She went on to
say that she "multiplied the base times the height and added the two on
because of the two extra." I could see the mismatch between what she
was saying and the formula that she had written, but how could I help
her see it? (I don't like to just correct mistakes. I don't think students
learn from this. I try to guide students to the right answer by asking
appropriate questions.)

24.   I asked Ning to use the formula to determine the number of tiles in
Step 5. She proceeded to show the following work:

$$(N + 1)(N − 1 + 2) = T$$
$$(5 + 1)(5 − 1 + 2) = T$$
$$(6)(6) = T$$
$$36 = T$$

When she was finished she had a curious look on her face and announced, "I think I messed up." This was confirmed when she counted
the number of tiles and found there were only 26 tiles in the fifth step. I
asked Ning what she was trying to do in her formula. She said she was
trying to find the area of a rectangle. I asked what the dimensions were
of the rectangle in Step 5. She said it was 4 times 6. I asked her to look at
her formula. Tonya, who had been working in the same group as Ning,
volunteered, "I think we put the two in the wrong place. We need to add
it last." I said this was an interesting observation and asked Ning if it
made a difference where the two was. She said it did—by putting 2
inside the parenthesis, instead of having N − 1 columns she had N − 1 +
2, or N + 1, columns. So, she announced, she found the number of tiles
in a 6 by 6 rectangle not a 6 by 4! I thanked Ning for working through
the problem with us. I pointed out to the class that this was a good
example of the importance of parentheses.

FIGURE 3.12. Ning's Diagram to Explain Her
Formula

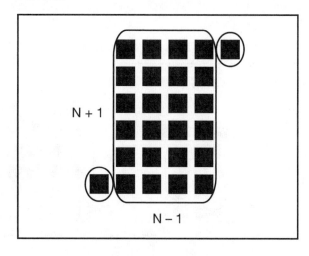

25.   Now that we had the revised formula, I asked Ning which observations she had used. She said that she used Kevin's observation about the rectangle and the two squares. Darrell said that she also must have used Observations 2 and 4 to get the number of rows and columns in the rectangle. Ning said that she hadn't thought about them, but agreed that she needed to get those numbers from somewhere!

26.   The next student to share his formula was David. He said that he thought about the arrangement the way Renee did—a square in the middle with two skinny rectangles—and wrote the formula $(N \times 2) + PN \times PN = T$. Before I could ask any questions, he explained that PN stood for "previous number." He went on to illustrate his formula, as shown in Figure 3.13. Using the third step in the pattern, he explained that "it is N times 2 because you have 2 rows of the step number. So in Number 3 you have 2 rows of three. Then PN times PN so for Step 3 it would be 2 times 2." He then went on to show how this would apply to Steps 4 and 5. I told David that this was an excellent observation and asked if we could write the second part of the formula—$PN \times PN$—a different way. Jamal suggested that we use $(N - 1)(N - 1)$. I asked David if this made sense to him. Before responding, David worked through the formula with the new component to see if it worked. After a minute or so he said, "Yeah, I think it is the same."

27.   Before going on I wanted to talk about what had just occurred. I told the class that the most important thing was that David came up with a formula that made sense to him. But if you want to communicate to everyone else, using N throughout the formula consistently will help everyone else understand it.

28.   Next Charles indicated that he had made a square out of the tiles. He went to the overhead to show us what he had done. As shown in Figure 3.14.a, he said that he moved the bottom row up to make a new column. On the overhead he drew in the tiles in their new position, as shown in Figure 3.14.b, and crossed out the last row. I asked, "Why is making a square a good thing to do?" He said that you could "multiply easier," almost as a question not a statement. I went on to say this was excellent thinking, but that I wanted him to explain it. I really believe that being able to explain how you get an answer and why it makes sense is as important as getting a correct answer. He said that if it was square, you could square the side to find out how many tiles were in the step the way Dwayne had said. I asked, "What is the length of the side in your

FIGURE 3.13. David's Diagrams to Explain His Formula

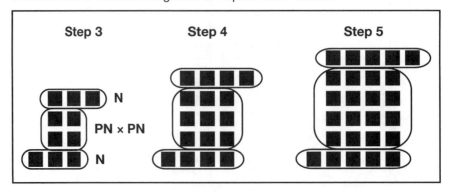

FIGURE 3.14. (a) Charles Illustrates How to Move the Tiles to Make a Square; (b) Charles Draws the Tiles in Their New Position

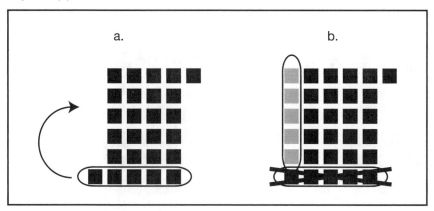

square?" He replied, "Five." I then asked how many tiles would be in the pattern, and he replied, "Twenty-six because you have to add the extra one." I then asked if he could find the number of tiles in any step in the pattern. Charles said, "Sure, just multiply the step number times itself and add one," and wrote the formula $T = N^2 + 1$ on the overhead. I told him this was excellent thinking.

29.   I asked if anyone had written a different description for the pattern. Beverly went to the overhead and wrote $N \times N + 1 = T$. I asked her what she meant by $N \times N$. Beverly explained that this meant "the step number times the step number." I asked her how she was seeing this in the pattern since, from my perspective, this was exactly what Charles had just done. Beverly explained, "In Step 2, two groups of two; in Step 3, three groups of three; in Step 4, four groups of four." I did not see this at all and asked her to show us this on the diagram. She said the words again and this time circled tiles on the steps, as shown in Figure 3.15— "one group of one in Step 1; two groups of two in Step 2; three groups of three in Step 3; four groups of four in Step 4, five groups of five in Step 5." I indicated that this was an excellent method.

30.   Tonya said that Beverly's approach was "sorta like what Charles did before except he moved the rows around." I asked Tonya if she would show us what she meant. Starting with Beverly's step, Tonya drew Figure 3.16, showing how you would just move the top row and get a square.

FIGURE 3.15. Beverly's Diagram to Explain Her Formula

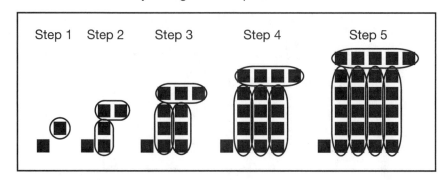

Step 1   Step 2   Step 3   Step 4   Step 5

FIGURE 3.16. Tonya's Diagram Showing How Beverly's Approach Is Similar to Charles's Approach

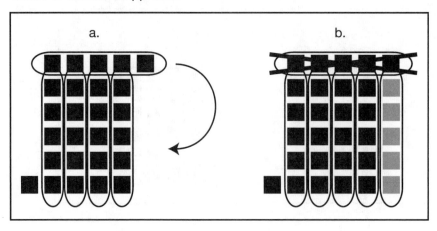

Then, she added, you could put that extra one anywhere you wanted, it didn't matter. I asked if both Charles's and Beverly's arrangements showed five groups of five. Jamar said they did, but one was a square and one wasn't.

31.   At this point I noticed that time was almost up. We had covered a lot of ground and I wanted students to reflect on the formulas that had just been suggested and to see if they could justify that they were in fact equivalent. As shown in Figure 3.17, I listed the four formulas on the board and added a fifth one for consideration that had been suggested by one of my other classes. I then asked students to take out their journals and spend the last 5 minutes writing an entry in which they discussed the different formulas and explained why they were equivalent. I reminded them that the next day we would be graphing both the S-pattern and the square pattern and making observations about the graphs.

FIGURE 3.17. Formulas Developed by Mr. Taylor's Students for the Number of Tiles in the S-Pattern

Formula 1	$T = (N - 1)(N + 1) + 2$ (Ning)
Formula 2	$T = (N - 1)(N - 1) + (N \times 2)$ (David)
Formula 3	$T = N^2 + 1$ (Charles)
Formula 4	$N \times N + 1 = T$ (Beverly)
Formula 5	$T = (N + 1)(N - 1) - 2N$

ANALYZING THE CASE

Now that you have read the case and have considered the mathematical understanding of one of the students in Ed Taylor's class, we encourage you to think about student learning more generally and about how Ed Taylor appeared to support students' learning. Here are a few suggestions about how to proceed.

- Identify the key pedagogical move(s) Ed Taylor made that appear to have supported students' learning. For each move identified, also discuss the following: why Ed Taylor might have made the move (rationale for move), and how it supported his students' learning of mathematics (implications of move). It is helpful to create a three-column chart showing "key pedagogical move," "rationale for move," and "implications of move." We encourage you to cite specific evidence from the case (e.g., paragraph numbers) to support each idea recorded in your chart. You might begin this process by focusing on the student you analyzed when you read the case and what he or she learned. Consider what Mr. Taylor did to support this student's learning and why you think he did it.
- If you have colleagues who also are reading this case, compare and contrast the ideas in your individual charts and possibly generate a master chart. Note points of disagreement since these are likely to be topics for ongoing discussion and debate. If you are working on this activity alone, we encourage you to refer to Appendix B, which includes a chart of pedagogical moves, rationales for moves, and implications of moves that was produced by teachers participating in a whole-group discussion of Ed Taylor's teaching practices. You may want to note points of agreement and disagreement and flag issues that you wish to pursue.

You may wish to continue your analysis of the case by considering the questions in the next section. Alternatively, you can skip the next section and proceed directly to the "Connecting to Your Own Practice" section in which you are encouraged to relate the analysis of the ideas and issues raised in "The Case of Ed Taylor" to your own teaching practice.

EXTENDING YOUR ANALYSIS OF THE CASE

The questions listed in this section are intended to help you focus on particular aspects of the case related to teacher decision-making and student thinking. If you are working in collaboration with one or more colleagues, the questions that follow can serve as stimulus for further discussion.

1. Rather than giving his students the original version of the task as it appeared in the curricular materials (the version that appears in the Opening Activity), Mr. Taylor and his colleagues adapted the task by adding Parts a through d. Why do you think they made this change? What impact do you think the changes in the task had on the level of difficulty of the task? What impact do you think the changes in the task may have had on student learning?

2. Consider the explanation to Part a given by Michael (para. 10). What does Michael's explanation tell you about what he understands and how he is thinking about the pattern? How is Michael's thinking about the problem similar to or different from the thinking of Ning, David, Charles, or Beverly? Can you create a generalization for the pattern based on Michael's way of thinking about how the pattern increases from one step to the next?

3. Mr. Taylor ends the class by asking students to discuss the five different formulas that were on the board and to explain why they were equivalent (para. 31). Why do you think Mr. Taylor added the fifth formula? How would you suggest Mr. Taylor use his students' journal reflections as the basis for a discussion the following day? How would this fit with what he had planned for the class—graphing both the S- and square patterns and making observations about them?

4. How would you expect Mr. Taylor's students to justify why the five formulas are algebraically equivalent?

5. Mr. Taylor comments, "I don't like to just correct mistakes. I don't think students learn from this. I try to guide students to the right answer by asking appropriate questions" (para. 23). Discuss whether you agree with Mr. Taylor and why. Cite examples from the case that are consistent or inconsistent with his stated belief and how Mr. Taylor's actions may have influenced student learning in positive or negative ways.

6. For the next class, Mr. Taylor wants students to graph both the S-pattern and the square pattern. What observations can his students make about these graphs? What mathematics will Mr. Taylor

be able to have his students explore during this lesson?

CONNECTING TO YOUR OWN PRACTICE

In this section, we offer ways to connect the specific ideas investigated in "The Case of Ed Taylor" to a set of larger issues that can be explored in your own classroom. Building on your analysis of "The Case of Ed Taylor," the activities presented in this section provide opportunities for focused reflection on issues that might be important to your own teaching of mathematics.

- In the "Analyzing the Case" section, you identified ways in which Ed Taylor supported students' learning. Choose one of the "key pedagogical moves" made by Ed Taylor during the lesson that currently is not part of your pedagogical repertoire. For example, you may be curious about the ways in which Mr. Taylor presses students for justifications and explanations. You might then plan and teach a lesson in which you make a concerted effort to press students for justifications and explanations. If possible, videotape your teaching of the lesson or have a colleague observe and take notes. Then reflect alone or with a colleague on the impact of the pedagogical move on students' learning or engagement. If no impact was noted, consider ways in which the pedagogy can be refined.
- Give your students the S-Pattern Task or a similar task from your curriculum in order to discover the strategies your students use to solve problems of this type. Review students' responses and identify the different strategies and representations used by students. Develop a set of questions you could use to help students make connections between different solution paths.

EXPLORING CURRICULAR MATERIALS

You may want to explore mathematics curricula for ideas related to nonlinear growth patterns by considering the following questions: Are nonlinear patterns found in your curriculum? If so, what opportunities do students have to compare linear and nonlinear patterns? How would making such comparisons help develop students' understanding of functions and functional relationships? If nonlinear patterns are not found in your curriculum, how and where could they be included so

as to provide students with opportunities to expand their view of functions?

You may want to solve additional tasks to continue to explore the mathematical ideas made salient in the case. The following list identifies resources that contain problems that are considered to be mathematically similar to the task used in Ed Taylor's class.

Billstein, R., & Williamson, J. (1999b). *Middle grades math thematics: Book 2.* Evanston, IL: McDougal Littell.

Of particular interest is an exploration activity (pp. 14–16) that encourages students to use tables and graphs to explore a visual pattern made from square tiles.

Education Development Center, Inc., (1998). *MathScape: Patterns in numbers and shapes: Using algebraic thinking* (Student guide). Mountain View, CA: Creative Publications.

Of particular interest is Lesson 4 (Letter Perfect, pp. 14–15), in which students explore several different visual patterns made of square tiles and are encouraged to make connections between the patterns and their symbolic representations.

Foreman, L. C., & Bennett, Jr., A. B., (1996). *Visual mathematics: Course II, Lessons 1–10.* Salem, OR: The Math Learning Center.

Of particular interest in Lesson 9 (Tile Patterns and Graphing) are Actions 2–5 in the Focus Teacher Activity (pp. 126–128). Students are asked to explore the same patterning task as featured in "The Case of Ed Taylor" and also are asked to create a bar graph and a coordinate graph based on their results.

Lappan, G., Fey, J., Fitzgerald, W., Friel, S., & Phillips, E. (1998). *Frogs, fleas, and painted cubes: Quadratic relationships. Connected mathematics.* Menlo Park, CA: Dale Seymour.

Of particular interest are Applications Problems 2, 3, 16, and 18 in Investigation 3 (pp. 45–50). Each of these problems asks students to analyze patterns consisting of geometric arrangements of dots.

The Mathematics in Context Development Team. (1998). Mathematics in context: Patterns and figures (Student guide). In National Center for Research in Mathematical Science Education & Freudenthal Institute (Eds.), *Mathematics in context.* Chicago: Encyclopaedia Brittanica.

Of particular interest are Problems 10–14 (pp. 6–9), in which students explore two visual patterns made from dots and create generalizations for both.

CONNECTING TO OTHER IDEAS AND ISSUES

If you have additional time, you may want to explore some aspect of the case in more depth. The resources identified in this section provide some possibilities for broadening or deepening the discussion of patterns and functions. For example, you might: (1) complete additional pattern activities such as those found in Arcidiacano and Maier (1993) or Phillips (1991); (2) compare student performance on the Extend Pattern of Tiles Task that appeared on the National Assessment of Educational Progress (Silver, Alacaci, & Stylianou, 2000) with the performance of Ed Taylor's students; (3) analyze the use of variable in Ed Taylor's class, drawing on the work of Schoenfeld and Arcavi (1988) or Usiskin (1988); (4) consider how the mathematical ideas in "The Case of Ed Taylor" serve as a transition between elementary school mathematics and students' future experiences in algebra, using Ferrini-Mundy, Lappan, and Phillips (1997) as an example; or (5) analyze "The Case of Ed Taylor" with respect to Thornton's (2001) discussion of the importance of visualizations and consider whether Mr. Taylor appears to have emphasized or missed the point of generalizing patterns. You also may want to revisit readings from Chapter 2 that are relevant to "The Case of Ed Taylor," such as English and Warren (1998), Friel and colleagues (2001), and Scanlon (1996).

Arcidiacano, M., & Maier, E. (1993). *Picturing algebra. Math and the mind's eye, Unit IX*. Salem, OR: The Math Learning Center.

> This is one of 13 units in the Math and the Mind's Eye series intended as replacement units for existing curricula. This unit features seven activities, each of which involves exploring patterns as a means for developing an understanding of algebraic concepts.

Ferrini-Mundy, J., Lappan, G., & Phillips, E. (1997). Experiences with patterning. *Teaching Children Mathematics, 3*, 282–289.

> This article discusses how patterning tasks can be used to develop algebraic thinking throughout the K–6 curriculum. The authors use the same pattern scenario in grades K–6, showing the algebraic concepts teachers can encourage their students to think about at each grade level. The pool border problem featured in the article is analogous to the Square Pattern Task used by Ed Taylor.

Phillips, E. (1991). *Patterns and functions*. Reston, VA: National Council of Teachers of Mathematics.

> This is one of six books in the Grades 5–8 Addenda series intended to support teachers' implementation of the *Curriculum and Evaluation Standards for School Mathematics* (NCTM, 1989). The book provides ex-

amples of pattern tasks drawn from a number of content areas (e.g., rational numbers, number theory, geometry) as well as suggestions for using the tasks in ways that will lead to the development of important mathematical understanding.

Schoenfeld, A. H., & Arcavi, A. (1988). On the meaning of variable. *Mathematics Teacher, 81*, 420–427.

> This article provides an interesting discussion on the meaning of variable and why this is a difficult idea for students to grasp. Three exercises are described that allow students to really grapple with the meaning of variable and how its definition changes depending on context. Three suggestions related to teaching the concept of variable also are discussed.

Silver, E. A., Alacaci, C., & Stylianou, D. A. (2000). Students' performance on extended constructed-response tasks. In E. A. Silver & P. A. Kenney (Eds.), *Results from the seventh mathematics assessment of the National Assessment of Educational Progress* (pp. 301–341). Reston, VA: National Council of Teachers of Mathematics.

> Included in this chapter is a discussion of student performance and an analysis of responses on the Extend Pattern of Tiles Task that appeared on the National Assessment of Educational Progress in 1992 and 1996. This task is almost identical to the S-Pattern Task featured in "The Case of Ed Taylor."

Thornton, S. (2001). New approaches to algebra: Have we missed the point? *Mathematics Teaching in the Middle School, 6*, 388–392.

> This article discusses how algebraic reasoning can be enhanced through alternative visualizations, symbolic manipulation, or a functional approach. The author points out that many times the algebraic value of an activity is lost because the important algebraic concept embedded in the activity has been missed. For example, the value in generalizing physical patterns is not in coming up with one correct formula but in finding alternative visualizations and connecting the symbols with the visual representation.

Usiskin, Z. (1988). Conceptions of school algebra and uses of variables. In A. F. Coxford & A. P. Shulte (Eds.), *The ideas of algebra, K–12, 1988 yearbook* (pp. 8–19). Reston, VA: National Council of Teachers of Mathematics.

> This article discusses different notions of variable and how they relate to different conceptions of school algebra, including algebra as generalized arithmetic, as the study of procedures for solving certain kinds of problems, as the study of relationships among quantities, and as the study of mathematical structures.

4

Comparing Linear Graphs

The Case of Edith Hart

Chapter 4 has been designed to engage readers in considering important issues in mathematics teaching and learning related to linear graphs.

Prior to reading "The Case of Edith Hart"—the centerpiece of this chapter—we suggest that all readers begin by completing the Opening Activity. The primary purpose of the Opening Activity is to engage readers with the mathematical ideas that will be encountered when reading the case.

OPENING ACTIVITY

The task found in the Opening Activity, shown in Figure 4.1, is the same task featured in "The Case of Edith Hart." Once you have completed the activity, you may want to refer to Appendix C, which contains solutions based on strategies generated by teachers who completed the Opening Activity as part of a professional development experience featuring "The Case of Edith Hart." You are encouraged to examine the different solutions provided and to consider the relationship between your solution and those produced by others.

READING THE CASE

As you read the case, we encourage you to make note of the mathematical ideas Edith Hart's students appear to be learning. (You may want to use a highlighter or Post-it notes to keep track of these as you read the case.) For example, you may identify something specific that you think Edith Hart's students are learning (e.g., what

the points of intersection mean in the context of the problem) or something more general (e.g., communicating mathematical ideas).

We encourage you to write down the "mathematics learned" that you identify and to cite evidence from the case (i.e., paragraph numbers) to support your claims. These can serve as topics for discussion with a colleague who also has read the case or as issues to investigate as you read additional cases. If you are currently teaching mathematics, issues that surface in reading "The Case of Edith Hart" might serve as starting points for exploration in your own classroom. For example, you might wonder what mathematical ideas your students could learn from solving the Cal's Dinner Card Deals Task and how you might facilitate a discussion that makes connections between different representations of the problem (e.g., the graph, the context of the problem, a table, or a symbolic formula). We will discuss additional connections to your own practice at the end of the chapter.

FIGURE 4.1. The Cal's Dinner Card Deals Task for the Opening Activity in "The Case of Edith Hart"

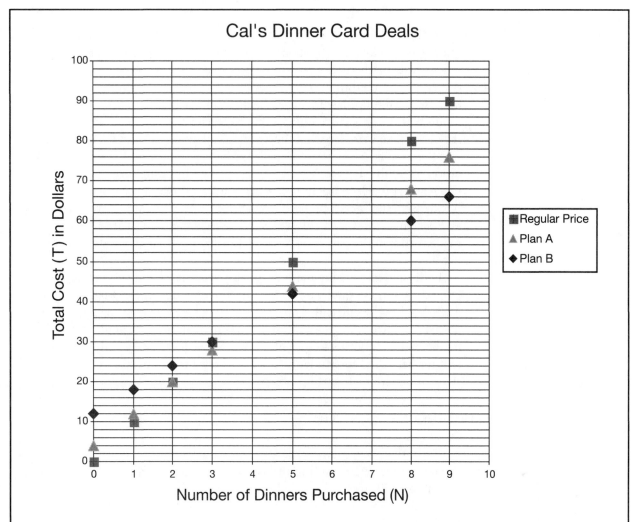

Solve

The graphs show data for three dinner plans. Make observations about each of the graphs. Find a way to determine the cost for any number of meals purchased on each dinner plan and explain your reasoning. Which dinner plan is best?

Consider

1. If you only had $5 to spend on food for the week, which dinner plan should you buy? How did you decide?
2. Does it make sense to connect the points in the dinner plan graphs? Why or why not?
3. Describe another situation besides dinner card plans that would generate a formula and a graph similar to the graph of Plan A or Plan B. Describe another situation that would give you a formula and a graph similar to the Regular Price Plan.

THE CASE OF EDITH HART

1.   Edith Hart, a 26-year teaching veteran, started teaching mathematics at Queenston Middle School about 5 years ago when Queenston began a school-wide mathematics reform project that involved using an innovative curriculum. Edith initially experienced a great deal of anxiety because she did not have a strong background in mathematics and she found that the new curriculum required teachers to deeply understand the conceptual basis for what they were trying to teach their students in a way that challenged her own knowledge base. Over the past 5 years, however, Edith has become one of the most enthusiastic proponents of this new approach to teaching mathematics. Through her participation in extensive staff development, her experience teaching the curriculum, and her interaction with colleagues, Edith feels she has learned as much mathematics in the past 5 years as she learned in all the previous years of her life.

2.   Edith started teaching math at the 6th-grade level and subsequently taught 7th and 8th grade. She has enjoyed seeing how mathematical ideas build in the curriculum over time. However, one area she feels does not receive enough attention in the curriculum is the application of mathematical concepts to real situations. She feels it is especially important for her 8th-grade students to see how algebra can be used to understand and solve real-world problems.

Edith Hart Talks About Her Class

3.   Up until now, my 8th-grade students have worked on solving linear equations and understanding and constructing graphs, but it has all been very abstract. They have focused mainly on building tables of values, evaluating formulas, and plotting points, and, in general, they are proficient with these skills. Part of what I want to do now is bring all of this algebra work into a context that involves graphing and using graphs to see patterns and make real-world decisions. I want the students to understand not only how to plot points, but also what a point on a graph represents in an applied context. I want them to have a sense that a graph represents a relationship between variables. I also want the students to relate numeric and graphical patterns to a situation.

4.   Toward that end, I developed a problem called Cal's Dinner Card Deals. In this problem, the students are given graphical information about three different dinner plans. They have to analyze which is the least costly dinner plan according to how often a person eats out, and also determine when the costs of the dinner plans are equal. The students should be able to use the procedures they have already learned for how a graph is constructed in order to do something they haven't had much experience with—constructing a formula from a graph. As they work through the task, I want students to focus on the reasoning processes they use to derive formulas from the original sets of points I give them. My hope is that a variety of methods or ways of reasoning will be generated across the class and that students will do a good job explaining their methods. I really want them to discover how the behavior of the

graph relates to the problem situation as well as the formula. Even though we are not yet dealing with these ideas formally, I hope they can see the relationship between the slopes and formulas of the three dinner plans. Last year I didn't provide students with enough opportunities to explore problems in context, and, as a result, they had difficulty making connections between graphs and the real-world situations they were intended to represent. Cal's Dinner Card Deals also gives students experience with a real-world situation involving discrete variables. All of our previous lessons have dealt with continuous variables and it's important that students don't think all functions are continuous.

5.   Through this activity I also hope to continue working on supporting and facilitating students' ability to articulate their thinking. The students will have to record their observations in writing and give a written explanation of how they decided which was the best dinner deal. As always, the students also will participate in the lesson as presenters. I believe the best way to improve students' ability to communicate their ideas is to actually have them write and talk about the mathematics they are doing. I hope to encourage them to elaborate on their own when they go to the overhead projector. Also, students at their seats are expected to question their peers, even if they understand the explanation. They need to press one another to explain their reasoning. I'm looking for my students to ask questions of themselves and one another.

6.   This year we started block scheduling at Queenston. With the new schedule we have a 90-minute block for math and science every day. Since I teach both subjects, I have the flexibility of using the time any way I choose. Today I want my students to have enough time to complete the activity so I decided to use the entire time for math. Although I have done similar activities in 45-minute classes—sometimes taking more than one day—it is nice to not feel rushed and to not lose time by stopping and starting.

The Class

7.   I passed out the Cal's Dinner Card Deals graphs (shown in Figure 4.1) and told students they would first consider the graphs on their own. I asked them to make and record in their notebooks as many observations as they could about the graphs. If they had time, I told them they could begin to work on determining the formula for each dinner deal. I then asked students to share with their groups what they came up with individually and to make some new observations. After about 15 minutes we shared these in the whole group. At the time, I didn't want to go into depth on each observation, but I wanted to get some ideas out in the open—ideas that we could potentially draw on during later discussions.

8.   *Making observations about the graphs.* I told students that as they listen to their peers, they should add the observations that were made to the list in their notebooks so we would all have them for future reference. Students began by making observations about specific values on the graph, such as, "Plan B costs $12 even if you don't have any dinners," and "the Regular Price Plan cost $90 for nine dinners." They also made comments about general characteristics of the graphs, for

example, "each graph has a different symbol," "each graph is a line," and "each graph goes up from the lower left to the upper right." Then Patrick, who was always very methodical, said, "What I noticed about this graph was that I wanted to see how far apart the triangles (Plan A) were, but I couldn't tell exactly, so what I did was I counted how many grid squares up they go. I noticed it keeps on raising by $8 as you go up." I repeated exactly what Patrick said so students could write it down. I asked him if he had tried to do this with the other plans as well. He said, "Well, I only had time to go through one plan so far, but you can tell they don't all go up by $8." At this point, I wanted to press students to think about the relationship between the graphs rather than focus on a single graph, so I asked students if they had made any observations that involved more than one graph.

9.   Ray said, "I noticed that the graphs seem to cross at certain places." I repeated this observation for the other students and asked Ray what it means when the graphs share a point. He said, "I don't know, but it must mean something." I chuckled to myself; I liked this answer much better than a simple, "I don't know." I didn't want to move on just yet because I wanted the students to understand the idea of intersection in this context, and here was an opportunity to put it on the table now.

10.   I asked if anyone else had any ideas about how to answer my question. Heather said, "If they have the same point then it means they have the same cost." I asked, "What do you mean by 'same cost'? How is the number of dinners involved?" Heather replied, "Well, like, OK, look at two dinners. If you have, like, Plan A and you buy two dinners and if you have the Regular Price and you buy two dinners, it's the same cost." I said, "So what does it mean in general when the graphs share a point, or intersect?" Ray excitedly raised his hand, "If you buy a certain number of dinners and it costs the same for both plans then they'll have the same point on the graph." I restated what Ray said, "OK, so when the graphs share a point, or intersect, in this case it means that the plans have the same total cost for the same number of dinners. See what we can come up with when we push a little harder and put our ideas together and listen to each other."

11.   I asked if there were other observations not already mentioned. Derrick said, "One of the lines crosses zero, the Regular Price, but the other two don't." This was another good observation that I hoped we could revisit later in the lesson after we had the formulas developed and could examine the differences in the y-intercept for each set of points. Sharee added, "No matter which plan you have, you can get nine dinners for less than $100. All the costs are from zero to $90." I repeated it for the class and mentioned that Sharee's idea might be related to a decision about which is the best dinner plan. Patrick raised his hand again. "We noticed that with a low number of dinners, the Regular Price is lower than the other two, but when you get more dinners, the Regular Price graph changes to being on top, higher than the other two. It starts out lower and ends up higher." I said, "That sounds like another observation that might help us decide which dinner plan is the best deal. We'll definitely come back to that later." I reminded students to add these ideas to their list of observations.

12.   Danielle spoke up and said she had another observation that she thought was different. "I notice they all have different slants." I asked her to say more about that. She gestured with her hand, moving it as she spoke. "The Regular Price one tilts like this, it's the steepest. Plan A tilts a little lower and Plan B is the least steep." I asked if anyone had any comments about what Danielle said. No one said anything, so I told the students we would get back to that idea later. These were some great observations, better than I expected. I guess since we did things like this often, they were getting better and better at making relevant observations.

13.   *Finding formulas.* We were now about 35 minutes into the class. I told the students they should now go back and try to determine the formulas that would generate each of the graphs. I really wanted students to be aware of the reasoning processes they were using to find the formulas. As students began working, I walked around the room. One of my concerns, too, was to be sure all the students were actively participating in their groups and students were questioning one another or asking their partners for help.

14.   Some students in one group were wondering how it was possible to have zero dinners cost $4 (for Plan A). I tried to think of a way to help them figure this out, without telling them directly. I asked them what would happen if they bought a card and never used it. Jamal said it would still cost $4. I then asked them to think about what would happen if they only used it once or twice, and so on. As it turns out, more than one group had this question, so I ended up having a similar conversation several times as I walked around the room. I was pretty sure I could expect it to come up in the whole-class discussion later.

15.   After about 15 minutes it looked like most students had a formula for at least one or two of the plans. I didn't want to just ask for the formulas outright; instead I wanted to ask a question that would require a formula to answer. I asked the class what the total cost for 100 dinners would be using Plan A—even though it clearly was not shown on the graph. Kyle said, "All you have to do is keep adding 8 for every dinner. So just take your calculator and keep doing 'plus 8.' So if nine dinners is $76, just keep adding 8, 91 times. Or take 91 times 8 and add it to $76. That would be $804." Although Kyle used a viable strategy, I was hoping that someone had found a formula that would allow you to calculate the cost for any number of dinners. I asked the class if anyone had solved the problem a different way. Jena said she thought it would be $804, too, and said she had come up with a formula. I asked her to come to the overhead to explain her process for finding the formula. She said, "I know from the graph of Plan A that 0 dinners cost $4, 1 dinner is $12, 2 dinners is $20, 3 dinners is $28. So I put this information into a table." She made a table of values, as shown in Table 4.1.a, containing the total costs associated with 0, 1, 2, and 3 dinners. "The first thing I noticed is that if zero dinners is $4 that means $4 is like a basic cost that is always going to be added. So I knew the formula for the total would be something plus 4."

16.   She continued, "So then I thought it would help to show the plus 4 which is always there for the dinner card. And you can put all of these as

TABLE 4.1. Jena's Tables of Values for Cal's Dinner Card Deals

a			b		
Jena's Original Table of Values for Cal's Dinner Card Deals			Jena's Expanded Table of Values for Cal's Dinner Card Deals		
# of Dinners N	Total Cost $T		# of Dinners N	Total Cost $T	Dinners + Dinner Card = $T
0	4		0	4	0 + 4
1	12		1	12	8 + 4
2	20		2	20	16 + 4
3	28		3	28	24 + 4

something plus 4." She then expanded her table to include the additional information (shown in Table 4.1.b).

17.　　I asked, "So how did that help you find the formula?" I wanted Jena to be explicit about how she reasoned from the patterns she found in the table to a formula. She said, "This made it easier to see that each time it is 8 times *something* plus 4. So 8 times the number of dinners plus 4, or 8N plus 4 equals T." And she wrote the formula.

18.　　I asked if anyone had any questions for Jena. I encourage the students to question one another as often as I can and I always want the student presenter to take on the role of "teacher for the moment," so it was Jena's job to call on students at this point. She called on Omar. Omar said, "I don't get how you knew it was plus 4 each time. How come the $4 stays there all the time?" Jena explained, "I looked at the graph for Plan A. I saw that even if you don't buy any dinners you still have to pay $4, so the $4 is always there from the beginning." Omar said he still didn't understand. Jena said, "OK, look back on the table." She pointed to the 0, 8, 16, and 24 and then the 4, 12, 20, and 28. "See, every time you add one dinner it goes up by the same amount, $8 per dinner." Then she pointed to the fours. "But the $4 is always part of the total because once you buy the card, no matter how many dinners you buy, you still started out spending $4, so it's always added in to the total." Omar said, "Oh, OK. I get it now." I asked if anyone else had other questions for Jena. There were none, so I thanked her. Omar's question brought out the idea that there is always a fixed cost independent of the number of dinners. So part of the total cost is not dependent on the number of dinners purchased and part of it is. Difficulty with this idea was apparent in some of the small groups, so I was glad Omar gave us a forum for discussing it as a class.

19.　　I felt it was important to get a variety of methods out on the table, so I asked, "Did anyone have a different method for finding the formula that they want to share? Did anyone use the graph to find the formula?" Danielle volunteered and went up to the overhead. She explained that she didn't make a table. She took an overhead pen and drew a horizontal line through the point (0, 4). She said, "Since you have to pay $4 no matter what, even if you don't buy any dinners, it's a given that you always have to add \$4 on to the cost because you have to buy the card. Then I looked at the points and each time you add on one more dinner, the cost goes up \$8." I asked her, "Can you show us what you mean on the graph?" She pointed to (2, 20) and said, "This one is 8 higher than this one [indicating the point (1, 12)]. Since it goes up by 8 for each additional dinner, the cost of the dinners is going to be 8 times the number of dinners, but you also have to remember to add the \$4, so it's 8N plus 4." I asked if anyone had any questions.

20.   Steven raised his hand and said he had a different way of using a table. Normally I would have made Steven wait until people asked questions of Danielle, but I needed to get things moving along, and I decided it would be better to have another method shared, so I let Steven go ahead and thanked Danielle for her explanation.

21.   Steven said, "I did a table, too. Then I looked for a pattern. I noticed the difference between each total and the next total is always 8 and I noticed that the difference between each total and the starting cost of \$4 is always the number of dinners times 8." He indicated these observations on a table of values he had drawn on the overhead (as shown in Figure 4.2).

22.   I interrupted for a second to ask Patrick if he could see how this related to the observation that had been made earlier, which was that as one more dinner is purchased, the total raises by \$8. He nodded yes. Steven continued, "The number multiplied by 8 each time is the same as N. So then I figured it was always going to be 8 times the number of dinners plus 4, or 8N plus 4, and it worked every time." I was pretty impressed with Steven's approach because I did not remember seeing this line of reasoning from my students in the past. I put Steven's table side by side with Jena's and we spent a few minutes brainstorming how the two methods were similar and different.

23.   I asked if anyone had any questions. No one did, so I gave them a few more minutes to finish finding the formulas for the other two graphs. When I could see that most groups had written formulas for all three graphs, I asked students to tell me the formulas so we could record them. I put a transparency of Cal's Dinner Card Deals on the overhead

FIGURE 4.2. Steven's Explanation of How He Used a Table to Develop the Formula 8N + 4

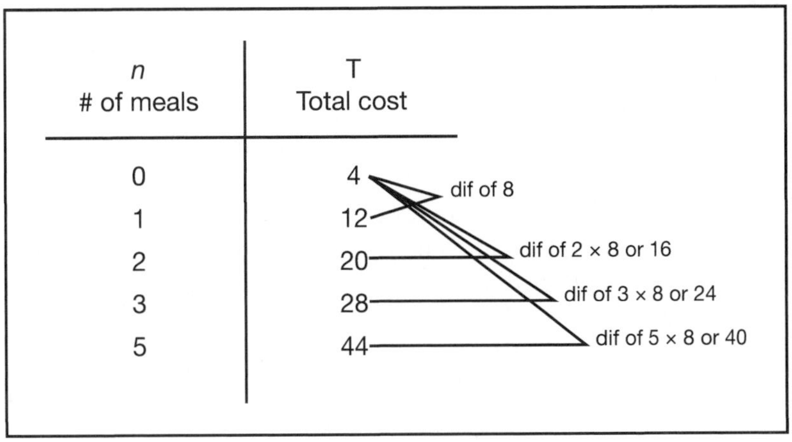

n # of meals	T Total cost	
0	4	dif of 8
1	12	
2	20	dif of 2 × 8 or 16
3	28	dif of 3 × 8 or 24
5	44	dif of 5 × 8 or 40

and wrote the formulas off to the side. I told students to record them the same way on their own sheets. We recorded $8N + 4 = T$ for Plan A, $6N + 12 = T$ for Plan B, and $10N = T$ for the Regular Price Plan.

24.   *Finding relationships and making decisions.* At this point we had less than 10 minutes left in the class. Before I could ask for any new observations, Carlos blurted out, "It seems like the bigger the number being multiplied by N the steeper the graph." I was kind of tickled that Carlos felt compelled to blurt out an observation before I even asked for any! Believe me, this was not normal. Josh said he thought of the same idea as Carlos. I asked if this had anything to do with Danielle's idea we had recorded earlier about the graphs all having different steepness or slant. I waited a few seconds and asked Danielle if she saw any relationship. Danielle said, "I think the number being multiplied by N tells you how steep it will be." I asked her to say more about that relationship. She said, "The number multiplied by N causes the total costs to go up faster the bigger it is. They are all going up as you buy more dinners, but the Regular Price goes up the fastest because it has the biggest number multiplied by N." I repeated what she said and told students to record it in their notebooks. I told them I wanted them to think about whether they agreed with this statement and that we'd talk more about it tomorrow.

25.   Annie said she wasn't sure if the number added had anything to do with it. She said, "But from these examples it looks like the larger the number you are adding to the N term the less steep it is." I told her that I didn't think her conjecture would always be true even though it worked for these three graphs. I realized that I might have to design another activity for the students in which her conjecture doesn't hold. I told her we would come back to it tomorrow when we talked about one of the homework problems.

26.   Now that we had the three graphs and the three formulas on the overhead, I asked students which dinner plan would be the best deal. Jena said it probably would depend on the number of dinners a person bought. Steven said, "If a person only bought two or three or four dinners then it doesn't make a big difference in the cost no matter which dinner plan you get." I recorded these ideas on the board. I asked if anyone had a different observation. I was happy to see Annie raise her hand. Annie came up to the overhead and said, "If you buy less than two dinners, the Regular Price is better than Plan A and if you get less than three dinners, the Regular Price is better than Plan B. But if you get more than two or three dinners then you start saving money with the other plans." I really praised her for coming up because I didn't want her incorrect conjecture from earlier to be the only thing she remembered about today.

27.   I asked if there was a different observation. I added, "What about the rate of savings?" Danielle said, "The graphs get farther apart as you buy more dinners—the more dinners you buy the more expensive the Regular Price Plan is." I asked, "Does everyone see what Danielle is saying?" Many students nodded yes, but I wasn't completely sure if the majority were following what she had said. I made a mental note that we

would have to come back to this idea tomorrow. I gave them three questions to grapple with for homework using the graphs.

1. If you only had $45 to spend on food for the week, which dinner plan should you buy? How did you decide?
2. Does it make sense to connect the points in the dinner plan graphs? Why or why not?
3. Describe another situation besides dinner card plans that would generate a formula and a graph similar to the graph of Plan A or Plan B. Describe another situation that would give you a formula and graph similar to the Regular Price Plan.

28.   I asked the third question because I wanted the students to make use of some of the ideas that had come out in the discussion and to take these ideas beyond the dinner deal problem. I felt if they could generate other situations that would have graphs that behaved similarly, then I would know they really understood the material.

ANALYZING THE CASE

Now that you have had an opportunity to "visit" Edith Hart's classroom and identify the mathematical ideas you thought students were learning, we invite you to consider how Edith Hart facilitated or supported students' learning of mathematics. Here are a few suggestions about how to proceed.

• Create a three-column chart indicating what mathematics Ms. Hart's students learned or were in the process of learning, what Ms. Hart did to facilitate or support her students' learning, and evidence (i.e., paragraph numbers) from the case to support your claims. (You might begin this process by reviewing the mathematics ideas that you identified as you read the case and determine what Edith Hart may have done to support students' learning of those ideas.)

• If you have colleagues who also are reading the case, compare and contrast the ideas in your individual charts. Note points of disagreement since these are likely to be fruitful topics for further discussion. If you are working on this activity alone, we encourage you to refer to Appendix C, which includes a chart of the mathematics students learned and the moves Edith Hart made that appeared to support her students' learning. This chart was produced by teachers who participated in a discussion of Edith Hart's lesson. You may want to note points of agreement and disagreement and identify issues that you wish to investigate.

You may wish to extend your analysis of the case by considering the questions in the next section. Alternatively, you can skip the next section and proceed directly to the "Connecting to Your Own Practice" section in which you are encouraged to relate the analysis of the ideas and issues raised in "The Case of Edith Hart" to your own teaching practice.

EXTENDING YOUR ANALYSIS OF THE CASE

The questions listed in this section are intended to help you focus on particular aspects of the case related to teacher decision-making and student thinking. If you are working in collaboration with one or more colleagues, the questions can serve as a stimulus for further discussion.

1. Ms. Hart was spurred to develop the Cal's Dinner Card Deals Task because she felt the algebraic skills she was teaching her students were too abstract and rarely connected to real-life applications. To what extent do you think Ms. Hart succeeded in developing a task for students that balances contextual features of a real-life situation with significant mathematical ideas? What contextual features and mathematical ideas do you see as important in the task?

2. In paragraph 22, Ms. Hart says she put Steven's table (Figure 4.2) side by side with Jena's table (Table 4.1) and had the class brainstorm how the two methods were similar and different. What might the students' responses have been to this activity? Why do you think Ms. Hart thought it was valuable to compare these two methods?

3. In paragraph 25, Annie wonders whether an increase in the constant added results in a decrease in the steepness of the line. Under what conditions would Annie's observation hold true? Is there a way in which Annie's observation might make sense in the context of this problem? In the context of Cal's Dinner Card Deals, what are the practical implications for increasing the initial price of the meal card?

4. Toward the end of the case (para. 25), Annie observes that the larger the constant being added, the less steep the line is. Ms. Hart expresses concern that Annie has drawn an incorrect conclusion that is unique to the three meal plans in the task and decides to come back to the point in a later lesson with some examples in which Annie's conjecture does not hold. Discuss the advantages and disadvantages of Ms. Hart's decision to table Annie's comment. In what other ways might Ms. Hart have responded to Annie's comment?

5. For homework, Ms. Hart asks students three questions (para. 27). The first question asks students to determine the best meal plan, the second question addresses whether the variables are discrete or continuous, and the third question pushes students to generalize beyond the particular graphs in the task. What other homework questions might have been appropriate given what happened during the lesson? Explain why you think your questions would be appropriate.

6. Suppose Ms. Hart's students arrive the next day and say the points on the dinner plan graphs should be connected. What kinds of questions

could Ms. Hart ask that might compel her students to reconsider this position?

CONNECTING TO YOUR OWN PRACTICE

The activities described in this section are designed to help you consider the ways in which the issues identified in Ms. Hart's classroom have implications for your own teaching of mathematics. Reflecting on one's own teaching is a valuable, and yet often neglected, activity. It is through reflection that "teachers can gain insight into how their actions and interactions in the classroom influence students' opportunities to learn mathematics" (Smith, 2001, p. 11). Here are a few activities that will help you move from consideration of Edith Hart's teaching to a focus on your own classroom practices.

- Review the list you created during the case analysis in which you indicated what Edith Hart did to support her students' learning. Select one of the moves from this list that you feel has implications for your own teaching. Plan and teach a lesson in which you purposefully address the identified pedagogical move. For example, you may be curious about the ways in which Edith Hart had students make, record, and refer to observations about the graphs. You could explore this by planning and teaching a lesson in which you make a concerted effort to promote the use of students' observations in your class discussions. If possible, audiotape or videotape the lesson or have a colleague observe and take notes. As you go back over the lesson, reflect on the changes you made and the impact these changes appear to have had on students' learning. Also indicate what you still need to work on with respect to this pedagogy.
- Plan and teach a lesson using Cal's Dinner Card Deals (or another task that has the potential to foster students' making connections between representations). If possible, record the lesson using videotape or audiotape, or by having a colleague observe and take notes. As you reflect on the lesson, consider the following questions: What questions did you ask that facilitated students' making connections between representations? In what ways was your enactment of the lesson similar to or different from the lesson portrayed in "The Case of Edith Hart"? What might you do differently the next time you teach (to further enhance stu-

dents' learning or to facilitate students' making connections between representations)?

EXPLORING CURRICULAR MATERIALS

You may want to explore mathematics curricula for ideas related to linear graphs. How is the Cal's Dinner Card Deals Task similar to and different from the problems in your curriculum? For example, in Cal's Dinner Card Deals students are given a graph and asked to develop the equations. Do any problems in your textbook have similar features? What might students' experiences with a task such as Cal's Dinner Card Deals "buy them" mathematically? In particular, consider the mathematical ideas that can be discussed with Cal's Dinner Card Deals and those that can be discussed via problems in your textbook. Are there differences? Are these differences important? Why or why not?

You also may want to solve additional tasks to continue to explore the mathematical ideas made salient in the case. The following list identifies resources that contain problems that are considered to be mathematically similar to the task used in Edith Hart's class.

Billstein, R., & Williamson, J. (1999c). *Middle grades math thematics: Book 3*. Evanston, IL: McDougal Littell.
> Of particular interest in Section 2 of Module 7 (Visualizing Change) are Exercises 1–10 (pp. 482–485), in which students can use a variety of representations to solve problems involving linear relationships situated in several contexts.

Education Development Center, Inc. (1998a). *MathScape: Exploring the unknown: Writing and solving equations* (Student guide). Mountain View, CA: Creative Publications.
> Of particular interest is an activity in Lesson 12 (pp. 32–33) in which students are asked to compare the charges of two CD clubs.

Foreman, L. C., & Bennett, A. B., Jr. (1998). *Math alive! Course III, Lessons 13–17*. Salem, OR: The Math Learning Center.
> Of particular interest in Lesson 14 (Analyzing Graphs) are Actions 12–15 in the Focus Teacher Activity (pp. 388–392). Students use tables, graphs, and equations to explore several real-world situations (e.g., comparing the pricing plans of two car rental companies; comparing two runners' positions on a track).

Lappan, G., Fey, J., Fitzgerald, W., Friel, S., & Phillips, E. (2002a). *Moving straight ahead: Linear relationships. Connected mathematics*. Glenview, IL: Prentice Hall.
> Of particular interest is Problem 3.4 (pp. 42–43), which asks students to compare the pricing plans of two roller rinks.

The Mathematics in Context Development Team. (1997c). Mathematics in context: Ups and downs (Student guide). In National Center for Research in Mathematical Sciences Education & Freudenthal Institute (Eds.), *Mathematics in context*. Chicago: Encyclopaedia Brittanica.

> Of particular interest is an activity (pp. 37–39) in which students must compare the pricing plans of two motorcycle rental companies.

CONNECTING TO OTHER IDEAS AND ISSUES

If you have additional time, you may want to explore some aspect of the case in more depth. The resources identified in this section provide some possibilities for exploring the mathematical and pedagogical issues raised in "The Case of Edith Hart." For example, you could: (1) use the activities that appear in Applebaum (1997), Cai and Kenney (2000), Friel and colleagues (2001), McCoy (1997), Swan, Bell, Burkhardt, and Janvier (1984), and Willoughby (1997) as a basis for discussing what Ms. Hart might have done prior to the task of Cal's Dinner Card Deals or what she might want to do next to help her students develop their ability to analyze graphs and identify the relationship between graphs and equations; (2) compare the thinking by students in Edith Hart's class with the types of student intuitions and misconceptions described by Leinhardt, Zaslavsky, and Stein (1990); or (3) analyze the connections made between equations and graphs in Edith Hart's class, drawing on the work of Knuth (2000). You also may want to revisit readings from Chapter 3 that are relevant to "The Case of Edith Hart," such as Schoenfeld and Arcavi (1988) or Usiskin (1988), as well as Van de Walle (2004), as described in Chapter 2.

Applebaum, E. B. (1997). Telephones and algebra. *Mathematics Teacher, 90,* 96–100.

> This article explores an application problem very similar to the task in the Edith Hart case, but more complex. The task in the article involves telephone calling plans and contains a discussion of deriving formulas from graphs and tables and making decisions based on the mathematics of the task.

Cai, J., & Kenney, P. (2000). Fostering mathematical thinking through multiple solutions. *Mathematics Teaching in the Middle School, 5,* 534–539.

> This article describes the importance of open-ended tasks in fostering students' mathematical thinking and communication. Three tasks are analyzed in detail to show the features that contribute to a deeper understanding and communication by students. The second

task involves video rental plans and is similar to the Cal's Dinner Card Deals Task in "The Case of Edith Hart."

Friel, S., Rachlin, S., Doyle, D., with Nygard, C., Pugalee, D., & Ellis, M. (2001). *Principles and standards for school mathematics navigations series: Navigating through algebra in grades 6–8.* Reston, VA: National Council of Teachers of Mathematics.

> This book is part of the Navigation Series intended to support teachers' implementation of the Principles and Standards (NCTM, 2000). The book focuses on algebra concepts in grades 6–8. Chapter 3, "Exploring Linear Relationships," offers activities for students to analyze the nature of changes in quantities in linear relationships and to investigate relationships between symbolic expressions and the graphs of lines, paying particular attention to the meaning of intercept and slope. The activities emphasize the importance of analyzing graphs and equations in relation to their situational context.

Knuth, E. (2000). Understanding connections between equations and graphs. *Mathematics Teacher, 93,* 48–53.

> This article describes a study of high school students' understanding of connections between equations and graphs. Results showed students were lacking in their understanding of a fundamental connection—a point satisfies an equation if and only if the point is on the graph of the equation. The author also discusses possible reasons for students' lack of understanding of connections between equations and graphs.

Leinhardt, G., Zaslavsky, O., & Stein, M. K. (1990). Functions, graphs, and graphing: Tasks, learning, and teaching. *Review of Educational Research, 60,* 1–64.

> This review of the literature on functions and graphs provides an analysis of the research on graph interpretation and construction tasks as well as an analysis of teaching and student learning. Students' common intuitions and misconceptions about functions and graphs (pp. 24–45) are described in detail and are similar to those encountered by Edith Hart's students. The article also provides an extensive list of references on this topic and could serve as a source for additional readings.

McCoy, L. (1997). Algebra: Real-life investigations in a lab setting. *Teaching Mathematics in the Middle School, 2,* 221–224.

> This article describes an activity for exploring linear relationships in a lab setting. There is a discussion about comparing more than one line and comparing slopes and intercepts, ideas that are salient in the Edith Hart case.

Swan, M., Bell, A., Burkhardt, H., & Janvier, C. (1984). *The language of functions and graphs: An examination module for secondary schools.* Shell Centre for Mathematical Education, University of Nottingham, United Kingdom.

> This module contains a set of instructional and assessment tasks related to functions and graphing. The

instructional tasks provide the opportunity to explore the qualitative meaning of graphs and to discover and explore patterns and functions arising from realistic situations.

Willoughby, S. (1997). Activities to help in learning about functions. *Mathematics Teaching in the Middle School, 2,* 214–219.

This article describes several classroom activities that promote an early introduction for students to the concept of function. The set of activities includes discussion of activities involving graphs and how students can use them to analyze real-life situations. There is also a brief discussion of the issue of the use of formal notation in building formulas.

 # Interpreting Graphs of Time versus Speed

The Case of Robert Carter

Chapter 5 has been designed to engage readers in considering important issues in mathematics teaching and learning related to graphs of time versus speed.

Prior to reading "The Case of Robert Carter"—the centerpiece of this chapter—we suggest that all readers begin by completing the Opening Activity. The primary purpose of the Opening Activity is to engage readers with the mathematical ideas that will be encountered when reading the case.

OPENING ACTIVITY

The Opening Activity, shown in Figure 5.1, is based on the graph of Keisha's Bicycle Ride, which is explored by students in the lesson featured in "The Case of Robert Carter." After you have created a story for Keisha's Bicycle Ride and a graph corresponding to Keisha's second bicycle ride, you are encouraged to complete the "Consider" portion of the activity in which you are asked to identify similarities and differences between the graphs for Keisha's first and second bicycle rides and to explore why these differences are important.

Once you have completed the activity, you may want to refer to Appendix D, which contains a set of solutions generated by teachers who completed the Opening Activity as part of a professional development experience featuring "The Case of Robert Carter." You are encouraged to compare your story and graph with those that are provided and to consider in what ways the similarities and differences that you notice are important mathematically and/or in the context of the bicycle ride.

READING THE CASE

As you read the case, we encourage you to identify the key instructional decisions that Robert Carter made during the lesson which appeared to influence his students' learning of mathematics. (You may want to use a highlighter or Post-it notes to keep track of these as you read the case.) For example, you might select a decision that Robert Carter makes during an interaction with a specific student (e.g., directing Tonya's question back to Crystal rather than answering it himself) or a more general instructional decision (e.g., having students work in groups of four to discuss the differences in the two graphs) that you feel influenced students' learning of mathematics in a significant way.

We encourage you to write down the decisions that you identify and specify where these decisions occur in the case (i.e., paragraph numbers). This list can serve as topics for discussion with a colleague who also has read the case or as topics to investigate as you read additional cases. If you currently are teaching mathematics, issues that surface in reading "The Case of Robert Carter" might serve as starting points for exploration in your own classroom. For example, you might consider how a decision to redirect a student's question back to a classmate or a decision to move on at a certain point in the lesson might influence student learning in your own classroom. We will discuss additional connections to your own practice at the end of the chapter.

FIGURE 5.1. The Keisha's Bicycle Ride Task for the Opening Activity in "The Case of Robert Carter"

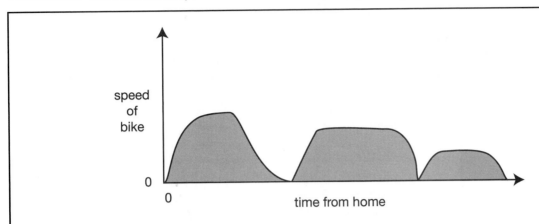

Solve

1. The graph represents the relationship between speed and time during Keisha's bicycle ride from home to school. Write a story about Keisha's bicycle trip that is consistent with the graph.

2. Now imagine that Keisha took a second trip on her bicycle that was different from the first one in two ways: (1) this time she slowed down but did not stop at the end of the first leg, and (2) her fastest speed for the entire trip was the constant part of the second leg. Sketch the new graph to portray the time/speed relationship for the second trip.

Consider

1. In what ways are the graphs of Keisha's first and second bicycle trips the same? In what ways are they different? Why are the similarities/differences important mathematically or in the context of the story?

2. Is the relationship between speed and time in Keisha's Bicycle Ride a functional relationship? Justify your position in at least two ways.

THE CASE OF ROBERT CARTER

1.   Robert Carter, an African American teacher, is completing his first year
at Justice Middle School. Justice Middle School has a history of poor
attendance, low test scores, multiple suspensions, and high student
mobility. The principal, who has been at Justice for 3 years, has made an
effort to create an academic, achievement-oriented atmosphere at the
school—student work is displayed throughout the hallways, the names
of students who have achieved a 4.0 grade point average during the
quarter are posted at the school's entrance, and each spring the school
hosts an Academic Exposition that focuses on student achievement and
accomplishments during the year.

2.   Neither his elementary education courses nor his student teaching
prepared Robert for the challenges of working in an urban district.
Moreover, he admittedly would have preferred to teach social studies
rather than mathematics because this had been his area of concentration
in college. Nevertheless, he undertook the challenges presented by the new
environment and content area with enthusiasm and optimism, ending his
first year of teaching with a sense of accomplishment. Robert attributes
much of his success to the support he received from Michelle Harris, a
retired high school mathematics teacher and supervisor, who worked with
him and his colleagues throughout the year. Robert views Ms. Harris as his
mentor—someone who shares ideas and materials, asks thought-provok-
ing questions, and listens to him "sound off" when he gets frustrated.

3.   Robert knows that his students face many obstacles in their lives and
that they need to believe in themselves if they are ever going to meet these
challenges. Hence, in addition to helping his students learn mathematics,
he also sees it as his responsibility to help them develop the self-esteem
and confidence they will need to be successful both in school and beyond.
According to Robert, competence plus confidence equals success.

Robert Carter Talks About His Class

4.   I've always felt that the ability to interpret graphs is an important life
skill that should be taught in school. After all, graphs are everywhere!
Also, when thumbing through the brand-new curriculum that our
school has just adopted for next year, I noticed that when my students
are in 7th grade they will be expected to use graphs in lots of different
situations. I wanted to lay some groundwork on interpreting graphs to
prepare them for this.

5.   Coincidentally, the topic came up in our weekly meeting with Ms.
Harris in which we received results from an assessment given to Justice
students last year. In one of the featured tasks, Tony's Walk (shown in
Figure 5.2), students were asked to tell a story about a graph that depicted the various speeds that a boy traveled during a 3-hour walk to his
grandmother's house. I found this task to be very intriguing. It was
certainly different from how I learned graphing—endless plotting of x
and y coordinates on a Cartesian grid followed by "connecting the dots."
I liked Tony's Walk much better, at least as a way to introduce graphing.
It seemed to me that kids would be more motivated by such a graph, and

FIGURE 5.2. The Tony's Walk Task.

Use the following information and the graph to write a story about Tony's walk.

At noon, Tony started walking to his grandmother's house. He arrived at her house at 3:00 p.m. The graph below shows Tony's speed in miles per hour throughout his walk.

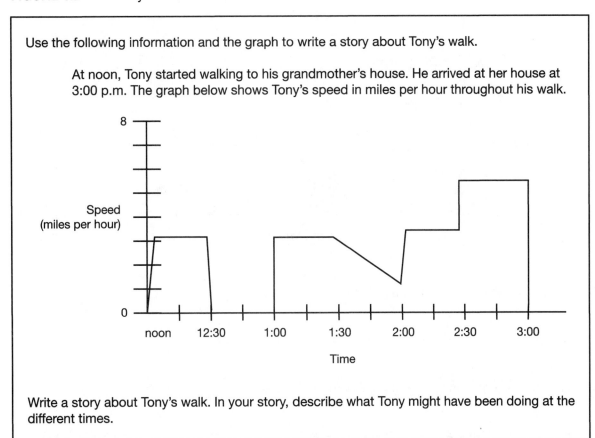

Write a story about Tony's walk. In your story, describe what Tony might have been doing at the different times.

Reprinted with permission from *Using Assessment to Improve Middle-Grades Mathematics Teaching & Learning CD,* copyright © 2003 by the National Council of Teachers of Mathematics.

that it would build on what they already knew and on their intuitions regarding how things happen in the world. The other thing that I liked about the task was that it was open-ended—there was not just one way to solve the problem and there were many possible solutions. This approach seemed to fit better with the ways in which my colleagues and I were trying to teach mathematics.

6.   My sense of excitement was tempered as my colleagues and I reviewed the student responses. Our students had done miserably on the task! Many students focused only on how fast or slow Tony was walking, and some others ignored the mathematical properties of the graph altogether, interpreting it instead as a picture. For example, some students interpreted a portion of the graph that showed an increase in speed, followed by a constant speed, followed by a decrease in speed, as changes in direction (going north one block, then east three blocks, then south one block) or as going uphill, traveling on flat ground, and then going downhill. Ms. Harris suggested that we might want to try these types of graphs in our classes, but initially give the students a little more help. Anticipating our reaction to students' poor performance, she had brought several graphing tasks with her to the meeting for us to consider. After exploring several of these, we selected the task called Keisha's Bicycle Ride, shown in Figure 5.3.

FIGURE 5.3. The Keisha's Bicycle Ride Task

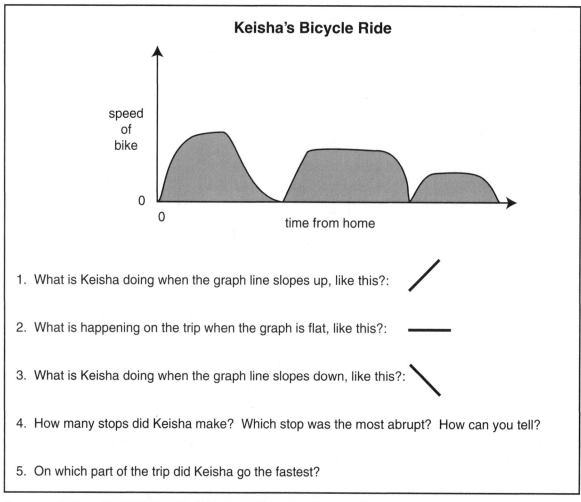

Keisha's Bicycle Ride

speed of bike

0

time from home

1. What is Keisha doing when the graph line slopes up, like this?:

2. What is happening on the trip when the graph is flat, like this?:

3. What is Keisha doing when the graph line slopes down, like this?:

4. How many stops did Keisha make? Which stop was the most abrupt? How can you tell?

5. On which part of the trip did Keisha go the fastest?

Problem p. 470 from ADDISON-WESLEY MATHEMATICS *Grade 7.* Copyright © 1991 by Addison-W esley Publishing Company, Inc. Reprinted by permission of Pearson Education, Inc.

7.   We thought that this task fit the bill because it was very similar to Tony's Walk except that it supplied a set of questions to help kids make sense of the graph. The questions, we thought, would draw students' attention to interpreting the lines as increases or decreases (or constancy) in speed. We thought that if kids learned to do tasks like this, we could move on to asking them to interpret graphs of complex relationships on their own.

The Lesson

8.   I distributed the task to each student and explained that they would be answering questions based on a graph that showed Keisha's bicycle trip to school (see Figure 5.3). I placed a transparency of the task on the overhead and explained that the vertical axis tells speed and that the horizontal axis tells time. I wanted to make sure that students had this basic information before they attempted the task. I then told students that they would have 5 minutes to answer the questions in their groups.

9.   Students began to work on the task, and I circulated quickly around the room. I like to make contact with each group during the early stages of working on a task so I can see if there are any difficulties that I need to address or if the students are likely to need more time to complete the assignment. The groups began working immediately and made good progress through the questions. One group seemed to be having trouble with Question 4 on Figure 5.3. They did not know what "abrupt" meant. I realized that this might be a problem for all of my students so I explained to the class that in this case "abrupt" referred to a quick stop— like when you were in a car and a dog runs out in front of the car and the driver slams on the brakes. They smiled and nodded at my explanation. After a few more minutes, I noticed that most groups had completed all the questions. I indicated that we would begin to go over the questions. Hands began waving around the room as students eagerly volunteered to answer the questions. I was happy to see this. Students seemed more willing to take risks now than they had been at the beginning of the year.

10.   *Discussing the initial questions.* For the first question in Keisha's Bicycle Ride, Crystal offered that when the line slanted up from left to right, Keisha was going faster and faster. I asked her if she could explain how she knew this. I like to ask my students to explain—it helps me get a better idea of what they really understand. She said that because the vertical part showed the bike's speed, when the line went up the speed was going higher. Although she had not used the most elegant language, it seemed that Crystal "got it." Tonya, though, seemed confused. I asked Tonya if she had a question about what Crystal had just said. Tonya said that she thought that Keisha was going up a hill. Several students chimed in that they agreed with Tonya. This was one of the problems I had noticed in student responses to Tony's Walk—misinterpreting an increase in speed as going up a hill.

11.   At this point, I felt that Crystal should respond to Tonya. In our sessions with Ms. Harris, we had talked a lot about trying to encourage more student-to-student talk. This is hard because I keep feeling that it is my job to step in when students are having trouble. But since Crystal seemed to get it, I decided that I would try this approach. Crystal explained the graph wasn't supposed to be a picture of the bike ride! At my invitation, she came up to the overhead and traced the first incline on the graph with her finger. She explained that when Keisha started her ride she went from not moving at all [her finger was on the point $(0, 0)$] to moving. Because the line keeps going up, she commented (she slowly moved her finger up from $(0, 0)$, tracing the graph), she was going faster and faster. When Tonya asked how Keisha could keep going faster as she was climbing a hill, Crystal responded, "You can't tell whether Keisha is going up a hill, down a hill, or riding on a flat road. But, it would be hard to go faster while you were climbing a hill." *I* was pleased with Crystal's explanation, but I still wasn't sure *Tonya* understood. Glancing around the room, however, I noticed that most of the other students were nodding in agreement with Crystal. I made a note to check in with Tonya later in the period.

12.   On Question 2 most of the students seemed to agree that the "flat" portion of the graph represented a constant speed. They described this

as "riding steadily" or at a "regular speed." I asked my students how they could tell this from the graph. James said that you could tell because "*it*" was the same. "*What* was the same?" I asked. He said that if you went over to the vertical line and put in numbers then you would see that the flat part was across from the same number. So that means it must all be the same speed. James's response caught me off-guard. In fact, it was just then that I realized that Keisha's Bicycle Ride had no numbers! Maybe, I thought, the numbers were omitted for a reason and that adding them could create another kind of problem.

13.　　　Although I was not exactly sure where this would take us, I took a deep breath and asked James to go to the overhead and explain his idea. James wrote the numbers 1 through 5 on the vertical axis of the graph as shown in Figure 5.4 and repeated his earlier explanation, adding that the constant speed for the "flat part" was about 2.5 miles per hour. After he finished, Daryl said that no speeds were given, so you couldn't just make them up. James said that you could because the actual speed didn't matter. He explained that he put in the numbers because they helped him understand the problem better. I asked James why he picked these particular numbers. James said that he thought Keisha could have ridden those speeds, but that he could have picked any numbers he wanted. I decided not to press further on this.

14.　　　Question 3 presented the next challenge. Travis suggested that the slanted line going down from left to right meant that Keisha was going downhill. Obviously Tonya wasn't the only one seeing the graph as a picture! I asked the class if everyone agreed with this explanation. Since we had discussed a similar misconception earlier in the class, I was interested in knowing how other students were interpreting this sloping line. Anthony said that at first he thought that Keisha was going downhill, but that after he heard Crystal explain the first part, he decided that this couldn't be true. He said that if when the line slanted up Keisha was increasing her speed, then when the line was going down she must be going slower or decreasing her speed—it had to be the opposite. I asked Travis what he thought of Anthony's explanation. Travis said that when you went downhill you went faster, not slower. Anthony agreed that this was true, but again went back to the fact that the graph didn't show hills. I then asked Travis to think about what the information on the vertical axis told us and

FIGURE 5.4. James Puts Numbers on the Vertical Axis to Explain His Thinking

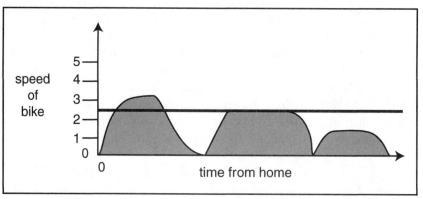

how that would help us read the graph. I decided to move on to the next question, hoping that this issue of slowing down versus going down a hill would come up again when we talked about abrupt stops.

15.   The fourth question proved to be even more difficult. In response to the first part, Tiffany came up to the overhead and drew little stop signs at the end of each of the legs as shown in Figure 5.5, indicating a total of three stops. I asked her how she could tell that Keisha had stopped at these points. She said that because the curves touched the horizontal line, the speed must be zero. "So," I said, "if you are going zero you aren't moving, right?" Tiffany nodded in agreement.

16.   Moving on to the next part, Tamika explained that she thought that the first stop was the most abrupt because the line "fell the greatest distance." William disagreed. He noted that the first stop "kinda curves," but that the second stop is a straighter line. Tamika countered that even though the second was straighter, Keisha wasn't going as fast when she decided to stop. Tamika asked me if she could go to the overhead to show what she meant. Not being quite sure what she intended to do, I said to go ahead. Tamika traced over the numbers that James had put on the vertical axis (see Figure 5.4), making them much bolder and darker. She then explained: "For the first stop, Keisha drops from 3 to 0; but for the second stop she only drops from 2.5 to 0." The first stop, she insisted, showed a more dramatic stop. This time I wasn't sure that the numbers would be quite so helpful since they seemed to be encouraging Tamika to look only at the one dimension of speed and not to consider how the change in speed was spread out over a period of time.

17.   I wanted to see if the other students were noticing that the change in speed and the amount of time that had passed needed to be considered together, an idea that was central to understanding this graph. In order to keep the conversation going, I indicated that Tamika had an interesting point and asked William what he thought about that. He said, "The numbers didn't matter." What was important, according to William, was how sudden the stop was, and the first stop was more gradual than the second. This convinced me that he understood the need to think about speed and time together.

FIGURE 5.5. Tiffany's Diagram for Question 4

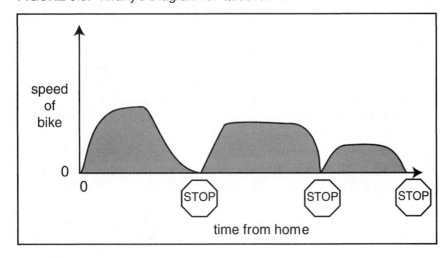

18.   As I glanced around the room, I noticed that most students seemed to be in agreement with William, and so I decided to ask about the third stop. Sarah said the third stop curved a little more than the second stop but not as much as the first. She added that Keisha was slamming on the brakes at the second stop, but at the first and third stops she just slowed down, perhaps by ceasing to peddle or using the brakes a little. I looked around the room to gauge students' reactions to Sarah's explanation. I couldn't see any visible signs of confusion, and so I asked the last question, "On which part of the trip did Keisha go the fastest?" Marsha said that she went the fastest in the beginning. I asked how she knew that, and she responded that the hill was the highest. One thing I was sure of was that I wanted my students to move beyond seeing this graph as a picture! I asked her if she could show us what she was talking about using the graph. Marsha went to the overhead and pointed to the first leg of the trip. She repeated that the hill was the highest. I repeated what she said as a question—"The *hill* is the highest?" She then corrected herself and said the *graph* was the highest. She said it was a little confusing because it did look like a hill. I said, "Yes, it does, but we just have to remember that this is a graph, not a hill. The vertical axis tells us how fast she is going and the horizontal how much time has passed."

19.   *Creating a new graph.* I explained that we were now going to work on the second part of the task, in which they were going to create a new graph. I asked students to imagine that Keisha took a second trip on her bicycle that was a little different than the first one—this time she slowed down but did not stop at the end of the first leg and that the fastest speed was the constant part of the second leg. I asked students to sketch the new graph on the back of their task sheet.

20.   Students got to work immediately. Again I traveled from group to group observing what they were doing, occasionally asking a clarifying question, and pressing students to explain why they were constructing the graphs in a particular way. After about 10 minutes I asked Jamal, Monica, and Terrance to put their groups' solutions (as shown in Figure 5.6) on the board. Although I noted that the groups had all made the changes correctly, there were differences in the graphs, which I wanted students to consider—some of which related directly to my earlier concern about the need to consider time and speed together.

21.   When the students were finished, I asked the class if the drawings were all the same. There was a mixed chorus of "yes" and "no." I asked Marilyn to explain why she thought they were the same. She said because they all curved up at the end of the first leg instead of touching and that they all had the second leg going fastest. Charles said that Marilyn was right, but that they didn't *look* the same. "What's different, Charles?" I asked, hoping he had noticed the steepness of Monica's group's graph versus the gradualness of the other two or that Jamal's group's graph showed the bicycle ride taking more time. Charles shrugged his shoulders and just repeated, "They just don't *look* the same." He added, "The horizontal part of Jamal's is longer."

22.   I wanted to press students to think harder about these graphs, so I asked them to get into their groups of four (each pair of students has a

FIGURE 5.6. The Graphs of Keisha's Second Bicycle Ride Produced by the Three Groups

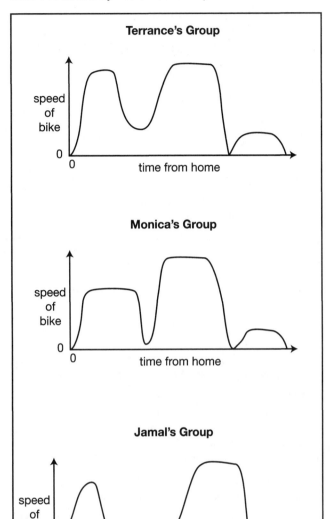

"partner pair" that they work with when I think that four heads might be better than two!) and to discuss what was the same and what was different on the three graphs. I decided that we could begin class the next day with a report from each group on their findings.

23.   As the groups began their work, I scanned the room quickly, trying to locate Travis and Tonya. They had both experienced some difficulty earlier in the period and I wanted to make sure that they were in groups with students who had moved beyond seeing the graph as a picture. I was pleased to see that they were both in groups with students who had provided good explanations earlier in the class. I made a note to touch base with them both tomorrow to see how they were doing.

The Next Day's Lesson

24.   I began the next class by returning to the question that the groups were considering at the close of the previous class—what was the same and what was different about the three graphs displayed on the board (Figure 5.6). Students made several comments that I was quite pleased with—ones that incorporated differences in how fast the bike was going *and* differences in how long of a period of time the bike remained at relative speeds (e.g., Miguel noticed that Monica's group's graph showed the bike slowing down very briefly before resuming a faster speed, while Jamal's group showed the bike riding at a slower speed for a little while, then gradually going faster and faster). Even the comments that focused only on speed or time without considering the two together provided evidence that students had moved beyond seeing the graph as a picture (e.g., no one referred to the graph as having "hills" when we discussed that, compared with the other two groups, Terrance's group made the second leg of the trip only a little faster than the first leg).

25.   I then had students work individually on Tony's Walk (Figure 5.2), the task that Ms. Harris had shared with us. I thought Tony's Walk was a good task because it required students to incorporate what they learned from our work on Keisha's Bicycle Ride. Since it is less structured than the previous task, I thought it would give students a chance to really dig in and make sense of the situation for themselves. Because of our earlier work, I also expected that my students would not have some of the same problems my colleagues and I had seen in the student work on Tony's Walk from the previous year's assessment. Specifically, I didn't think my students would make the mistake of seeing the graph as a picture of Tony going up and down hills.

26.   This assignment also would let me know the extent to which my students were successfully integrating both variables when interpreting graphs. Our session with Ms. Harris really brought this to my attention. She commented that qualitative graphs, such as Keisha's Bicycle Ride and Tony's Walk, help students to think about variables in a way that "went beyond rule-based notions of functional relationships." I definitely agreed—in the graphs of Keisha's Bicycle Ride and Tony's Walk, speed didn't seem to depend on time in the way that, for instance, sales tax depends on the amount of the purchase. Instead, both time and speed varied together so that for any point in time shown on the graph, there was only one corresponding speed. With Tony's walk, I wanted to see whether my students would consider how both variables were changing together. Armed with this information, I could then decide on the next course of action.

Reflecting on Students' Work on Tony's Walk

27.   In looking at my students' work on Tony's Walk, I was pleased to see that many students were able to integrate time and speed in their interpretations and appropriately describe what Tony might have been doing during each time interval of his walk. William's story (shown in Figure 5.7) is representative of the best responses. It is both accurate and complete because it addressed each segment of the graph, noted differ-

FIGURE 5.7. William's Work on Tony's Walk

> Tony left his house at noon. From noon to 12:30 he was walking about 3½ miles per hour because he was trying to catch ants. At about 12:30 Tony stopped to rest and eat lunch. Then at 1:00 he started walking again, he was walking about 3½ miles per hour until about 1:30 because he was daydreaming. At 1:30 he saw five birds hopping along the sidewalk so he watched them while he was walking which slowed him down a little. Then at 2:00 he finally caught up with his regular pace until 2:30 when he realized the time then he ran the rest of the way.

Reprinted with permission from *Using Assessment to Improve Middle-Grades Mathematics Teaching & Learning CD*, copyright © 2003 by the National Council of Teachers of Mathematics.

ences between the segments, and provided relevant activities for each time interval. For example, William identified when Tony was walking, stopped, was running, "caught up with his regular pace," and "slowed down a little." William also correctly interpreted the speed using miles per hour and considered speed and time together in statements such as, "he was walking about 3½ miles per hour until about 1:30" (indicating that he realized the speed was constant over this time interval). One thing that concerned me, though, was that even in the best responses, students didn't account for the difference between speed versus acceleration. Not that I expected them to use technical language—but I thought that our discussion during Keisha's Bicycle Ride about the "abruptness" of a stop might have influenced at least some students to comment on instant changes in speed (such as at 1 P.M.) versus gradual changes (such as between 1:30 and 2:00 P.M.). William indicated that watching birds slowed Tony down a little, but he did not address the gradual deceleration over the 1:30–2:00 interval.

28.   Although there were only a few responses like William's, most of the students showed the ability to integrate time and speed at some point in their response, attending to most (if not all) aspects of the graph. Tiffany's story of Tony's Walk (shown in Figure 5.8) is representative of what the majority of students did. Tiffany correctly interpreted the graph by indicating relative speeds (i.e., "rested," "slowed down a little bit," "speeded up"), and she included relevant activities for some time intervals ("rested," "getting tired"). However, she did not give a reason why Tony might have "speeded up" or "went even faster." Tiffany began by referring to the interval from noon to 12:30, but (like many other students) often described what was happening only at the point on the graph at which the speed changed rather than describing what was happening over the entire time interval. For example, she did not indicate that the speeds for the time intervals 12:00–12:30, 1:00–1:30, and 2:00–2:30 were all constant and equal to each other (recall that William referred to the speed at these intervals as "3½ miles per hour" and as the "regular pace"). In thinking about what Tiffany's response indicated about what she *did* understand, it appeared that she was able to consider both speed and time for specific points on the graph and to

FIGURE 5.8. Tiffany's Work on Tony's Walk

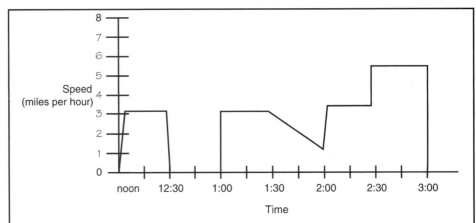

Write a story about Tony's walk. In your story, describe what Tony might have been doing at the different times.

One day tony decided he wanted to go to his grandmother's he started walking at noon til 12:30 he rested and started again at 1:00 Then he started getting tired at 1:30 and slowed down a little bit. At 2:00 he speeded up at 2:30 he went even faster at three we was where he wanted to go.

compare relative speeds for different intervals. I made a point to ask Tiffany some questions that would require her to discuss changes in time and speed over an entire time interval, to determine whether she simply wasn't thorough in her written response or whether she needed more opportunities to consider changes in both variables together.

29.   A few students seemed not to completely understand the need to consider both time and speed. For example, although Marsha's response (shown in Figure 5.9) indicated that Tony stopped walking from 12:30–1:00, there are other indications that she did not integrate time and speed in the interpretation of the graph. She didn't mention the change in speed at 1:30 or that the speed continued to decrease until 2:00. She indicated that "by 2 P.M. he was getting a bit tired," which might provide a reason for the decrease in speed. However, she then wrote, "But he ate the rest of his lunch and drank the rest of his Pepsi and was on his way again." This sounded to me like she thought Tony stopped walking, but the graph indicates only a decrease in speed, not a stop. It is unclear from Marsha's story whether she understood that. Another part of Marsha's story concerned me. She wrote, "At 2:30 Tony found his grandmother's dog wandering by himself. The dog was so small, Tony picked it up and carried it the rest of the way to Grandma's." You might expect that if Tony was carrying the dog, he would stop to pick it up, then walk slower rather than faster. This makes me wonder whether she understood the increase in Tony's speed at 2:30, or whether she was seeing each vertex as a stop. Like Tiffany's story, Marsha's story does not attend to the constant rates and equal speeds of the three time intervals.

FIGURE 5.9. Marsha's Work on Tony's Walk

> Tony gets off work at noon, and that day he promised his grandmother he would come over. He stopped at a resturant on the way, at about 12:30, to get lunch and got going again at 1:00. By 2:00 he was getting a bit tired. But he ate the rest of his lunch and drank the rest of his Pepsi and was on his way again. At 2:30 Tony found his grandmother's dog wandering by himself. The dog was so small, Tony picked it up and carried it the rest of the way to Grandma's, just in case she got too worried. She was glad to see both of her boys.

Reprinted with permission from *Using Assessment to Improve Middle-Grades Mathematics Teaching & Learning CD*, copyright © 2003 by the National Council of Teachers of Mathematics.

30.   Although students were no longer interpreting speed versus time graphs as hills, Travis and Tonya still missed key points. They made limited meaningful references to the graph in their stories. For example, Tonya (whose work is shown in Figure 5.10) correctly identified that Tony walked 3 mph from noon to 12:30. However, she went on to say that "between 12:30 and one o'clock he was bouncing [a] ball still walking 3 mph." A correct interpretation would have Tony doing an activity so that he was not walking. Perhaps she mistakenly looked at the time interval between 1:00 and 1:30, since she said "still walking 3 mph," but even so, her description did not account for the stop between 12:30 and 1:00 P.M. In fact, Tonya ignored the segments between 1:00 and 2:30 P.M., as her story then skipped to the last half hour of the graph and said, "For the next one half hour he only got up to 6 mph." Although Tonya did not discuss any increases or decreases in speed or that Tony stopped walking for half an hour, I was pleased that Tonya was able to interpret the speed axis to give a speed that corresponded with some of the time intervals and that she had moved beyond seeing the graph as a picture.

31.   After looking at all of the responses to Tony's Walk, I am pleased with the progress my students have made in interpreting graphs of speed versus time. I think the work we have done has really helped my students to move beyond seeing these types of graphs as pictures of hills.

FIGURE 5.10. Tonya's Work on Tony's Walk

> One day this bright little boy wanted to go on a nature walk. at noon he left to start his journey. By 12:30 he was going 3 mph during that time he was sing the blues between 12:30 and one o'clock he was bouncing his ball still walking 3mph. For the next one half hour he only got up to 6 mph. he's a slow walker. But at least he got to Grandmother's house. Although it took him 3 hours. He got there.

Reprinted with permission from *Using Assessment to Improve Middle-Grades Mathematics Teaching & Learning CD*, copyright © 2003 by the National Council of Teachers of Mathematics.

However, there are still some students who did not consider the changes in both variables together when they interpreted Tony's Walk, so we need some more practice. It will be interesting to see how my students deal with qualitative graphs in other contexts (perhaps a roller coaster ride or a car on a racetrack) and that involve other variables (such as distance versus time or height versus time).

32.   For the next lesson, I think I will select a few responses to Tony's Walk, remove students' names, then distribute the responses along with a rubric we have used and have students score the work. I think this will raise many issues for the students, helping them to see the important aspects of the graph and how to integrate both variables in their interpretations as we explore more qualitative graphs in future lessons.

ANALYZING THE CASE

Now that you have had the opportunity to read the case and to identify instructional decisions that Robert Carter made throughout the lesson, we invite you to consider why Robert Carter might have made these decisions. Here are a few suggestions about how to proceed.

- Using the list of instructional decisions that you identified as you read the case, consider what might have influenced Robert Carter to make each decision at that particular point in the lesson. Cite specific evidence from the case (i.e., paragraph numbers) to support your claims.
- If you have colleagues who also are reading this case, compare and contrast your ideas about what influenced Robert Carter's instructional decisions. Note points of disagreement since these are likely to be fruitful topics for ongoing discussion and debate. If you are working on this activity alone, we encourage you to refer to Appendix D, which includes a decisions/rationale chart that was produced by teachers participating in a whole-group discussion of Robert Carter's teaching practices. You may want to note any decisions that you did not identify and consider whether or not you would add the decision to your own list.

You may wish to continue your analysis of the case by considering the questions in the next section. Alternatively, you can skip the next section and proceed directly to the "Connecting to Your Own Practice" section in which you are encouraged to relate the analysis of the ideas and issues raised in "The Case of Robert Carter" to your own teaching practice.

EXTENDING YOUR ANALYSIS OF THE CASE

The questions listed in this section are intended to help you focus on particular aspects of the case related to teacher decision-making and student thinking. If you are working with one or more colleagues, the questions can serve as a stimulus for further discussion.

1. Robert Carter selected Keisha's Bicycle Ride because it supplied a set of questions to help students make sense of the graph (para. 7). What do you see as the costs and benefits of using this task (as opposed to a more open-ended task such as Tony's Walk or the Opening Activity) in terms of opportunities for student learning?

2. Consider James's introduction of numbers on the y-axis in order to explain what was happening on the trip when the graph line was flat (paras. 12–13). Why do you think James used numbers to explain what "riding steadily" or "at a regular speed" means? In general, what are some advantages and disadvantages of omitting numbers from the axes of the graph of Keisha's Bicycle Ride?

3. Robert Carter makes the point that "Jamal's group's graph showed the bicycle ride taking more time" (para. 21). Is this a valid interpretation of the graph? Explain your reasoning.

4. Mr. Carter encourages his students to communicate their thinking in many ways. To what extent do you think Mr. Carter holds his students accountable for providing good mathematical explanations? Find specific examples in "The Case of Robert Carter" to support your judgment.

5. Identify Mr. Carter's goals for his students' learning. To what extent do you think Mr. Carter's goals were met during the lesson? Cite specific evidence from the case to support your judgment.

6. At several points during the lesson, Mr. Carter notices some students are still struggling with a concept, but makes the decision to move on (e.g., Tonya, end of para. 11; Travis, end of para. 14). What are the advantages and disadvantages of this decision? If Robert Carter had decided to attend to the students who were struggling, in what ways might he have supported their thinking?

7. While discussing the initial questions, Mr. Carter has Crystal respond to Tonya, making a deliberate decision to encourage student-to-student talk rather than intervening himself (para. 11). In what circumstances might teacher intervention be appropriate?

8. When Robert Carter first considered Tony's Walk, he stated that it was "certainly different from how I learned graphing—endless plotting of x and y coordinates on a Cartesian grid followed by 'connecting the dots'" (para. 5). How might Robert Carter connect his students' work with qualitative graphs such as Keisha's Bicycle Ride and Tony's Walk to work with quantitative graphs?

9. When looking at Tiffany's response, Robert Carter considers "what Tiffany's response indicated about what she *did* understand" (para. 28). Why is this important? What questions would you like to ask Tiffany to further her understanding? In what

ways do you agree or disagree with Mr. Carter's assessment of his students' work?

CONNECTING TO YOUR OWN PRACTICE

In this section, we offer ways to connect the specific ideas investigated in "The Case of Robert Carter" to a set of larger issues that can be explored in your own classroom. Building on your analysis of "The Case of Robert Carter," the activities presented in this section provide opportunities for focused reflection on issues that might be important to your own teaching of mathematics.

- In the "Analyzing the Case" section, you identified instructional decisions that Robert Carter made that influenced his students' learning and considered why he might have made those decisions. Videotape a lesson in your own classroom. As you view the tape, identify the instructional decisions you made during the lesson and reflect on your reasons for making those decisions. Consider whether your decisions were based on students' understanding of mathematical ideas throughout the lesson and whether, in hindsight, you would make different decisions based on students' mathematical understandings.
- Robert Carter makes several decisions about what his students did and did not understand about the mathematical ideas in Keisha's Bicycle Ride and Tony's Walk based on students' written responses to Tony's Walk. According to NCTM's *Principles and Standards for School Mathematics* (2000), assessment should "furnish useful information to both teachers and students" (p. 22) and be a "valuable tool for making instructional decisions" (p. 23). Robert Carter appears to have assessed his students' work on Tony's Walk in a way that met both of these goals. Give your students an open-ended task (such as Keisha's Bicycle Ride, Tony's Walk, or another task of your choosing) and collect their responses. Sort the responses into piles of high, medium, and low. Choose two responses from each category to serve as representative samples. For each response that you have chosen, consider the following questions: What does the student appear to understand? What would you like to ask the student in order to get a better idea of what the student understands? (You also may want to analyze the set of responses in each category and make a list of the criteria that make a response "high," "medium," or "low.")

EXPLORING CURRICULAR MATERIALS

You may want to explore mathematics curricula for ideas related to qualitative graphs by considering the following questions: Are qualitative graphs found in your curriculum? If not, is there a natural place in the curriculum to include qualitative graphs in order to develop your students' abilities to integrate two variables in order to make sense of a situation? In what ways can qualitative graphs be used to expand students' ideas on what function is and how two variables are related?

You also may want to solve additional tasks to continue to explore the mathematical ideas made salient in the case. The following list identifies resources that contain problems that are considered to be "mathematically similar" to the task used in Robert Carter's class.

Billstein, R., & Williamson, J. (1999c). *Middle grades math thematics: Book 3*. Evanston, IL: McDougal Littell.
> Of particular interest in Section 1 of Module 7 (Visualizing Change) are Exercises 1–11 (pp. 468–472). Students are asked to create or interpret qualitative graphs of change over time in a variety of contexts.

Education Development Center, Inc. (1998b). *MathScape: Mathematics of motion: Distance, speed, and time* (Student guide). Mountain View, CA: Creative Publications.
> Of particular interest is Lesson 6 (pp. 18–19), which asks students to make connections between stories, maps, and distance–time graphs.

Lappan, G., Fey, J., Fitzgerald, W., Friel, S., & Phillips, E. (2002c). *Thinking with mathematical models: Representing relationships. Connected mathematics.* Glenview, IL: Prentice Hall.
> Of particular interest is Problem 4.1 (pp. 48–49), which provides students with two qualitative graphs and asks students to determine what events from the story are being modeled by the graphs.

The Mathematics in Context Development Team. (1997b). Mathematics in context: Tracking graphs (Student guide). In National Center for Research in Mathematical Sciences Education & Freudenthal Institute (Eds.), *Mathematics in context.* Chicago: Encyclopaedia Brittanica.
> Of particular interest is Section D (Graphs Depicting Speed, pp. 29–32), which provides several opportunities for students to explore graphs of speed versus time.

CONNECTING TO OTHER IDEAS AND ISSUES

If you have additional time, you may want to explore some aspect of the case in more depth. The resources identified in this section provide some possibilities for exploring the mathematical and pedagogical issues raised by the case. For example, you might: (1) discuss how

Robert Carter could use the holistic scoring rubric and the resulting scores to improve his teaching and his students' learning according to the Cai, Lane, and Jakabcsin (1996) and Parke and Lane (1996) articles and the Parke, Lane, Silver, and Magone (2003) book; (2) use the activities that appear in Lambdin, Lynch, and McDaniel (2000), Nickerson, Nydam, and Bowers (2000), and Van Dyke (1994) as a basis for discussing what Mr. Carter might have done prior to the Keisha's Bicycle Ride Task or what he might want to do next to help his students alleviate misconceptions and develop their ability to interpret graphs; or (3) complete additional qualitative graph activities such as those found in Van de Walle (2004). You also may want to revisit readings from Chapter 4 that are relevant to "The Case of Robert Carter," such as Friel and colleagues (2001), Leinhardt and colleagues (1990), or Swan and colleagues (1984).

Cai, J., Lane, S., & Jakabcsin, M. S. (1996). The role of open-ended tasks and scoring rubrics in assessing students' mathematical reasoning and communication. In P. C. Elliott (Ed.), *Communication in mathematics: K–12 and beyond, 1996 yearbook* (pp. 137–145). Reston, VA: National Council of Teachers of Mathematics.

This article discusses the role of open-ended tasks and holistic scoring rubrics in assessing students' mathematical communication and reasoning, and features two tasks that appeared on the QUASAR Cognitive Assessment Instrument. One of these tasks, Tony's Walk, is discussed in "The Case of Robert Carter." Student work on this task is shown as examples of the five different levels on the holistic scoring rubric.

Lambdin, D. V., Lynch, R. K., & McDaniel, H. (2000). Algebra in the middle grades. *Mathematics Teaching in the Middle School, 6,* 195–198.

This article describes a 4-day, mini-unit designed to have 6th-grade students develop a deeper understanding of the relationships between rates of change and the shapes of graphs that represent change over time. Students used a variety of hands-on activities related to the Keisha's Bicycle Ride Task in "The Case of Robert Carter."

Nickerson, S. D., Nydam, C., & Bowers, J. S. (2000). Linking algebraic concepts and contexts: Every picture tells a story. *Mathematics Teaching in the Middle School, 6,* 92–98.

This article describes an instructional sequence using a computer software package that incorporates animation with position and velocity graphs. The article provides the website where the lessons and software package can be downloaded for free. A variety of activities are described. An activity that makes salient the relationship between position and velocity graphs could be useful in dispelling the misconception of Robert Carter's students that the velocity graph represents a position graph.

Parke, C. S., & Lane, S. (1996). Learning from performance assessments in math. *Educational Leadership, 54,* 26–29.

This article discusses how performance assessments were used to improve mathematics instruction and student achievement within the QUASAR Project, using three tasks from the QUASAR Cognitive Assessment Instrument. One of these tasks, Tony's Walk, is discussed in "The Case of Robert Carter." An example of students using a holistic scoring rubric to grade another student's work on Tony's Walk demonstrates the value of having students use a rubric to further understand what constitutes a good mathematical solution.

Parke, C. S., Lane, S., Silver, E. A., & Magone, M. E. (2003). *Using assessment to improve middle-grades mathematics teaching and learning: Suggested activities using QUASAR tasks, scoring criteria, and students' work.* Reston, VA: National Council of Teachers of Mathematics.

This book provides a set of six activities intended to illustrate the potential of using open-ended tasks as performance assessments in the classroom. Tony's Walk is featured on the CD that accompanies this book as one of 16 tasks that could engage teachers in using performance tasks, developing rubrics, and assessing students' learning.

Van de Walle, J. (2004). *Elementary and middle school mathematics: Teaching developmentally.* Boston: Pearson Education/ Allyn & Bacon.

In Chapter 23, the section "Graphs Without Equations" discusses how having students work with qualitative graphs, similar to Keisha's Bicycle Ride or Tony's Walk depicted in "The Case of Robert Carter," offers the advantage of focusing on how graphs can express functional relationships. Several different activities using qualitative graphs are described.

Van Dyke, F. (1994). Relating to graphs in introductory algebra. *Mathematics Teacher, 87,* 427–432.

This article features a set of activities designed to help students make connections between graphical and verbal representations of functions by identifying, interpreting, and creating graphs. The graph identification activity—matching a graphical representation with a verbal description—is likely to bring to the fore the most frequently cited errors with respect to interpreting and constructing graphs—interpreting the graph of a situation as a literal picture of the situation.

Part II

FACILITATING LEARNING FROM CASES

In Part II of this book (Chapters 6–10), we turn our attention to providing support for case facilitators. Chapter 6 serves as an opening to this part of the book, which describes how to facilitate learning from the cases. Chapters 7 through 10 provide support materials intended to assist facilitators in utilizing the cases and related materials provided in Chapters 2 through 5, respectively. Part II is intended primarily for those readers who will be facilitating discussions around the cases and related materials found in Part I. These facilitators may include any professionals who contribute to improving the quality of mathematics teaching and learning through their work in diverse settings: schools (e.g., teacher leaders, coaches, mentors, administrators); school district offices (e.g., curriculum coordinators, staff developers); regional intermediate units and state agencies; or colleges and universities (e.g., instructors of mathematics or methods courses).

6

Using Cases to Support Learning About Teaching

The cases found in Part I of this book embody a vision of mathematics teaching and learning that is very different from how most teachers have learned mathematics and learned to teach mathematics. The vision calls for students who can think and reason about challenging and complex problems that give rise to significant mathematical understandings. It also calls for teachers who can appropriately scaffold and support students' learning by creating environments that foster communication, inquiry, and investigation. It is now widely accepted that meeting these goals and standards will require a great deal of learning on the part of teachers.

The kind of learning that is required of teachers has been described as transformative (i.e., sweeping changes in deeply held beliefs, knowledge, and habits of practice) as opposed to additive (the addition of new skills to an existing repertoire) (Thompson & Zeuli, 1999). Teachers of mathematics cannot successfully develop their students' thinking, reasoning, and communication skills simply by adopting a new curriculum or by using more hands-on materials. Rather they must thoroughly overhaul their thinking about what it means to know and understand mathematics and how they can best provide support as their students struggle to learn deeper and more complex mathematics.

One approach to helping teachers transform their practice involves situating the professional education of teachers "in practice" (Smith, 2001). In a seminal chapter on this topic, Ball and Cohen (1999) argue that "teachers' everyday work could become a source for constructive professional development" through the development of a curriculum for professional learning that is grounded in the tasks, questions, and problems of practice (p. 4). They propose that teachers' instructional practice be seen both as a site for professional learning and also as a stimulus for developing inquiry

into practice from which many teachers could learn. To accomplish this goal, they argue that records of authentic practice—curriculum materials, narrative or video summaries of teachers planning for and/or engaging in instruction, samples of student work—should become the core of professional education, providing a focus for sustained teacher inquiry and investigation.

This book represents such an approach to teacher education. The materials and activities in Part I encourage teachers and other readers to construct knowledge central to teaching by engaging in activities that are built around artifacts of classroom practice. The narrative cases provide the opportunity to analyze how teacher and student interactions in the classroom influence what students learn. The instructional tasks that appear in the Opening Activity of each case (which are drawn from actual classroom practice) invite teachers and other readers to explore important mathematical ideas. Finally, activities such as the comparison of the cases and/or instructional tasks to teachers' own practice, or to other curricular materials, provide yet more opportunities for teachers or other readers to learn about practice from the actual work of practice.

WHY CASES?

Similar to many other teacher educators, we have been drawn to cases because they capture the complexity and situatedness of instructional practice. Unlike theories, propositions, principles, or other abstractions, the particularities of cases vividly convey the profusion of events, actions, and thought that constitute the moment-by-moment lived experience of a classroom lesson. Told through the voice of the classroom teacher, our cases offer the additional advantage of allowing the reader to "listen in" as the teacher in the case struggles with the multitude of decisions and dilemmas that make up the lived experience of the middle school mathematics classroom.

Cases are also an effective medium for capturing the *interdependence* of teachers' knowledge of mathematics, pedagogy, and students. By exposing how these different kinds of knowledge are accessed and used in the decisions that teachers make, cases portray how teachers simultaneously think about and pull from mathematical knowledge, pedagogical expertise, and knowledge of how students learn mathematics, in order to reach an instructional goal.

LEARNING FROM CASES

To learn from cases, readers must do more than simply read them. We have found it useful to distinguish between two classes of activities in which participants engage in order to learn from cases: analysis and generalization. Analysis involves the careful examination of a case teacher's decisions and interactions with students in light of the goals that the teacher wishes to accomplish. Generalization involves viewing the particularities of case-based episodes as instantiations of a broader set of ideas about mathematics, about teaching, and about learning. The following sections discuss analysis and generalization in more detail.

Analysis

Analyzing the instructional practice in a case involves the interpretation of teacher thinking and action in the context of the overall lesson. For example, a case facilitator might want participants to analyze how the teacher in the case drew students' attention to the mathematical ideas that constituted his or her goals for the lesson. This would involve paying attention to the teaching moves that built upon certain student responses (and not others) and instances in which the teacher took a more directive role. In "The Case of Ed Taylor" (Chapter 3), for example, the teacher focuses his students' attention on making connections between the diagram, which showed the physical arrangement of square tiles, and different ways of symbolically representing the pattern by pressing students to use the diagram to explain their symbolic representation, recording their equations, and asking students to spend the final portion of the lesson writing a journal entry in which they discussed the different equations and explained why they were equivalent. Analyzing Ed

Taylor's moves involves paying attention to what he did, and how and why he did it in order to accomplish his goals for the lesson.

Because they appear as narratives in print form, narrative cases represent a controlled way for readers to learn these skills of lesson analysis. Unlike observations of real teaching, readers can stop the action at any moment to ponder the implications of a particular decision. They can even revisit a particular part of the lesson in order to check the facts and deepen their analysis. And, finally, narrative cases that appear in print form allow the reader to more easily keep the entire lesson in view while interpreting the teacher's action at a given point in the lesson.

Generalization

The ultimate goal of reading and analyzing cases is for readers to recognize specific situations in the cases as instances of something larger and more generalizable. In order for readers to be able to move from a specific instance of a phenomenon to a more general understanding, they need multiple opportunities to consider an idea, to make comparisons across situations, and ultimately to examine their own ideas, beliefs, and, if currently teaching, their own instructional practice.

Our goal for all readers, through reading and discussing cases, is for them to connect the events depicted in the cases to an increasingly elaborated knowledge base of mathematics, teaching, and learning, and, when applicable, to their own practice. For example, consider "The Case of Catherine Evans and David Young" (Chapter 2). Although events in either Mrs. Evans's or Mr. Young's classroom could be elevated to a discussion of larger, more generalizable ideas, considering Catherine Evans and David Young together illustrates the power of two contrasting examples of the same big idea. When, for example, both teachers try to get students to develop generalizations for finding the perimeter of any sized pattern-block train, they do so in different ways and with different results. By comparing the two approaches, participants can engage in a more general discussion of classroom factors that impact students' opportunities to learn.

For classroom teachers particularly, extracting general principles from the specific instances in a case is necessary so that they can begin to formulate new ways of acting and interacting in *their own classrooms* that are based on thoughtful, principled, sharable, and effective decisions (Shulman, 1996). To achieve this goal, teachers must learn to connect the specifics of deeply contextualized, case-based moments with a broader set of ideas about mathematics, about teaching, and about learning. Generalizing allows teachers to view the specific incidents within the cases as instantiations of larger patterns and principles that will have applicability to their own practice.

In order to foster the development of this kind of skill, our cases are situated within a larger, more general set of mathematical and pedagogical ideas that we intend for current or future teachers to understand and to utilize in making sense of new situations that they will encounter in their own practice. Toward this end, well-conducted case discussions are crucial because they highlight the question, "What is this a case of?" thus stimulating learners "to move up and down, back and forth, between the memorable particularities of cases and powerful generalizations and simplifications of principles and theories" (Shulman, 1996, p. 201).

WHAT CAN BE LEARNED FROM OUR CASES

In addition to learning the skills of analyzing and generalizing, there is also specific mathematical content that can be learned through engagement with our cases. As noted in Chapter 1, the cases were designed to instantiate a broader set of ideas about mathematics, algebra as the study of patterns and functions, and ways in which teachers may support and inhibit students' learning in the context of cognitively challenging mathematical tasks. Each of these ideas is discussed briefly in the following sections.

Algebra as the Study of Patterns and Functions

Algebra has been viewed as an important topic in secondary school, but the development of algebraic thinking has emerged in recent years as a topic of interest and import in grades K–8, and especially in grades 6–8. Much of this shift has been associated with a view of algebra not only as a set of procedures for symbolic manipulation but also as a process of representing and generalizing observed regularities in patterns and relationships. For example, the *Principles and Standards for School Mathematics* (NCTM, 2000) notes the importance of developing middle-grades students' ability to represent, analyze, and generalize patterns using tables, graphs, words, and symbolic rules; relating and comparing different representations for a relationship; and solving problems using various representations.

The newer middle-grades curricula reflect this view of algebra as the study of patterns and functions. Yet, middle school teachers who learn mathematics content in university mathematics courses may not be exposed to patterns as a precursor of algebraic thinking or to the manner in which analyzing and describing qualitative functions can lay the foundation for later algebraic reasoning. Research on teacher knowledge of functions (Even, 1989, 1990, 1993; Sánchez & Llinares, 2003; Stein, Baxter, & Leinhardt, 1990; Wilson, 1994) suggests that teachers would benefit from a deeper understanding of the nature of a function, the import of function as a mathematical concept, and the variety of ways in which functions can be represented.

Situations aimed at encouraging teachers and other readers to revisit and question their own understanding of patterns and functions have been purposefully built into the cases in this volume. We have embedded multiple opportunities for readers to actively explore, identify, and characterize how two variables that have a functional relationship relate to one another. These include situations in which readers are encouraged to generate and use a variety of representational forms to solve problems (e.g., language, tables, equations, graphs, context); to recognize the equivalence of different representations of a functional relationship both within and between forms; and to develop flexible reasoning within and across a variety of representational forms (i.e., by recognizing changes in the symbolic representation of linear equations and the corresponding changes in the graphical representations). Readers are expected to develop deeper understandings of variables and functions by encountering these situations in our cases again and again, in different contexts, and in slightly different forms.

Ways of Supporting and Inhibiting Student Learning

After years of focusing on the mastery of non-ambiguous, procedurally oriented skills, skills that are easy to mimic and apply successfully without much thought, many students find high-level tasks intimidating and anxiety provoking. As increasing numbers of middle schools have taken up the challenge of using more ambitious tasks, it has become clear that many teachers need assistance in learning how to support students to engage with and successfully complete these tasks. Those who are most effective are able to both retain high-level expectations for how students should tackle such tasks and provide the right kind and amount of assistance to allow students to succeed. Other, less effective teachers either supply too much assistance, essentially taking the difficult pieces of thinking away from the students, or fail to provide enough direction and assistance, allowing students to flounder in unsystematic and nonproductive ways.

Situations aimed at encouraging teachers to identify and understand ways of supporting students' learning of complex mathematical ideas have been purposefully built into the cases. We have embedded multiple opportunities for readers to notice and analyze how student thinking can be supported during a lesson. These include situations in which the teachers in the cases keep expectations high by pressing students to explain and justify their thinking and reasoning; situations in which the case teachers assist students as they generate and make connections between different ways of representing the same functional relationship; and situations in which the case teachers uncover and use student responses to problems in pedagogically productive ways for all students. As with the mathematical ideas, readers can develop deeper understandings of ways of supporting student thinking by encountering these ideas in our cases again and again, in different contexts, and in slightly different forms.

PREPARING FOR AND FACILITATING CASE DISCUSSIONS

Although we recognize that individual readers may elect to use the cases on their own (and Part I is written to allow them to do so), we feel that engaging readers as a group around the central ideas of the cases has even greater potential to lead to robust learning and improved teaching practice. The success of group sessions, however, is directly dependent on the skill and preparedness of the facilitator. In this section, we describe how facilitators can prepare for and carry out effective learning experiences using our cases.

Preparing for Case Discussions

Similar to the wisdom of teachers preparing for lessons by anticipating how their students will approach planned instructional tasks, it is a good idea for facilitators to prepare for case discussions by reading and thinking about the case from the perspective of the learners. We encourage facilitators to begin their preparations by completing the problems presented in the Opening Activity and then reading the case. By keeping in mind how the specific group with whom they will be

working might approach the Opening Activity and case, the facilitator often can predict what issues will arise and prepare for how to deal with them.

The next preparation step is to study the facilitation materials that have been prepared for each case (found in Chapters 7 through 10 of Part II). These materials have been specifically designed to help facilitators assist readers as they interact with the case materials. As the facilitation chapters were being written, we were keenly aware of the fact that the cases will be used in a variety of settings and with a variety of individuals (i.e., with teachers at different points in their careers, future teachers of mathematics, or school administrators, or with other individuals interested in mathematics teaching and learning). Moreover, we expect that facilitators will have a variety of backgrounds and will be pursuing a multitude of important and worthwhile goals. As such, the facilitation chapters do not prescribe certain formats or routes through case discussions. Rather they have been designed to make explicit what is embedded in the cases so that facilitators can make their own decisions regarding how to connect learning opportunities in the cases to the particular group with whom they are working and the goals that they have for their work.

The heart of each facilitation chapter is the "Case Analysis." This section indexes the main ideas embedded in the cases; more specifically, it allows the facilitator to prepare for case discussions that connect particular, case-based incidents to larger, more generalizable sets of ideas. The "Case Analysis" has two major components. First, the key mathematical ideas are more fully described in an easy-to-access fashion *and*, for each idea, the specific places in the case that contain incidents related to that idea are identified. The incidents are identified by paragraph numbers in the case and by a short explanation of how the incident relates to the mathematical idea. Next, the key pedagogical ideas are identified and accompanied by, as in the mathematics section, markers of specific places in the case that contain incidents related to those ideas and a brief explanation of how the incident relates to the pedagogical idea.

A complaint sometimes raised about case discussions is that they can be all over the board, with the facilitator appearing to have only loose control over what gets talked about and how. Becoming familiar with the materials in the "Case Analysis" section of the facilitation chapter will enable facilitators to avoid this pitfall and to lead a focused and productive case discussion. By studying both the mathematics and pedagogy sections of the "Case Analysis," facilitators will become familiar with the big ideas of the case and exactly where examples of those ideas are embedded in the case. This knowledge will help them to recognize when readers are grappling with case incidents that have the potential to lead to deeper insights, to encourage readers to consider specific episodes of the case at opportune moments, and to help readers to look across various instances to surface the big ideas.

Other sections of the facilitation chapter will help the facilitator to prepare for activities related to the case discussions. For example, a section entitled "Facilitating the Opening Activity" provides suggestions for orchestrating the mathematical problem-solving session that utilizes a task related to the mathematical task featured in the case. In "Facilitating the Case Discussion," suggestions are provided for how to have participants prepare for case discussions and for various strategies for conducting the discussion. Finally, in "Extending the Case Experience," we provide facilitators with ideas regarding how they might extend explorations of the mathematical and pedagogical ideas on which the cases are based.

Facilitating Case-Based Experiences

We recommend having participants work on the problems in the Opening Activity prior to reading the case. In our experience, having participants complete and reflect on ways of solving the tasks in the Opening Activity is critical to an informed reading of the case and to a rich and successful case discussion. By grappling with the mathematics in the tasks, participants become familiar and confident with the underlying mathematical ideas in the case and are therefore better prepared to think flexibly about the solution strategies that students produce as the case unfolds.

The role of the facilitator during the Opening Activity is to elicit a variety of solution strategies to the problems and, to the extent possible, help participants to identify how those strategies are both similar to and different from one another. We have found it useful to have participants work on the tasks first individually, then in small groups, and finally to participate in a large-group discussion in which various solution strategies are made public.

We also have found that case discussions are most productive when participants have read the case on their own prior to the session in which the case will be discussed. In this regard, reading the case with a guiding question in mind appears to lead to more active reading of the case and more thoughtful and focused participation in the case discussion. Toward this end, we

have provided suggestions in the facilitation chapters for ways to focus the participants' initial reading of the case.

Facilitating the case discussion itself is a learned skill. Not unlike classroom teachers, facilitators must listen intently to the participants and learn how to steer the conversation in useful directions. Toward this end, it is important for the facilitator to have specific learning goals in mind for the case discussion. With respect to "The Case of Edith Hart" (Chapter 4), for example, a facilitator may want participants to be able to learn what effective teachers do to support student learning. To accomplish this goal, the facilitator might ask participants to break into small groups and create a three-column chart indicating what Ms. Hart's students learned or were in the process of learning, what Ms. Hart did to facilitate or support her students' learning, and evidence (i.e., paragraph numbers from the case) to support their claims. Afterwards, the facilitator can bring the groups together to generate a master chart and reach consensus regarding what was learned and how the learning was supported. Points of disagreement also could become the focus of the discussion, as they are likely to be fruitful topics for further analysis.

Extending Case-Based Experiences

Finally, facilitators sometimes choose to extend the case-based experiences by providing participants with additional opportunities to explore the mathematical and pedagogical ideas on which each case is based. By moving beyond the specifics of a case and task, participants can begin to generalize the ideas and issues raised in the case discussion. Specifically, teachers can begin to examine their own practice in light of new understandings about mathematics, instruction, and student learning. The following activities suggest ways in which facilitators might extend the case experience.

Connecting to teachers' practice. Several suggestions are made in the section entitled "Connecting to Your Own Practice" (Chapters 2 through 5) for how to draw linkages to the teacher's own practice. Facilitators may wish to assign one or more of these activities as follow-up assignments for teachers to explore in their own classrooms.

Facilitators also might consider asking teachers to identify an issue that the case raised for them and collect these ideas into a master list of issues with which their particular group of teachers is grappling. Facilitators then could ask teachers to identify one issue that they would like to work on and begin working collaboratively on planning a lesson in which the issue can be addressed. By focusing on an issue, teachers will be able to base the lesson on whatever mathematical content they currently are teaching.

Exploring the mathematical ideas in curricular materials. Facilitators also can have participants examine the manner in which the mathematical ideas portrayed in the case play out in mathematics curricula, by asking them to identify similar tasks in the curricula and the kind of thinking required to solve them, how the tasks build on students' prior knowledge, and how the tasks collectively shape students' learning of the mathematical content.

Alternatively, facilitators could ask participants to compare two different curricula. By comparing and contrasting curricula, participants have the opportunity to see how different texts develop a particular mathematical idea or set of ideas and to analyze the extent to which the texts are designed to engage students in mathematical thinking and reasoning. (When working with preservice teachers, facilitators may want to have them compare the curriculum that is used in the school in which they will be doing their student teaching with one that reflects an alternative view of mathematics teaching and learning.)

In addition, facilitators may want to have participants engage in solving additional mathematical tasks. The tasks identified and described in the section entitled "Exploring Curricular Materials" in Chapters 2 through 5 are mathematically similar to the tasks featured in each case.

Using professional readings to enhance and extend learning. In the section entitled "Connecting to Other Ideas and Issues" in Chapters 2 through 5, several suggestions are made for how to use the resources that are identified and described. Facilitators can assign one or more of the suggested activities and readings as follow-up assignments in order to help participants broaden or deepen their understanding of algebra and/or the teaching of algebra as the study of patterns and functions.

PUTTING THE PIECES TOGETHER

Based on our own experiences in using the cases and the experiences of colleagues, we can recommend their use in preservice mathematics methods and content courses, in professional development efforts for practicing teachers, and in workshops with various school administrators. However, it is important to note the cases in this volume are not meant to represent a complete curriculum for middle school mathematics teacher education.

Depending on one's circumstances, the cases can be used in a variety of ways. For example, facilitators may want to build a focused course around all four cases in this volume. We have designed and offered such a course on algebraic reasoning to practicing and prospective elementary, middle, and high school teachers, using the cases in this volume as the backbone and supplementing them with related readings and activities. Details about this course can be found at *www.cometproject.com.* This website provides information regarding the goals for the course, specific activities used in the course, and details regarding the ways in which course activities were sequenced. In addition, the website contains instruments that we developed to measure what teachers learned about the teaching and learning of algebra from the course as well references to papers that describe what teachers appeared to learn.

In other situations facilitators may want to select one or two specific cases to blend into an existing teacher education agenda in order to address an identified need. Whatever the situation-of-use, facilitators will find in the facilitation chapters the support that they need to make optimal use of each case.

Facilitating Learning from The Case of Catherine Evans and David Young

"The Case of Catherine Evans and David Young" is a dual case portraying how mathematically challenging tasks unfold under different classroom conditions. In each classroom, students are working on a set of pattern tasks. Each pattern begins with one regular figure (e.g., square, hexagon) and for each subsequent train in the pattern one additional figure is added. The students are asked to find the perimeter of the first four trains, which are already drawn, and then to find the perimeter of the tenth train without constructing it. The first part of the case features Catherine Evans, an experienced teacher in the initial stages of teaching mathematics in a new way. Mrs. Evans's deep concern for student success during her first year of using a reform-oriented curriculum leads her to simplify and proceduralize tasks. Over time, Mrs. Evans progresses toward reform-oriented mathematics teaching, and she and her colleagues serve as mentors to newcomer David Young. The second part of the case portrays Mr. Young's experience in teaching a similar lesson involving pattern tasks, where the experiences and insights of his colleagues convince Mr. Young to provide students with time to struggle and to make sense of mathematical ideas for themselves. When considered together, the teaching episodes of Catherine Evans and David Young make salient ways in which a challenging task can be implemented so as to afford different opportunities for student engagement with the task and, ultimately, for student learning.

In the following sections, we provide support for case facilitators' use of the materials in Chapter 2, "Examining Linear Growth Patterns: The Case of Catherine Evans and David Young." Sample responses for the Opening Activity and for the "Analyzing the Case" activity are provided in Appendix A.

CASE ANALYSIS

In this section, we provide detailed analyses of the mathematical and pedagogical ideas that are found in "The Case of Catherine Evans and David Young." These analyses may help the case facilitator determine which aspects of the case to highlight during the case discussion.

Considering the Mathematics in the Case

The Square-Pattern and Hexagon-Pattern Tasks—the foci of the lessons featured in "The Case of Catherine Evans and David Young"—are designed so as to move students from a concrete activity (calculate the perimeter of the first four trains) to a more abstract activity (calculating the perimeter of the tenth, twentieth, and one-hundredth trains). The tasks require students to apply their understanding of perimeter to count the perimeter of the first few consecutive trains. Then students explore the relationship between the perimeter and train number by observing patterns in the perimeters of the trains they have built, subsequently developing noncounting procedures for determining the perimeter of larger trains. As several useful patterns emerge in each train sequence, students are given the opportunity to consider and to discuss multiple solution methods. Students are also free to employ a variety of representations to create, explain, and justify their solutions.

In the following paragraphs, we identify several important mathematical ideas that surface in the case, and we provide examples of where these ideas appear in "The Case of Catherine Evans and David Young."

Identifying patterns. Students identify geometric patterns in the structure of the trains and use these patterns to construct larger trains in the sequence. Students also notice patterns in the procedures used to determine the perimeters of the first few trains and apply these patterns in determining the perimeters of larger trains. Students eventually generalize these procedures to any train in the sequence (see examples under "Generalizations"). Recursive and relational patterns also arise in the numeric values of the perimeters. The following list provides examples from the case where students identify and use patterns:

- In Mrs. Evans's class, Zeke builds the fourth train in the square pattern, and Tracy notices that a hexagon is added to every subsequent train. (paras. 16 and 24)
- Several students in Mr. Young's class are able to predict the perimeter of the next consecutive train in the sequence by identifying and applying a recursive pattern. (Jamal, para. 45; Katie, para. 53; and Derek, para. 59)
- In Mr. Young's class, Michele indicates that she built the tenth train and then counted. (para. 47)
- Based on her table, Janelle notices a pattern relating the train number to the numeric value of the perimeter. (para. 54)

Generalizations. Students apply the patterns presented in the previous examples to create generalized procedures for finding the perimeter of any train in the sequence. Students' generalizations are expressed verbally, which is foundational to expressing generalizations with symbolic notation. Students in Mrs. Evans's classroom, however, do not explicitly generalize their procedures as applying to *any* train in the sequence. While students seem to realize that any train number can be substituted into a verbal "formula," their thinking remains tied to a numeric referent and to a memorized series of steps. The following list shows where generalizations surface in "The Case of Catherine Evans and David Young":

- In Mrs. Evans's classroom, Angela and others apply Angela's procedure for finding the perimeter of the third train in the sequence to quickly state the perimeters of larger trains. (para. 19)
- Mrs. Evans leads Devon, Tommy, and Jeremy to apply Devon's method for finding the perimeter of the second train to the tenth, twentieth, and thirtieth trains, respectively. (paras. 25, 26, and 27).

- In Mr. Young's classroom, although Travis offers essentially the same solution method as Angela did in Mrs. Evan's class, Mr. Young's questioning prompts Travis to express the general relationship between the train number and the value of the perimeter. (para. 47)
- Several students in Mr. Young's classroom give verbal generalizations that move beyond requiring a numeric referent. (Joseph, para. 48; Alicia, para. 50; Janelle, para. 54; and Carmen, para. 61)

Intuitive notions of variable. While symbolic notation or variables are not used explicitly in "The Case of Catherine Evans and David Young," students encounter several foundational notions of variable (Usiskin, 1988) through grappling with the pattern-train tasks. Students appear to understand that any number can be substituted into a given procedure and thus are able to evaluate a verbal "formula" for a specific value of the unknown. In Mr. Young's class, Alicia uses a variable as a generalized number when applying Travis's pattern to create a formula that can be used to determine the perimeter of any train in the sequence. Note that while Alicia does not use a single letter to represent the variable quantity, she uses the phrase "train number" as symbolic notation in her diagram. Students also develop the notion of variable as a parameter in recognizing and applying the relationship between the train number and the perimeter. Examples of students' intuitive notions of variable from the case are identified in the following list:

- In Mrs. Evans's class, Angela and Devon make observations that can lead to generalizations of larger trains. (paras. 18 and 25)
- In Mr. Young's class, Alicia uses a variable as a generalized number when applying Travis's pattern to create a formula that can be used to determine the perimeter of any train in the sequence. (para. 50)
- In Mr. Young's class, several students use verbal phrases to express variable quantities. For example, Travis notices that the "number of units on the top and bottom were the same as the number of the train"; Janelle indicates that "the perimeter was always two more than the train number"; and Carmen states, "The number on top is double the train number." (paras. 47, 54, and 61)

Functions. A function is a relationship between two variables. In the context of the pattern-train tasks, the perimeter of the trains is a function of the train number (or the number of shapes). For each train number (the value of the first variable) there is only one perimeter (the value of the second number). Although Mrs. Evans, Mr. Young, and their students do not explicitly address the functional relationship that exists between train number and perimeter, the students demonstrate an understanding of the relationship between these quantities as they successfully determine the perimeter for the tenth and one-hundredth trains. The following list provides examples of the ways in which the notion of function surfaces informally in "The Case of Catherine Evans and David Young":

- Mrs. Evans and Mr. Young both identify a goal of the unit on pattern trains as developing a generalization for the perimeter of any train in a pattern. Such generalizations could help students to identify the functional relationship between the perimeter and the train number. (paras. 8 and 42)
- Both the Square- and Hexagon-Pattern Tasks (Figures 2.2 and 2.1, respectively) involve a relationship where the perimeter is a function of the train number (or number of blocks).
- In Mr. Young's class, several students identify a relationship between the train number and the number of units in some aspect of the pattern train. (Travis, para. 47; Joseph, para. 49; and Carmen, para. 61)
- In Mr. Young's class, Janelle explains through her table of values for the triangle pattern that the perimeter is always two more than the train number. (para. 54)
- Mr. Young encourages students to find a connection between the train number and the perimeter. He asks students, "How are those two numbers related?" (paras. 52 and 58)

Connections among representations. Proficiency in translating between various representations is an essential component of students' understanding of the concept of function (Leinhardt, Zaslavsky, & Stein, 1990). In using the geometric structure of the pattern sequence to determine the perimeter of larger trains, students in Mrs. Evans's and Mr. Young's classes, make frequent connections between visual models, verbal descriptions, and numeric data when solving the pattern-train tasks. The following list identifies where connections among representations occur in "The Case of Catherine Evans and David Young":

- In Mrs. Evans's class, Angela uses a diagram to explain her rule for finding the perimeter of the trains (para. 17), and Devon refers to the structure of the hexagon train diagram to explain his method for finding the perimeter (para. 25).
- Mrs. Evans uses the diagram to demonstrate an alternative method for finding the perimeter of any train in the square-pattern train. (para. 21)
- In Mr. Young's class, several students use diagrams to explain their strategies for finding the perimeter of larger trains in the patterns. (Jamal, para. 45; Travis, para. 47; Alicia, para. 50; and Kirsten, para. 60)
- In Mr. Young's class, Janelle uses a table and notices a pattern (that the perimeter is always two more than the train number) to find the perimeter of the tenth train. (para. 54)

Perimeter. Perimeter is the measure of the distance around a figure. In "The Case of Catherine Evans and David Young," students determine the perimeters of the pattern trains using the side of a square-pattern block as the unit of measure. Perimeter, however, is not the central focus of the lesson. Rather, it is a prior understanding needed in order to determine the pattern of growth. The following list provides instances in which the notion of perimeter arises in "The Case of Catherine Evans and David Young":

- In Mrs. Evans's classroom, Jake demonstrates his method of counting out the perimeters of the trains. (para. 12)
- Zeke counts the number of sides in the figure rather than the number of units in the perimeter, but Zeke's misconception is clarified by Nick's solution and Zeke correctly counts out the perimeter of the fourth train. (paras. 13, 14, and 16).
- Derek demonstrates the same method in Mr. Young's class. (para. 44)
- In Mr. Young's classroom, Jamal's explanation that "two sides of the new square are on the inside not on the perimeter," relies on and reinforces a solid understanding of the concept of perimeter. (para. 45)
- Joseph's method of "subtracting the sides that were in the inside" also relies on and helps to reinforce a solid understanding of the concept of perimeter. (paras. 48, 55, and 62)

Considering How Student Thinking Is Supported

Catherine Evans and David Young see the pattern-train lessons as a vehicle for helping students visualize and describe geometric patterns, make conjectures about the patterns, and, ultimately, explore functional relationships by developing generalizations about the perimeters of any train in the pattern. While sharing these broad goals, each teacher approaches the lesson with specific personal goals in mind. Mrs. Evans wants to ensure that her students experience success and organizes her lesson to accomplish this goal. By contrast, Mr. Young's goal is to allow students "time to think, to struggle, and to make sense of things for themselves." The lesson unfolds very differently in the two classrooms, with Mrs. Evans's students having fewer opportunities than Mr. Young's students to engage in high-level thinking, reasoning, and communication.

In the following paragraphs, we identify several pedagogical moves that Catherine Evans and David Young made that may have influenced students' opportunities for high-level engagement, and we provide examples of where these ideas appear in "The Case of Catherine Evans and David Young" in Chapter 2.

Continuing to press students for explanation and meaning. Mr. Young expects his students to explain their thinking and consistently presses them to do so. For example, in Mr. Young's classroom, Derek, Jamal, Michele, Travis, and Alicia are all asked to explain their answers. (paras. 44, 45, 47, and 50)

Mrs. Evans, on the other hand, does not consistently ask her students to explain their solution strategies. When she does ask students to explain (e.g., asking Jake how he got his answer in para. 12), she is satisfied with responses that may not fully describe their solution strategy. In addition, Mrs. Evans consistently focuses the discussion on providing correct answers and/or following correct procedures, and does not press students to make sense of what they are doing. Examples of this are provided in the following list:

- Mrs. Evans engages the class in a rapid question and answer exchange because she wants everyone to use and understand Angela's observation. (para. 19)
- Mrs. Evans has students apply the pattern she presented. (para. 22)
- Mrs. Evans asks Tommy to apply Devon's method to the twentieth train (para. 26), and then asks Jeremy to do the thirtieth train because she wants to make sure that everyone has all the steps that Tommy explained (para. 27).

Maintaining the complexity of the task. Mr. Young supported student thinking in a way that maintained the

complexity of the task, as illustrated by the examples provided in the following list:

- When students are "stuck" Mr. Young suggests that they try to see if they can find a connection between the train number and the perimeter. (paras. 52 and 58)
- Mr. Young gives students the opportunity to develop and use their own strategies for solving the problems—ones that are sensible to them. Joseph's method for finding the perimeter and Alicia's model for the generalization are two examples of this. (paras. 48 and 50)

By contrast, Mrs. Evans simplifies the task to the point where it is no longer challenging for her students by asking students to simply provide a numerical response to her questions (paras. 19, 22, and 27) rather than to find the perimeter of any train. In addition, Mrs. Evans does not expect students to make generalizations and is surprised when this occurs (para. 18).

Having capable students model high-level performance. Students in both Mrs. Evans's and Mr. Young's classrooms model high-level performance, although this occurs more consistently in Mr. Young's class. For example, in Mrs. Evans's classroom, Angela explains her thinking (para. 17). Several students in Mr. Young's classroom model high-level performance, such as Travis, Joseph, Alicia, Kirsten, and Carmen (paras. 47, 48, 50, 60, and 61).

Providing an appropriate amount of time. Mr. Young provides his students with ample time to explore and think about the task, as indicated by the examples provided in the following list:

- Mr. Young enters the lesson with the goal of providing the students with an appropriate amount of time to explore the task, think, and make sense of the mathematics themselves. (para. 41)
- Mr. Young provides several opportunities for students to engage in the task with a partner (e.g., on the square pattern, para. 43; on the triangle pattern, para. 51; and on patterns 2, 3, and 4, para. 57).
- Mr. Young pauses twice during the discussion of the square-pattern train to allow students time to think. (paras. 46 and 50)

By contrast, Mrs. Evans does not give her students enough time to explore the task, to think, and to make sense of the mathematics themselves. Specifically, during the entire class students are given only 5 minutes to think about the hexagon pattern with a partner (para. 24). The remainder of class is conducted in whole-group format with no time for individual, pair, or small-group work or reflection.

The teacher or capable students drawing conceptual connections. Mr. Young's use of questioning helps students make explicit connections between the figures in the pattern and students' verbal formulas. The following list provides examples of students making connections between the figure and their verbal formulas and Mr. Young's encouragement to relate the perimeter to the train number:

- Jamal explains the pattern between the second and third train. (para. 45)
- Travis explains how he predicted the perimeter of the tenth train. (para. 47)
- Mr. Young encourages students to "find a connection between the train number and the perimeter," and to determine "how those two numbers are related." (paras. 52 and 58)
- Kirsten explains how she predicted the perimeter of the three-hexagon train. (para. 60)

Mrs. Evans and several of her students describe methods for calculating the perimeter that make connections between the pattern figures and their verbal formulas. However, she often follows students' descriptions with questions that are leading and focus on the process of calculating the perimeter rather than on highlighting the connections. Instances in which Mrs. Evans focuses on procedures rather than on conceptual connections are provided in the following list:

- In the beginning of the lesson, Mrs. Evans's focus is on finding the perimeters of trains two and three. She then questions several students to see if they understand the method. (paras. 12–16)
- Angela explains how to find the perimeter of the third and fourth trains. Mrs. Evans then questions Angela and the whole class to see if they can apply Angela's method to other trains. (paras. 17 and 19)
- Devon describes how to find the perimeter of the fourth and tenth train. Mrs. Evans then asks leading questions of Tommy and Jeremy to see if they understand Devon's method. (paras. 25–27)

Building on students' prior knowledge. Building on prior knowledge gives all students an opportunity to explore the mathematics in the lesson. Both Mrs. Evans and Mr. Young made an effort to build on students' prior knowledge, as shown by the examples in the following list:

- Mrs. Evans talks about what her students have been working on from the beginning of the unit through the previous lesson. (paras. 8 and 9)
- Mr. Young talks about what his students have been working on from the beginning of the unit through the previous lesson. (paras. 40 and 42)
- Mr. Young encourages students who are "really stuck" to think about the solution methods for the previous pattern train. (para. 52)

FACILITATING THE OPENING ACTIVITY

The primary purpose of the Opening Activity is to engage participants with the mathematical ideas that they will encounter when they read "The Case of Catherine Evans and David Young." The task found in the Opening Activity is similar to the Hexagon-Pattern Task featured in "The Case of Catherine Evans and David Young" (Figure 2.1). In order to complete this task successfully, participants must look for the relationship between the train number and the perimeter and use this relationship to represent the general case for any figure in the pattern. The complexity of the task is derived from the fact that no particular pathway to finding a pattern is suggested and the aspects of the sequence to which participants should attend (e.g., the number of hexagons in each train, the number of sides of each hexagon that should be counted in the perimeter, etc.) are not specified. In this section, we provide the case facilitator with suggestions for using the Opening Activity.

1. Begin by having participants work individually on the Hexagon-Pattern Task for 5 to 10 minutes and then continue to work on the task with a partner. We have found that beginning with "private think time" ensures that each participant has a chance to grapple with the task prior to engaging in collaborative work. You may want to provide participants with the following materials: hexagon tiles (for building subsequent figures in the train); calculators (for determining the perimeter of larger trains); graph paper (for depicting the relationship

between train number and perimeter graphically); and a transparency or poster of the first four trains in the hexagon pattern (for recording their solutions).

2. Assist participants in their work on the task if they appear to be having difficulty. Consider the following suggestions:

• If some participants have difficulty getting started, suggest that they sketch (or build) the next two figures in the hexagon pattern and find the perimeter. Alternatively, you might ask participants to predict the perimeter of the next train, and then to check their prediction by sketching it. You also may want to continue to support participants' work on the task by asking them to make observations about the relationship between the train number, sides of the hexagons, and the perimeter.

• Watch for recursive approaches to finding the perimeter of the next train. For example, participants may conclude, "You just add 4 each time," since the perimeter of the first train is 6; of the second train, 10; of the third train, 14; and of the fourth train, 18. Although this is true, a recursive formula does not allow participants to find the perimeter of the tenth train without first knowing the perimeter of the ninth train. Recursive strategies are difficult to use for large train numbers and do not lead to a general description of how to find the perimeter of *any* train in the pattern. To help participants use this approach to develop a general formula, you might ask them to think about what happens numerically as they use the "add 4 each time" strategy to find the perimeter of the one-hundredth or one-thousandth train and whether they can develop a short-cut to adding 4 each time. Alternatively, you might (1) suggest that they describe the relationship between the train number, sides of the hexagons, and perimeter; or (2) ask two groups to exchange descriptions, determine if the description produced by the other group works, and explain why it is or is not a valid description.

• Some participants may provide a verbal or written description of any train in the sequence rather than a formula. Given a participant's mathematics background this may be an appropriate starting point for the discussion. You may want to make note of groups that did not use

algebraic notation and discuss how to move from the verbal description to a more algebraic one.

• Some participants may produce an algebraic formula by creating a data table for the train number and its perimeter and then determining the pattern of growth. You may want to encourage these participants to consider another approach that uses the figures in the pattern train or to use a visual-geometric approach to justify why their formula works.

3. Orchestrate a whole-group discussion to allow participants to share various solution strategies and approaches. During the discussion you may want to:

• Solicit responses that portray both visual-geometric approaches and arithmetic-algebraic approaches to solving the problem. (Examples of solutions for solving the Opening Activity are provided in Appendix A. These solutions may help you prepare for the emergence of methods you might not use yourself in solving the problems.) If you ask the small groups to record their solutions on an overhead transparency, this will facilitate the presentation of solutions during the whole-group discussion. You may wish to ask specific groups to share unique strategies to ensure that a range of approaches will be represented. It is important to discuss at least two different visual-geometric approaches and at least one arithmetic-algebraic approach. If all the solutions you would like to discuss do not emerge, you may want to suggest these approaches for the participants to consider, by providing a solution on a transparency or handout.

• If participants do not produce a graph as a solution to this task, you might want to give them time to actually construct the graph of the pattern-train numbers and their perimeters. Alternatively, participants could be presented with the solution shown in Figure 7.1 and asked to determine if the solution makes sense. This also could lead to a discussion of whether the graph can be drawn outside the first quadrant and whether or not the points on the graph should be connected (i.e., determining whether the data are discrete or continuous).

• You also may want to ask participants to make connections between the different approaches that are discussed. For example, in Table A.1, the perimeter increases by 4 for each consecutive train. This +4 in the table represents the slope of the line shown in Figure 7.1 and it is the coefficient of *x* in the equation $P = 4x + 2$ discussed in Solution B of the arithmetic-algebraic approaches. This +4 also can be connected to the diagram since it represents the four sides that each newly added hexagon contributes to the perimeter.

- You also may want to use this discussion as an opportunity to focus explicitly on functions. You may want to begin by presenting participants with the following statement and asking them to indicate whether it is true or false and to explain their reasoning: "The perimeter of a train of hexagons is a *function* of the number of hexagons in the train."

- You may then want to have participants begin to articulate a definition of function that they can modify and test out on subsequent problems. If participants simply say that a relationship is a function if it passes the vertical line test, you may want to press them to explain what that means and what conditions must be met in order to pass the test. (See the "Case Analysis" section for a brief discussion of functions. You also may find the article by Sand, 1996, which is described at the end of Chapter 2, to be helpful in the discussion of functions.)

FIGURE 7.1. Graph of the Perimeters of the Hexagon-Pattern Trains

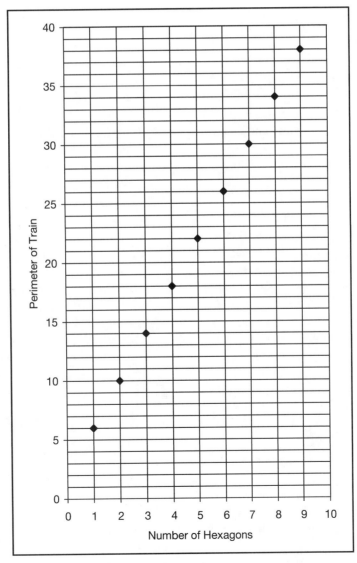

- Finally, you may wish to extend the discussion by focusing on issues of planning for instruction around the use of this task. The following discussion questions may be helpful in this regard: (1) What mathematical ideas can be explored through work on this task? (You may want to actually have participants investigate their state or local standards documents in answering this question.) (2) What prior knowledge and experience would students need in order to successfully engage with this task? (3) What difficulties might students encounter while working on this task? (4) What questions could you ask students in order to support their work on this task? (5) How could you verify that all the expressions are equivalent?

FACILITATING THE CASE DISCUSSION

The case discussion is intended to help participants analyze the mathematical and pedagogical ideas in "The Case of Catherine Evans and David Young." The "Case Analysis" should be of assistance in identifying the key ideas in the case and how each idea "plays out" in the details of the case. In this section, we provide the case facilitator with suggestions for launching and facilitating the discussion of "The Case of Catherine Evans and David Young," and for various follow-up activities that might be pursued.

1. If possible, have participants read and reflect on the case before meeting as a group to discuss the case. We have found it helpful to provide participants with a question or issue on which they can focus as they read the case. As participants read the case, we suggest that you ask them to consider what they think students in each class were learning. By considering what students learned, participants will be prepared for subsequent discussions of the similarities and differences between the classes. Alternatively, you may want to select one of the questions found in Chapter 2 (see the section entitled "Extending Your Analysis of the Case") to guide the reading of the case.

2. Have teachers work in groups of three or four to create a two-column chart in which they indicate the ways that they think Mrs. Evans's and Mr. Young's classes are similar and the ways that they think the two classes are different. Teachers should be encouraged to review the lists of what students appeared to learn, which they created while reading "The Case of Catherine Evans and David Young," and to consider whether there are similarities and differences in what was learned that should be included in the chart. In completing this task, group members should be encouraged to reach consensus on what is placed in their group's chart and to cite specific evidence from the case (using paragraph numbers) to support each idea recorded in their chart.

3. During the whole-group discussion, you may want to develop a master chart that draws on the work of all the individual groups. You might begin building this chart by asking the groups to identify the most important similarity and the most significant difference they identified and to justify their choices by citing evidence from the case. Encourage participants to argue respectfully if they do not agree that an identified similarity or difference is the most important or the most significant. This can lead to a rich discussion that draws on evidence used to support claims being made. After each group has contributed one similarity and one difference to the list, open up the conversation by asking if there are any other similarities and differences that should be included. See Appendix A for a sample similarities and differences chart that was created by a group of teachers. We encourage you to develop your own chart prior to reviewing the one we have provided.

   You may wish to end the discussion by asking teachers if the identified differences really matter and why. This may lead to a discussion of how the same task can be implemented differently and result in different opportunities for student learning. This moves the discussion from the particulars of what occurred in Catherine Evans's and David Young's classes to a more general discussion of classroom factors that impact students' opportunities to learn what mathematics is and how one does it.

4. Following the discussion, you may want to have participants reflect individually by writing about some aspect of the case experience. We have found it productive to ask participants to identify lessons learned from the case that can be applied to teaching more broadly. This also helps participants think about the case in more general terms.

EXTENDING THE CASE EXPERIENCE

If you have additional time, you may want to continue to explore the mathematical and pedagogical ideas on which the case is based. The section "Extending Case-Based Experiences" in Chapter 6 suggests three types of activities you might want to assign for these purposes.

Specifically, if you are working with participants who currently are teaching, you may want to provide opportunities for teachers to consider their own practice in light of the issues that surfaced in reading and discussing "The Case of Catherine Evans and David Young." This will help teachers to generalize the issues beyond the specific events of the case.

8

Facilitating Learning from The Case of Ed Taylor

"The Case of Ed Taylor" focuses on a 7th-grade teacher and his students at Richland Middle School. The case portrays the work of Mr. Taylor and his students during a lesson in which students explore a growth pattern involving arrangements of square tiles. This exploration involves sketching figures in the pattern, making observations about the pattern, and ultimately describing a method for finding the total number of tiles in larger arrangements in the pattern. Students in the class are eager to share their approaches to the task with their peers and take center stage at the overhead projector in order to do so. During these student presentations, Mr. Taylor questions students in order to clarify aspects of their solutions, to refocus a student when an error is made, and to help students consider alternative ways of representing their solutions. Students succeed in developing formulas for representing the total number of tiles in any step in the pattern and in making connections between visual, verbal, numeric, and symbolic representations. At the conclusion of class, students are left with the task of justifying the equivalence of the formulas that have been presented.

In the following sections, we provide support for case facilitators' use of the materials in Chapter 3, "Examining Nonlinear Growth Patterns: The Case of Ed Taylor." Sample responses for the Opening Activity and for the "Analyzing the Case" activity are provided in Appendix B.

CASE ANALYSIS

In this section, we provide detailed analyses of the mathematical and pedagogical ideas that are found in "The Case of Ed Taylor." These analyses may help the case facilitator determine which aspects of the case to highlight during the case discussion.

Considering the Mathematics in the Case

The mathematics in this case unfolds as Mr. Taylor and his students work on the S-Pattern Task. The S-Pattern Task is designed to move students from a concrete (sketching the next two steps in the pattern) to a more abstract activity (writing a generalized formula for the total number of tiles). In order to complete this task successfully, students must look for the underlying mathematical structure of the pattern and use this structure to represent the general case for any step in the pattern. The complexity of the task is derived from the fact that no particular pathway to finding a pattern is suggested, and the aspects of the sequence to which students should attend (e.g., the number of tiles in each arrangement, the number of tiles in each row, the shape of each arrangement, etc.) are not specified.

In the following paragraphs, we identify several important mathematical ideas that surface in the case, and we provide examples of where these ideas appear in "The Case of Ed Taylor."

Generalization. The underlying structure of the pattern sequence is used to generalize the number and arrangement of tiles for any step in the pattern. The following list provides examples of generalizations made by Mr. Taylor's students throughout the case:

- Sorrell, Angela, Sharla, Maria, Dwayne, Renee, and Kevin share observations that make generalizations about the S-pattern. (paras. 12, 13, 14, and 15)
- Lamont discusses his diagram that describes what the twenty-fifth step would look like. (para. 19)
- Ning, David, Charles, and Beverly provide general descriptions or formulas that could be used to determine the number of tiles in any step

in the pattern sequence. (paras. 23–24, 26, 28, and 29)

Variable. In the case, there are two variables: step number (independent—N) and total number of tiles in the arrangement (dependent—T). Students observe relationships between the two variables and summarize their observations verbally, in tables, and symbolically. They construct formulas that describe the relationship and relate them to the visual-geometric arrangement of the pattern. The list that follows shows examples of students' notions of variable from the case:

- Dwayne discovers a relationship between N and T using a table of values. (para. 14)
- Ning, David, Charles, and Beverly use N to represent the step number and T to represent the total number of tiles in the step, and then create algebraic formulas to represent the relationship between N and T. (paras. 23–24, 26, 28, and 29)

Functions. A function is a relationship between two variables. In the context of the square pattern and S-pattern, the total number of tiles is a function of the step number. For each step number there is only one corresponding value for the number of tiles. Although neither Mr. Taylor nor his students explicitly address the functional relationship that exists between the number of tiles and the step number, the students demonstrate an understanding of the relationship between these quantities as they successfully determine the number of tiles for larger steps and, more generally, for any step. The following list provides examples of the ways in which the notion of function surfaces during the lesson:

- Michael shows how he got from the fifth step to the sixth, introducing the idea of describing the change between two steps. (para. 10)
- Dwayne makes the first explicit connection between the step number and total number of tiles. (para. 14)
- David expresses his formula as a function of both step number and previous step number. (para. 26)
- Mr. Taylor, Jamal, and David work to revise David's solution using only step number and eliminating previous step number. (para. 26)
- Mr. Taylor establishes the reasons for using only step number in the formula. (para. 27)
- Multiple formulas are given that represent the same functional relationship. (Figure 3.17)

Connections among representations. Visual models, verbal descriptions, tables, and symbolic rules are used to represent patterns, and each of these representations is connected to the others. Students use all of the representation throughout the class, as illustrated in the examples shown in the following list:

- Michael uses visual models to build the next steps in the pattern. (para. 10)
- In explaining his solution, Dwayne makes a connection from picture to formula, using a table as an intermediate representation. (para. 14)
- The list of observations connects the visual models with students' verbal descriptions. (Figure 3.9)
- In analyzing the observations, Jamie notes that the verbal descriptions tell you the number of tiles in each step, but not what the arrangement would look like. (para. 17)
- When describing the twenty-fifth step, Lamont moves from verbal descriptions to a pictorial representation. (paras. 19–20)
- Myesha uses a sketch to clarify her reasoning in describing the three-hundredth step. (para. 22)
- The symbolic rules that Ning, David, Charles, and Beverly derive are connected to a specific way of looking at the visual model of the pattern. (paras. 23–24, 26, 28, and 29)

Recursion. Each successive step in a pattern can be built by altering the previous arrangement in a particular way. In the S-Pattern Task, each new step can be found by adding a row and a column to the previous arrangement. Michael's description of the sixth and seventh steps (para. 10) reflects a recursive approach.

Equivalent expressions. The various ways of describing the number of tiles in any step in the pattern are equivalent algebraically. At the end of the class, Mr. Taylor asks students to show that the five formulas created in class are equivalent (para. 31).

Considering How Student Thinking Is Supported

Ed Taylor believes that early experiences with patterns can lay the groundwork for exploring ideas such as variables and functions. As a result, he provides his 7th-graders with opportunities to work with patterns, first writing directions for finding the total number of tiles for any step in the pattern sequence and then moving to using symbols instead of words for these descriptions.

During the lesson, Mr. Taylor has his students extending a pattern and describing a method for finding the total number of tiles in a larger arrangement in the pattern. He focuses his students' attention on making connections among different ways of representing the pattern: visually, verbally, numerically, and symbolically.

In the following paragraphs, we identify several pedagogical moves that Ed Taylor made that may have influenced his students' opportunities to engage in high-level thinking, reasoning, and communication during the lesson, and we provide examples of where these ideas appear in "The Case of Ed Taylor."

Selecting a task that builds on students' prior knowledge. Mr. Taylor chooses a task that he feels his students will be able to engage in, given their experiences in 6th grade and their experiences in his classroom. His students' experience in 6th grade involved exploring patterns and writing descriptions for finding the total number of tiles for a specific step in the pattern (para. 5). Mr. Taylor currently has his 7th-graders exploring variables and functions by writing directions for finding the total number of tiles for any step in a pattern sequence, which moves the students from verbal to symbolic descriptions (para. 6).

Allowing students time to grapple with the mathematical ideas in the task. Ed Taylor provides an appropriate amount of time for students to explore the task, to think, and to discover mathematical relationships for themselves. Mr. Taylor allows time in class for students to think about the problem individually and within a small group, and to share ideas in a whole-class setting (paras. 8 and 9).

Pressing students for explanations and meaning. Mr. Taylor presses students for explanations and meaning throughout the lesson. Mr. Taylor often asks students to explain their thinking and use a diagram of the pattern to show what they mean. This provides Mr. Taylor and all students with an opportunity to make sense of each student's approach and to make connections between a student's explanation and the diagram of the pattern. The following list provides instances in which Mr. Taylor presses students for explanations and meaning:

- Mr. Taylor presses Michael to explain how he determined what the sixth and seventh steps would look like. (para. 10)
- Mr. Taylor asks Angela to go to the overhead and explain her thinking. (para. 12)

- Mr. Taylor presses Sharla to consider the bottom row in her observation. (para. 13)
- Mr. Taylor asks Dwayne to explain his observation that "if you square the step number and add one you get the total number of tiles." (para. 14)
- Mr. Taylor elicits an explanation from Jamie about whether her observation about Dwayne's solution mattered. (para. 17)
- Mr. Taylor asks Myesha to go to the overhead and explain her thinking. (para. 22)
- Mr. Taylor presses Ning to work through her solution and find her own error. (paras. 23–24)
- Mr. Taylor asks a series of questions to press Charles to explain his thinking. (para. 28)
- Mr. Taylor asks Beverly to show how her formula relates to the arrangement of tiles in the pattern. (para. 29)
- Mr. Taylor presses Tonya to explain what she means. (para. 30)

Making, recording, and using observations. By recording students' observations in a public place, Mr. Taylor facilitates opportunities for students to continually reflect on their observations about the S-pattern. He encourages students to refer to student observations whenever he sees an appropriate connection. The act of recording students' observations is important in facilitating student learning because it can be used both to share thinking and as a common object of reflection for the class. Recorded observations also may be used to keep track of progress on the task and to build new ideas from previous observations. The following list provides examples of when observations were recorded and used during the lesson:

- Jason numbered and recorded the class observations on a sheet of newsprint on the easel in the front of the room. (para. 11)
- Mr. Taylor repeats Sorrell's observation so Jason can record it for the class. (para. 12)
- Mr. Taylor asks the class to identify similarities and differences between the observations they made. (para. 16)
- Mr. Taylor asks students to think about what observations they were drawing on as they described how to find larger steps in the pattern. (paras. 19, 22, and 25)
- Mr. Taylor suggests Lamont go back to the observation list to see if his description of the twenty-fifth step worked. (para. 19)
- Dwayne applies his observation in finding the number of tiles in the twenty-fifth step. (para. 21)

- Myesha identifies that she used Renee's observation to find the number of tiles in the three-hundredth step. (para. 22)
- The class discusses which observations (2 and 4) Ning used in her approach to finding a formula for the number of tiles in any step. (para. 25)
- David claims that he used Renee's observation when finding a formula. (para. 26)

Having capable students model high-level performance. Mr. Taylor provided multiple opportunities for students to share their thinking with their peers, not only in small groups, but also in whole-class discussions. Initially, several students had the opportunity to make public observations about the S-pattern. Mr. Taylor solicited more than one extensive student explanation of how to find the total number of tiles in any step. Instances of capable students modeling high-level thinking and reasoning occur when Michael, Angela, Dwayne, Lamont, and Charles share their observations and solutions with the class (paras. 10, 12, 14, 19–20, 21, and 28).

Encouraging many different solution strategies. Mr. Taylor encouraged a variety of observations about the pattern and approaches to finding the total number of tiles in any step of the pattern. The variety of solution strategies offered by Mr. Taylor's students represented different cognitive approaches to the problem, and each was associated with a different, but equivalent, algebraic representation. The following list indicates where Mr. Taylor encouraged different observations and solution strategies:

- Mr. Taylor asks for students to share their observations. (paras. 11–15)
- Mr. Taylor solicits Maria to share her group's observation because he knew it was different from those already shared. (para. 13)
- Ning, David, Charles, and Beverly share their formulas with the class. Each solution is based on a different way of viewing the visual model. (paras. 23–24, 26, 28 and 29)

FACILITATING THE OPENING ACTIVITY

The primary purpose of the Opening Activity is to engage participants with the mathematical ideas that they will encounter when they read "The Case of Ed Taylor." The task found in the Opening Activity (Figure 3.1) asks participants to write a description that

could define any figure in the square pattern and the S-pattern. The Opening Activity is similar to, but less structured than, the activity in Parts a–e used by Mr. Taylor in the case.

In order to complete the task in the Opening Activity successfully, participants must identify the underlying geometric structure of the patterns and use this structure to represent the general case for any step in the pattern. The complexity of the task is derived from the fact that no particular pathway to finding a pattern is suggested, and the aspects of the sequence to which participants should attend (e.g., the number of tiles in each arrangement, the number of tiles in each row, the shape of each arrangement, etc.) are not specified. In this section, we provide the case facilitator with suggestions for using the Opening Activity.

1. Begin by having participants work individually on the Square- and S-Pattern Tasks for 5 to 10 minutes and then continue to work on the tasks with a partner. We have found that beginning with "private think time" ensures that each participant has a chance to grapple with the tasks prior to engaging in collaborate work. You may want to provide participants with the following materials: square tiles (for building subsequent steps); calculators (for determining the number of tiles in larger steps); graph paper (for depicting the relationship between the step number and the total number of tiles graphically); and transparencies of the square and S-patterns (for recording their solutions).

2. Assist participants in their work on the tasks if they appear to be having difficulty. Consider the following suggestions:

   - If some participants have difficulty getting started, suggest that they sketch (or build) the next two steps in the pattern. (This often helps participants focus on how the pattern grows from one step to the next.) You also may want to continue to support participants' work on the tasks by asking them to make observations about the pattern that help describe larger steps in the pattern and to describe two steps in the pattern that are larger than the twentieth step.
   - If some participants are thinking about the pattern in only an arithmetic or algebraic way, encourage them to consider a visual-geometric approach. Visual-geometric approaches focus on describing the appearance of any shape in the

pattern in relation to its step number, where algebraic or arithmetic approaches focus on determining the total number of tiles. You may want to ask participants if they could use their approach to sketch any step in the pattern. (See Appendix B for a range of solutions that use a visual-geometric approach.)

- If participants have determined a formula for the total number of tiles by creating a table, you might ask them to find a relationship between the step number and the shape of the arrangement or to justify their formula using the geometric structure of the pattern.

- Watch for incorrect descriptions resulting from focusing on a subset of steps (e.g., based on observing the growth in the S-pattern from Step 1 to Step 2, some participants might conclude that each step has three tiles more than the previous step), incorrectly counting the number of tiles in a step, or misinterpreting some aspect of the problem. If participants produce incorrect descriptions, try to help them focus on the source of the error by applying the description to other steps in the pattern or by recounting the number of tiles. Alternatively, ask two groups to exchange descriptions, determine if the description produced by the other group works, and explain why it is or is not a valid description.

3. Orchestrate a whole-group discussion to allow participants to share various solution strategies and approaches. During the discussion you may want to:

- Begin by soliciting solutions for the square pattern followed by solutions to the S-pattern. Solicit responses that portray both visual-geometric approaches and arithmetic-algebraic approaches to solving the problem. If you ask the small groups to record their solutions on an overhead transparency, this will facilitate the presentation of solutions during the whole-group discussion. It is important to discuss at least two different visual-geometric approaches for each pattern and at least one arithmetic-algebraic approach for each pattern. If all the solutions you would like to discuss do not emerge, you may want to suggest these approaches by providing a solution on a transparency or handout for group consideration.

(Examples of different solution methods that participants have used to solve the tasks can be found in Appendix B. This may help you prepare for the emergence of methods you might not use yourself in solving the problems.)

- During the discussion, press participants to relate their formulas to the geometric structure of the pattern and to relate their descriptions of any step in the pattern to the step number.

- Keep a running list of formulas for each pattern produced by the participants. You may want to ask participants to justify that these formulas are equivalent. You also may want to discuss the value in not simplifying all the formulas to the same expression, since the simplified form no longer reflects how each formula was derived from visual-geometric aspects of the tile arrangements.

- If participants do not produce a graph as a solution to these tasks, you might want to give them time to construct graphs of the step numbers and the total number of tiles. Alternatively, participants could be presented with the graph shown in Figure 8.1 and asked to determine if the solution makes sense for each of the patterns. This also could lead to a discussion of whether the graphs for each pattern can be drawn outside the first quadrant and whether or not the points on the graphs should be connected (i.e., determining whether the data are discrete or continuous).

- Discuss the "Consider" question, "How are the patterns the same and how are they different?" You may find it helpful to record participants' responses in a two-column chart of "similarities" and "differences." This would provide an opportunity for participants to consider the similarities and differences between linear and nonlinear growth patterns. A key similarity that you should focus on is that both patterns are functions (see the following paragraph for suggestions on continuing the discussion of functions). A key difference that you should pursue is that the square pattern is a linear function and the S-pattern is a quadratic function. The discussion of linear and quadratic functions also will provide an opportunity to discuss rate of change and how it is manifested in various representations of function (i.e., table, equation, and graph).

FIGURE 8.1. Graph of the Step Number and Total Number of Tiles for the Square and S-Patterns

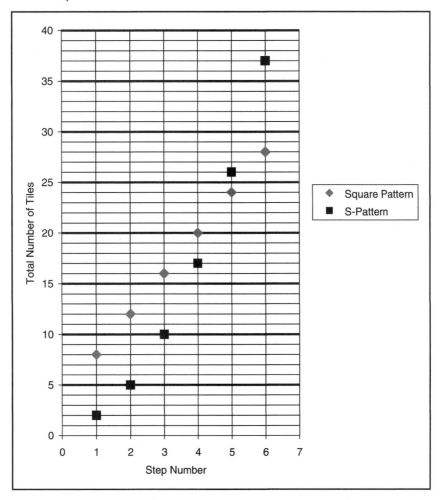

• You also may want to continue the discussion of functions by having participants refer to the definition of a function they created as a part of their previous work with the Hexagon-Pattern Task found in Chapter 2. Discussing functions in light of a quadratic function (the S-pattern) may bring about the need to explicitly clarify and define what it means for each *x*-value (input) to have exactly one unique *y*-value (output). Some participants may confuse the definition of a one-to-one function with that of a function in general and think that a function must have one unique *x*-value (input) for each *y*-value (output). Discussing a quadratic function with respect to the definition of a function will address this misconception and further build on the definition of a function that participants have created.

FACILITATING THE CASE DISCUSSION

The case discussion is intended to help participants analyze the mathematical and pedagogical ideas in "The Case of Ed Taylor." The "Case Analysis" should be of assistance in identifying the key ideas in the case and how each idea plays out in the details of the case. In this section, we provide the case facilitator with suggestions for launching and facilitating the discussion of "The Case of Ed Taylor," and for various follow-up activities that might be pursued.

1. If possible, have participants read and reflect on the case before meeting as a group to discuss the case. We have found it helpful to provide participants with a question or issue on which they can focus as they read the case. As participants read the case, we suggest you ask them to pick one

student in Ed Taylor's class and think about what the student understands, what they are not sure the student understands, and what questions they would like to ask the student. (This activity is described in more detail in the section of Chapter 3 entitled "Reading the Case.") This individual activity will help participants to think deeply about the student learning that is occurring in "The Case of Ed Taylor" and prepare them for the small- and large-group discussions. Alternatively, you may want to select one of the questions found in Chapter 3 (see the section entitled "Extending Your Analysis of the Case") to guide the reading of the case.

2. In small groups, ask participants to identify the key pedagogical moves Ed Taylor made that appeared to support his students' learning of mathematics. For each move identified, have participants also discuss the following: why Ed Taylor might have made the move (rationale for move), and how it supported students' learning of mathematics (implications of move). This activity requires participants to determine the pedagogical moves Ed Taylor made and make connections between those moves and the implications they have for students' learning.

    It is helpful to have each small group create a three-column chart of "key pedagogical move," "rationales for move," and "implications of move" in preparation for a whole-group discussion. Participants should be encouraged to cite specific evidence from the case (e.g., paragraph numbers) to support each idea recorded in their charts. This will ensure that participants ground their discussion in the actual events that unfold in "The Case of Ed Taylor."

    You should suggest that the small groups begin the process of creating their charts by focusing on what the students they analyzed when they read the case learned and by considering what move(s) Ed Taylor made that may have fostered students' learning. This will give participants an opportunity to discuss what they think was learned in the class, how the teaching supported student learning, and what might have guided Mr. Taylor's decisions.

3. Once the small groups have completed their work, you should create a master chart that draws on the work of all the groups. One way to facilitate the development of a master chart is to ask each small group to share with the whole group the one move they think had the greatest impact on students' learning. Encourage participants to argue respectfully if they do not agree that an identified move had the greatest impact on students' learning. The key in the discussion is to connect teacher actions (either implicit or explicit) with students' learning opportunities. (See Appendix B for a sample chart that was created by a group of teachers who participated in a discussion of "The Case of Ed Taylor." You may find this chart helpful in anticipating and making use of responses from participants.)

    Conclude the discussion by asking participants to consider whether or not the identified moves are applicable to teaching in general (i.e., beyond Ed Taylor's students and this particular lesson). The goal here is to help participants generalize the pedagogy used by Ed Taylor to mathematics teaching beyond the specific lesson that is the focus of the current analysis.

4. Following the discussion, you may want to have participants plan a lesson that Ed Taylor could use the day after the one portrayed in the case. (The questions raised in question 6 in the "Extending Your Analysis of the Case" section of Chapter 3 may provide a starting point for the design of the lesson.

EXTENDING THE CASE EXPERIENCE

If you have additional time, you may want to continue to explore the mathematical and pedagogical ideas on which the case is based. The section "Extending Case-Based Experiences" in Chapter 6 suggests three types of activities you might want to assign for these purposes. Specifically, if you are working with participants who currently are teaching, you may want to provide opportunities for teachers to consider their own practice in light of the issues that surfaced in reading and discussing "The Case of Ed Taylor." This will help teachers to generalize the issues beyond the specific events of the case.

9

Facilitating Learning from The Case of Edith Hart

"The Case of Edith Hart" focuses on an 8th-grade teacher and her students at Queenston Middle School. One of Ms. Hart's overall goals for her students is that they learn how to apply algebraic concepts in understanding and solving real-world problem situations. In the lesson portrayed in "The Case of Edith Hart," the students work on a task called Cal's Dinner Card Deals, in which students are given graphical information about three different dinner plans and asked to compare and contrast the cost of the dinner plans, and determine which of the plans is best. The task was developed by Ms. Hart in order to focus students' attention on developing algebraic formulas through analyzing graphs of a situation involving discrete variables. The problem also was intended to provide students with an opportunity to discuss informally the idea of slope and how it relates to both graphs and formulas. Through a rich discussion, several students share their reasoning with the whole class using multiple representations. Ms. Hart consistently asks students to explain their reasoning and also encourages students to question one another. Many students successfully make connections among the graphs, the formulas they develop, and the real-world situation depicted in the problem.

In the following sections, we provide support for case facilitators' use of the materials in Chapter 4, "Comparing Linear Graphs: The Case of Edith Hart." Sample responses for the Opening Activity and for the "Analyzing the Case" activity are provided in Appendix C.

CASE ANALYSIS

In this section, we provide detailed analyses of the mathematical and pedagogical ideas that are found in "The Case of Edith Hart." These analyses may help the case facilitator determine which aspects of the case to highlight during the case discussion.

Considering the Mathematics in the Case

The mathematics in this case unfolds as Edith Hart and her students work on the Cal's Dinner Card Deals Task. Cal's Dinner Card Deals is designed to have students use prior knowledge about how a coordinate graph is constructed in order to do something they have not had much experience with—constructing a formula from a graph. The problem situation is also novel for students because it deals with relationships between discrete, rather than continuous, variables. The complexity of the task is derived from the fact that students are expected to look for patterns or regularities in how the three graphs behave (i.e., discover how the variables depicted are related to one another). The students then must relate those patterns to the problem situation, as well as develop symbolic formulas to describe the relationships they have discovered. The task also affords students the opportunity to informally interact with the ideas of slope (i.e., rate of change) and y-intercept.

In the following paragraphs, we identify several important mathematical ideas that surface in the case, and we provide examples of where these ideas appear in "The Case of Edith Hart."

Variable. In "The Case of Edith Hart," there are two variables: number of meals (independent) and cost of meals (dependent). Students observe relationships between the two variables as points on the graphs and summarize their observations verbally, in tables, and symbolically. They construct formulas that describe the relationship and use the formulas to make decisions related to the contextual situation. The following list provides examples of students' notions of variable from the case:

- Ms. Hart asks Heather to elaborate on her observation in order to highlight how the number of meals relates to the cost. (para. 10)
- Jena explains her reasoning about a method for determining the total cost for a certain number of meals and then how she translated her reasoning into a symbolic formula. (paras. 15–17)
- When students compare all three meal plans, they explicitly note that the cost of a meal is a parameter that affects the behavior of the graphs. (para. 26)

Functions. A function is a relationship between two variables. In the context of Cal's Dinner Card Deals, the cost of each plan is a function of the number of dinners purchased. For each number of dinners there is only one corresponding cost. Although neither Edith Hart nor her students explicitly state the functional relationship that exists between cost of the plan and number of dinners, the students demonstrate an understanding of the relationship between these quantities as they successfully determine the formula for each plan. The following list provides examples of the ways in which the notion of function surfaces in the lesson:

- Kyle's strategy to determine the cost of 100 dinners with Plan A suggests that he understands that the cost changes as the number of dinners increases. (para. 15)
- Jena, Danielle, and Steven express their formulas as a function of the number of dinners purchased. (paras. 16–17, 19, and 21–22)
- For homework, Ms. Hart asks students to describe a situation that can be represented by a relationship that is similar to Cal's Dinner Card Deals. (para. 27)

Slope and rate of change. Slope is the rate of change—that is, the change in y as a comparison to the change in x. In this context, the slope, or rate of change, is the increased cost for each additional meal purchased. Students begin to relate their qualitative understanding of the steepness of the graphical models to the symbolic formulas in which slope is a parameter. Slope and rate of change are explored informally through the discussion of student observations. Through an examination of the three lines simultaneously, students explore informally the dynamic effects of varying the slope. The following list provides instances in which the idea of slope and rate of change arise in the lesson:

- Danielle notices that the lines all have different steepness. (para. 12)
- Carlos observes a relationship between the size of the coefficient of N and the steepness of each line and Danielle elaborates further. (para. 24)
- Ms. Hart asks students about rate of savings for the three dinner plans, and Danielle notes that the cost of the three plans increases at different rates. (para. 27)

Y-intercept. The y-intercept is the point where a graph intersects the y-axis. The x value of this point is zero. In an equation in slope–intercept form ($y = mx + b$) the y-intercept is the constant value (b). In the context of Cal's Dinner Card Deals, the y-intercept represents the initial fee for the dinner card (i.e., the cost of the card if no meals are purchased). Students begin to relate their understanding of the y-intercept within the graphical model, symbolic formulas, and the problem situation. Instances in which the concept of y-intercept arises in the case are shown in the following list:

- Derrick observes that the Regular Price Plan crosses zero and the other two plans do not. Edith Hart hopes to revisit this later on, examining the differences in the y-intercepts for each plan. (para. 11)
- Small groups struggle with the meaning of the y-intercept in the context of the problem, wondering how it is possible to have zero dinners cost \$4 (for Plan A). (para. 14)
- Jena explains to Omar where the "+4" in her formula can be found on the graph and in the table and what it means in the context of the problem. (para. 18)

Connections among representations. Proficiency in translating back and forth between various representations is an essential component of students' understanding of function (Leinhardt, Zaslavsky, & Stein, 1990). One interesting aspect of Cal's Dinner Card Deals is that the problem situation is presented in the form of a graph and students are asked to determine the formula. (By contrast, in most algebra problems, students are presented with the equation or a word problem first.) Many students in Edith Hart's class also create a table as an intermediate step in determining formulas for the three dinner plans. The following list identifies where connections among representations occur during the lesson:

- Heather and Ray connect the graph to the dinner card context by explaining the meaning of the points where the graphs intersect. (para. 10)

- Jena uses her table to generate a formula for Plan A. (paras. 15–17)
- In responding to Omar's question about where the "+4" in her formula comes from, Jena shows the "+4" on the graph and in her table. (para. 18)
- Danielle explains how she determined the formula from the graph. (para. 19)
- Steven explains how he determined the formula from his table. (paras. 21–22)
- Carlos and Danielle make observations about the relationship between the N in the formula and the steepness of the line. (para. 24)
- Annie makes an observation about the relationship between the *y*-intercept and the steepness of the line. (para. 25)
- Danielle comments about the relationship between the graphs of the dinner plans and the rate of savings for the plans. (para. 27)

Considering How Student Thinking Is Supported

Edith Hart believes that students' understanding of mathematics is deepened when they are able to apply mathematical ideas in contextualized situations. Therefore, she designed Cal's Dinner Card Deals so that students could use the algebraic ideas they were learning to help them work together to understand, analyze, and solve a real-world problem situation. Ms. Hart's aim is to encourage students to share publicly a variety of ways of reasoning about the relationships among the problem situation, the graphs, and the formulas they create. Ms. Hart believes there is great value in having students articulate their mathematical understanding and provides her students with many opportunities to share and elaborate their reasoning processes and to question one another directly.

In the following paragraphs, we identify several pedagogical moves that Edith Hart made that may have influenced her students' opportunities to engage in high-level thinking, reasoning, and communication during the lesson, and we provide examples of where these ideas appear in "The Case of Edith Hart."

Consistently pressing students for explanations and meaning. In the initial discussions of student observations (beginning at para. 8), Ms. Hart often asked students to elaborate on their observations, particularly observations that related specifically to her goals for the lesson. Also, when students gave extensive explanations for the whole class, Ms. Hart either pressed them to

elaborate or invited students in the class to ask questions in order to make the explanations as meaningful as possible. Examples of Ms. Hart pressing students for explanations and meaning are found in the following list:

- Ms. Hart presses Heather to explain what "same cost" means. (para. 10)
- When Jena completes her initial explanation of how she thought about the formula for one meal plan, Ms. Hart encourages students to question Jena, and there was an ensuing discussion between Jena and Omar. (para. 18)
- Ms. Hart presses Danielle to show how the cost goes up by 8 on the graph. (para. 19)
- Ms. Hart asks Danielle "to say more about that relationship," as Danielle explains how the numbers in the formula relate to the steepness of the graphs. (para. 24)
- During the discussion of which plan is the best, Ms. Hart presses students further to think about the rate of savings. (paras. 26–27)

Having capable students model high-level thinking and reasoning. Ms. Hart structured the lesson so that there were multiple opportunities for students to share their thinking with their peers, not only in small groups, but also in whole-class discussions. Initially, several students had the opportunity to make public observations about the graphs. Ms. Hart also solicited more than one extensive student explanation about how to find the formula for Plan A. The following list provides instances of when capable students modeled high-level thinking and reasoning duing the lesson:

- Jena explains how she built her formula. (paras. 15–17)
- Danielle explains how she used the graph to build her formula. (para. 19)
- Steven explains how he built his formula. (paras. 21–22)

Making, recording, and using observations. By asking students to record observations, Ms. Hart facilitates opportunities for students to continually reflect on their observations about the graphs. Ms. Hart frequently reminds students to record everyone's observations, not just their own, and she makes a point of referring to student observations whenever she sees an appropriate connection. The act of recording students' observations is important in facilitating student learning because it can be used both to share thinking and as a common object of reflection for the class. Recorded observations also may be used to keep track of progress on the task and to build new ideas from previous analyses. The following list provides examples of when observations were recorded and used in the class:

- Ms. Hart reminds students to record observations and questions in their notes. (paras. 7, 8, 11, and 23)
- Ms. Hart repeats students' observations and explanations so other students can record them in their notes. (paras. 8, 10, and 11)
- Ms. Hart makes a point to stop and ask Patrick if he can see how what they are doing that moment in the lesson relates to an earlier observation. (para. 22)
- Ms. Hart asks Danielle if she can see how her earlier recorded idea is related to the observation made by Carlos. (para. 24)

Allowing students time to grapple with the mathematical ideas in the task. During the lesson students had ample opportunity to make observations about the graphs, build formulas from the graphs, and use their formulas and observations to make decisions about the problem situation. Examples of students having time to grapple with the mathematical ideas in the task are identified in the following list:

- Ms. Hart decides to use 90 minutes for this lesson so students have enough time to complete the activity. (para. 6)
- Ms. Hart provides time for individual, small-group, and whole-class discussion. (para. 7)
- After a discussion of students' observations, Ms. Hart allows students time to grapple with the task in order to find formulas for each dinner plan. (paras. 13 and 15)
- After discussing Plan A as a class, Ms. Hart gives students time to finish finding formulas for the other two dinner plans. (para. 23)

FACILITATING THE OPENING ACTIVITY

The primary purpose of the Opening Activity is to engage participants with the mathematical ideas they will encounter when they read "The Case of Edith Hart." The task found in the Opening Activity, Cal's Dinner Card Deals (see Figure 4.1), is the task featured in "The Case of Edith Hart." Participants are asked to make observations about the three graphs shown in the task, to develop a way to determine the cost of each plan, and

to make a decision about which plan is the best. The complexity of the task is derived from the fact that no particular pathway for finding the cost of each plan is suggested, and participants must use the graphs to find a relationship between the quantities represented in the problem situation. In the "Consider" questions, participants also are challenged to explore the nature of the variables in the problem (as discrete or continuous) and to go beyond the task by generating other problem situations that might produce graphs similar to those in Cal's Dinner Card Deals. In this section, we provide suggestions for using the Opening Activity.

1. Begin by having participants individually make observations about each of the graphs of Cal's Dinner Card Deals (Figure 4.1), then share their observations with a partner or small group. Have participants continue to work with their small groups to determine the cost for any number of meals purchased on each dinner plan and to decide which plan is best. You may want to ask each group to record their solution on newsprint to post for the whole-group discussion. You may want to provide participants with the following materials: graphing calculators (for calculating cost and graphing the average cost per meal in the extension activity); a piece of spaghetti (for checking to see if all data points of the same shape are on the same line); and newsprint (for recording their solutions). You also may want to have a transparency or poster of Cal's Dinner Card Deals graph to refer to during whole-group discussions.
2. Assist participants in their work on the task if they appear to be having difficulty determining the cost of any number of dinners purchased on each meal plan. Consider the following suggestions:

   - If participants are having difficulty getting started, you may want to ask them to identify the variables they are trying to relate and to consider how the variables are related in the problem situation (i.e., identify patterns they notice on the graph). Encouraging participants to find a way to describe the relationship between the number of meals and the cost of the dinner plan using natural language (i.e., talking about what is happening in the graphs) may facilitate their ability to develop a formula (verbal or symbolic) to determine the cost of each dinner plan for any number of meals. Alternatively, you may suggest that participants first focus on what is happening in the Regular Price Plan and then move on to observing how Plan A and Plan B differ from the Regular Price Plan and from each other. Beginning with the Regular Price Plan may be beneficial because it is easier to describe than Plans A and B since the starting cost, or y-intercept, is zero.

- If further support is needed, you might suggest that participants build a chart or a table of data from the graphs in order to discern patterns and develop formulas.

- If participants connect the data points to form lines (i.e., treat them as continuous rather than discrete data) and identify the slope and y-intercept to create a formula for each dinner plan, you may want to encourage them to articulate how their symbolic formula describes the data in the context of the dinner plans. Since Ms. Hart's students do not use the slope–intercept formula for solving Cal's Dinner Card Deals, you may want to encourage participants to try developing the formula another way (e.g., using a table or interpreting the graph within the context of the problem). You also may want to encourage participants to look for connections between their slope–intercept strategy and other strategies.

3. Orchestrate a whole-group discussion to allow participants to present their solutions and discuss their reasoning about how they determined the cost of each meal plan. During the discussion you may want to:

- Begin by having participants offer observations about each graph and the relationships between the graphs. You might want to record these observations on newsprint so they can be referred to later in the discussion.

- Have participants present strategies that represent different ways of determining the cost of each dinner plan for any number of meals (e.g., putting the data into a table, seeing the graph as a line and identifying the slope and y-intercept, or using the graph in the context of the problem). A list of different solution methods we have seen teachers use to solve the Opening Activity can be found in Appendix C. This may help you prepare for the emergence of methods you might not use yourself in solving the problem.

- Make connections between strategies that use different representations. For example, if participants make a table from the graph, ask

them to choose a row in their data table and discuss what the information says about each of the meal deals and where the information is represented on the graph. You might ask participants who used a formula to explain where the numbers in their formula can be seen on the graph and what these numbers mean in the context of the dinner plans. For participants who used the graph and the context of the problem (but did not create a table or a symbolic formula), you might ask where the cost per meal and the initial cost for each dinner plan can be seen in the table or in the formula.

4. Discuss the "Consider" portion of the Opening Activity. During this whole-group discussion, you may want to:

- Focus the discussion on how participants decided which plan is best. This can be approached by simply asking, "Which is the best plan?" Alternatively, you could ask participants to share their responses to the first "Consider" question. This question may lead participants to discuss the ideas of slope, or rate of change, and the y-intercept if they have not already been discussed and to compare and contrast these ideas with respect to each of the three meal plans. You may want to connect this discussion to the observations recorded at the outset of the session. You may want to push the discussion by asking participants to consider the features of a meal plan they could create that would be a better deal for lots of meals.

- Discuss the second "Consider" question. This question highlights some differences between discrete and continuous data. Cal's Dinner Card Deals involves discrete data since a person cannot buy portions of meals. Teachers and students often have little experience working with discrete data and the graphs they produce, so it is important to make this distinction. You might approach this discussion by asking participants to connect the points on the graph to form a line, and to consider questions about this new graph (e.g., What values are represented along the line? Is it appropriate in this context to have a graph where the points are connected? Would a line be useful in determining the missing points for 4, 6, and 7 dinners? Is it necessary to connect the points in order to find these missing values?)

- Discuss the third "Consider" question. This question challenges participants to generalize beyond the Cal's Dinner Card Deals Task. Depending on how much time you have, pairs or groups could share the new problem situations they generated and compare them with Cal's Dinner Card Deals. Examples of different problem situations we have seen teachers come up with can be found in Appendix C.

5. If you had participants create a definition for function as part of their work on the cases in Chapters 3 and/or 4, you should revisit the definition and ask participants if the dinner card deals are functions.

6. As an extension, you may want participants to consider the average cost per meal (i.e., the total cost divided by the number of meals) for each of the plans. Have participants graph (by hand or with a graphing calculator) the average cost per meal as a function of the number of meals for each dinner card plan. Graphs that depict this relationship are shown in Figure 9.1. You may want to have participants compare the graphs of Cal's Dinner Card Deals (Figure 4.1) with the graphs of the average cost per meal (Figure 9.1) and explain the relationship between them. For example, the graphs in Figure 4.1 are all linear, yet only one of the graphs in Figure 9.1 is linear. This should lead to a discussion of how the proportional relationship between the number of meals and the cost in the Regular Price Plan (shown in Figure 4.1) results in a constant function for the average cost per meal (Figure 9.1). For Plans A and B, which were originally linear functions (Figure 4.1), the graphs in Figure 9.1 show the nonlinear change in the average cost per meal, with the average cost per meal decreasing as additional meals are purchased (and the initial card fee distributed over an increasingly larger number of meals). You may want to ask questions that get at the changes in the average cost per meal with the number of meals purchased for each meal plan (e.g., Why do the graphs of the average cost per meal for Plans A and B approach $8 and $6, respectively? Will the average cost per meal for Plan A or Plan B ever equal $8 or $6, respectively? Why is the graph of the average cost per meal for the Regular Price Plan constant?). You also may want to revisit the definition of function and have participants determine whether or not the graphs in Figure 9.1

show functional relationships. Depending on the mathematical backgrounds of the participants with whom you are working, you also may want to discuss the graphs of the average cost per meal for Plans A and B in terms of the limits of the functions. (The functional relationships and the limits of the graphs in Figure 9.1 are discussed in more detail in Appendix C.)

7. Discuss the mathematics found in the Opening Activity. The following question may be useful in eliciting a whole-group discussion about the mathematics: What mathematical ideas or concepts *could be learned* from engaging in Cal's Dinner Card Deals Task? A list of mathematical ideas we have seen teachers identify can be found in Appendix C. The "Considering the Mathematics in the Case" portion of the "Case Analysis," found earlier in this chapter, also may be helpful in preparing for this discussion. You may want to conclude the discussion by asking participants, "What influences students' opportunities to *actually learn* these ideas or concepts?" This question makes a connection between the potential mathematics in a task and the pedagogical moves a teacher makes that may support or inhibit the realization of that potential. This discussion also leads into the focus question that participants are asked to think about when reading the case.

FACILITATING THE CASE DISCUSSION

The case discussion is intended to help participants analyze the mathematical and pedagogical ideas in "The Case of Edith Hart." The "Case Analysis" should be of assistance in identifying the key ideas in the case and how each idea plays out in the details of the case. In this section, we provide the case facilitator with suggestions for launching and facilitating the discussion of "The Case of Edith Hart," and for various follow-up activities that might be pursued.

1. If possible, have participants read and reflect on the case before meeting as a group to discuss the case. As participants read the case, we suggest that you ask them to identify the mathematics students appear to be learning during the lesson depicted in "The Case of Edith Hart." (This activity is described in more detail in the section of Chapter 4 entitled "Reading the Case.") This individual activity will help participants think deeply about

FIGURE 9.1. Graphs of the Average Cost Per Meal for Each Plan

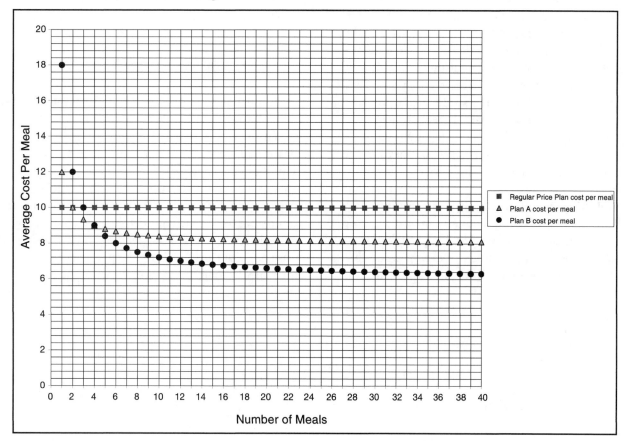

the student learning in "The Case of Edith Hart" and help them prepare for the small- and large-group discussions. Alternatively, you may want to select one of the questions found in Chapter 4 (see the section entitled "Extending Your Analysis of the Case") to guide the reading of the case.

2. In small groups, ask participants to indicate how Edith Hart facilitated or supported students' learning of each of the mathematics ideas they identified, when they read the case, as being learned by students and to cite evidence to support their claims. It is helpful to have each small group create a three-column chart of what students learned or were in the process of learning, what Ms. Hart did to facilitate or support students' learning, and evidence.

You should suggest that participants begin the process of creating their charts by reexamining the passages they identified as providing evidence of student learning. By focusing first on what was learned, they can then discuss what the teacher did either explicitly or implicitly to support the learning.

3. Once the small groups have completed their work, you may want to begin the whole-group discussion by first asking participants to identify the mathematics ideas that students appeared to be learning. Making a list of the ideas on newsprint will allow you and the participants to keep track of the ideas that have been suggested. You may want to take a poll in order to get a sense of the number of groups that identified the same ideas. This will help you in deciding which ideas to pursue.

At this point you should create a master chart, using the identified subset of the math ideas that were learned in order to focus the discussion on what Ms. Hart did to facilitate or support her students' learning. One idea that is particularly important to discuss is connections among representations. The "Case Analysis" earlier in this chapter, as well as a chart produced by a group of teachers who engaged in this task provided in Appendix C, may be helpful in identifying both math ideas on which to focus and passages in the case that provide evidence of how student learning of specific ideas was supported by Edith Hart.

Conclude the discussion by asking participants to consider whether the things Edith Hart did to support her students' learning (e.g., asking questions that helped students make connections between different representations of the dinner card plans) are applicable to teaching in general (i.e., beyond Edith Hart's students and this particular lesson). The goal here is to help participants generalize the pedagogy used by Edith Hart to mathematics teaching beyond the specific lesson that is the focus of the current analysis.

4. Following the discussion, you may want to have participants reflect individually in writing about the next steps Ms. Hart might take to help students to continue to develop an understanding of slope (rate of change)—in particular, when and how she might introduce formal language.

EXTENDING THE CASE EXPERIENCE

If you have additional time, you may want to continue to explore the mathematical and pedagogical ideas on which the case is based. The section "Extending Case-Based Experiences" in Chapter 6 suggests three types of activities you might want to assign for these purposes. Specifically, if you are working with participants who currently are teaching, you may want to provide opportunities for teachers to consider their own practice in light of the issues that surfaced in reading and discussing "The Case of Edith Hart." This will help teachers to generalize the issues beyond the specific events of the case.

10

Facilitating Learning from The Case of Robert Carter

"The Case of Robert Carter" focuses on a 6th-grade teacher and his students at Justice Middle School. The case portrays the work of Mr. Carter and his students during two consecutive lessons in which students interpret qualitative graphs. The students are given a graph of the Keisha's Bicycle Ride Task showing speed versus time (see Figure 5.3) and are asked to interpret what Keisha is doing when the graph slopes up, is flat, and slopes down. Students also are asked to draw a new graph that represents changes in Keisha's Bicycle Ride, such as having her slow down, but not stop at the end of the first leg of her trip. The task was structured to provide students with specific questions that addressed the important aspects of the graph and to alleviate students' misinterpretations of the graph as a picture of Keisha riding up and down hills. The case ends by presenting Mr. Carter's analysis of his students' work on Tony's Walk (shown in Figure 5.2), a similar but more open-ended qualitative graphing task that his students work on immediately following their exploration of Keisha's Bicycle Ride.

During the lessons featured in "The Case of Robert Carter," students work in groups and share their solutions with the whole class. Mr. Carter presses students to explain their reasoning and encourages student-to-student communication. Mr. Carter also makes many decisions that appear to influence his students' learning, and these decisions are often based on his assessment of students' thinking and understanding of the mathematical ideas in the tasks.

In the following sections, we provide support for case facilitators' use of the materials in Chapter 5, "Interpreting Graphs of Time versus Speed: The Case of Robert Carter." Sample responses for the Opening Activity and for the "Analyzing the Case" activity are provided in Appendix D.

CASE ANALYSIS

In this section, we provide detailed analyses of the mathematical and pedagogical ideas that are found in "The Case of Robert Carter." These analyses may help the case facilitator determine which aspects of the case to highlight during the case discussion.

Considering the Mathematics in "The Case of Robert Carter"

In order to arrive at the meaning of the graph in Keisha's Bicycle Ride and Tony's Walk, students need to consider the relationship between two variables (speed and time), keeping both active in their minds simultaneously as they relate the changes in one to the changes in the other. The tasks lay the groundwork for discussing concepts such as function, variable, slope, and rate of change. The task also requires that students access relevant real-world knowledge regarding bicycle riding and walking in a way that appropriately describes the information being portrayed on the graph. According to several research studies (e.g., Leinhardt, Zaslavsky, & Stein, 1990), students often overgeneralize that knowledge and interpret the graph as a picture of riding a bicycle over hills (or as changing directions while walking). Students must keep that pictorial representation at bay while they struggle to learn the new, more abstract representation of a graph as the relationship between two variables.

In the following paragraphs, we identify several important mathematical ideas that surface in the case, and we provide examples of where these ideas appear in "The Case of Robert Carter."

Function. The tasks used in "The Case of Robert Carter," Keisha's Bicycle Ride and Tony's Walk, allow students to explore graphs of functions that represent real-life situations without using specific numerical data. These types of qualitative graphs allow students to focus on the relationship between variables and how the variables change together. In "The Case of Robert Carter," Mr. Carter's students frequently use an implicit notion of function as a relationship between variables to make sense of the relationship between speed and time in the graphs of Keisha's Bicycle Ride and Tony's Walk. These two functions in particular are different from graphs that typically are explored in the context of function in that they are not defined by a numeric rule or formula. The following list provides instances in which the concept of function arises implicitly in "The Case of Robert Carter":

- Crystal elaborates on the relationship between speed and time, explaining why the graph is not a picture of the ride. (para. 11)
- James introduces numbers to help explain the idea of "riding steadily" or at a "regular speed." (paras. 12 and 13)
- Tamika and William's discussion about the abruptness of the stops leads the class to thinking about speed and time together. Following this discussion, Mr. Carter reflects on the importance of students noticing that the change in speed and the amount of time that had passed needed to be considered together. (paras. 16–17)
- Miguel's comment is an example of a response that integrated time and speed in interpreting the graphs of Keisha's second bicycle ride. (para. 24)
- Mr. Carter comments on how he sees the graphs of Keisha's Bicycle Ride and Tony's Walk as representing functional relationships and how these are different from rule-based notions of functions. (para. 26)
- Mr. Carter comments that William and others were able to demonstrate the ability to integrate time and speed in interpreting the graph of Tony's Walk. (para. 27)

Slope. An accurate interpretation of the graphs of Keisha's Bicycle Ride and Tony's Walk requires recognition that a positive slope represents increasing speed, a negative slope represents decreasing speed, and a horizontal line represents constant speed. Furthermore, thinking about slope as a rate of change requires students to consider changes in speed and time together, which is central to understanding the functional relationship in the graph. The rate of change is discussed in Mr. Carter's

class in terms of the "abruptness" of stopping. The following list contains examples of how the ideas of slope and rate of change surface in the case:

- Crystal answers Question 1, explaining that a line going up (positive slope) means Keisha is going faster and faster. She explains to Tonya why this is so. (paras. 10 and 11)
- Most students understand a flat line represents a constant speed. (para. 12)
- Anthony provides a reason for Question 3: A negative slope represents a decrease in speed. (para. 14)
- Tiffany explains that when the graph touches the horizontal line, Keisha stopped. (para. 15)
- Students discuss the abruptness of the stops. (paras. 16, 17, and 18)
- Student work on Tony's Walk indicates that students are considering the slope and rate of change of the graphs. (para. 27)

Variable. The variables of time and speed in Keisha's Bicycle Ride and Tony's Walk have a functional relationship in that for any point in time shown on the graph, there is only one corresponding speed. Time and speed co-vary, changes in time affect changes in speed, and they need to be considered simultaneously in accurately interpreting the graph. Speed is thus dependent on time, but not in the numeric, rule-based way that functions and graphs usually are presented. For example, you cannot substitute a numeric value for time into a formula to determine the corresponding speed, nor can you predict how fast Keisha or Tony will be going at a time not shown on the graph. Both variables are continuous, with a domain and range restricted to what is portrayed on the graph, and neither variable has any specific numeric value in these tasks. The following list identifies places in the case where the notion of variable arises:

- Crystal, Anthony, and others interpret the graph as portraying changes in the variables speed and time. (paras. 11 and 14)
- Tonya and Travis are not able to interpret the graph as portraying changes in the variables speed and time and instead see the graph as a picture. (paras. 10–11 and 14)
- James seems to understand that the actual speed can remain unknown, even though he put in numbers in order to help him think about the problem. (para. 13)

- In the student work on Tony's Walk, William's work is representative of students who could consider both speed and time together. Tiffany's response indicated that she was able to interpret speed and time for specific points on the graph and to identify changes in speed. (paras. 27 and 28)
- Marsha's response does not consistently interpret the variable of speed accurately, as she provides activities that do not correspond to changes in speed shown on the graph. (para. 29)

Connections among representations. Keisha's Bicycle Ride and Tony's Walk are qualitative graphs whose interpretation requires translation back and forth between the *graph* (where speed and time are variables), the *context* of the bicycle ride or walk, and the real-world activities that might affect changes in speed and time. The following list provides examples from the case in which Mr. Carter's students make connections among representations:

- James explains that when the line is flat, the bicycle is going at a constant speed, because the speed of the "flat part" of the graph will be the same number. (paras. 12–13)
- James adds numbers to the vertical axis and explains that he could choose any numbers since none were given, but he chose speeds that he thought Keisha could have ridden at. (para. 13)
- Sarah gives plausible real-world explanations for the differences in rate of change for the three stops Keisha makes. (para. 18)
- Many students demonstrate the ability to create a verbal description based on the new graph of Tony's Walk. (paras. 27 and 28)

Considering How Student Thinking Is Supported

Robert Carter sees the lesson on Keisha's Bicycle Ride as laying the groundwork for interpreting graphs and understanding concepts such as variable, slope, and rate of change. In the lesson portrayed in "The Case of Robert Carter," Mr. Carter provides opportunities for his students to move away from seeing the graph of Keisha's Bicycle Ride as a picture of her riding up and down hills and to correctly interpret the qualitative graph as depicting speed versus time. Robert Carter attempts to provide a learning environment where students are encouraged to question one another and make sense of the ideas of their classmates. In the following

paragraphs, we identify several pedagogical moves that Robert Carter made that may have influenced his students' opportunities to engage in high-level thinking, reasoning, and communication during the lesson, and we identify specific places where these moves can be seen in "The Case of Robert Carter":

Pressing students for explanation and meaning. Mr. Carter presses students to explain their thinking and to question one another. After students respond to a question, Mr. Carter often asks the responding students to "explain how they knew that," or "explain how they could tell that from the graph." The following list identifies instances in which Mr. Carter presses students for explanation and meaning:

- Mr. Carter asks Crystal to explain how she knew that when "the line slanted up from left to right, Keisha was going faster and faster." (para. 10)
- Mr. Carter asks students how they could tell that Keisha was riding at a "regular speed" from looking at the graph. (para. 12)
- Mr. Carter asks James to go to the overhead and explain his idea, even though he was not sure where James was going to lead them (James wanted to add numbers to the vertical axis). (para. 13)
- Mr. Carter asks Tiffany how she could tell that Keisha had come to a stop. (para. 15)
- Mr. Carter asks Marsha how she knew that Keisha went the fastest in the beginning and continues to press her to consider what the graph represents. (para. 18)

Although Mr. Carter presses individual students to elaborate on their ideas, he often does not press for more than one response to each question. Except in the instances where a student has a question or a misunderstanding, Mr. Carter does not ask other students to rephrase an idea, to put it in their own words, or to explain how they thought about the question. The following list identifies points at which Mr. Carter moves on after soliciting ideas from only one student:

- Crystal is the only student to express accurate ideas about Question 1. (para. 11)
- Anthony is the only student to express accurate ideas about Question 3. (para. 14)
- Tiffany is the only student who offers ideas about when Keisha stopped, and Marsha is the only student who describes how she knew when Keisha went the fastest. (paras. 15 and 18)

Having capable students model high-level performance. Mr. Carter asks capable students to go to the overhead and explain their solutions. Mr. Carter provides class time for students to model successful solutions to the problems, as shown in the following list:

• Crystal goes to the overhead to explain how the positively sloping portion of the graph represents a progressive increase in speed, thus modeling the accurate way of thinking about the graph of Keisha's Bicycle Ride. (para. 11)

• Another example occurs when James mounts an argument to support his position that the flat portion of the graph represents a constant speed. (paras. 12 and 13)

Scaffolding students' learning. Mr. Carter provides scaffolding for students' learning in at least two ways: (1) by providing a set of questions that help students focus on the salient features of the graph (e.g., positive and negative slope, rate of change); and (2) by engaging students in more localized efforts to help them make sense of the task without simply telling them the answer or giving step-by-step procedures. The following list identifies instances in the case where Mr. Carter scaffolds students' learning:

• Questions about the graph of Keisha's Bicycle Ride focus students' attention on the salient features of the graph (e.g., positive and negative slope, rate of change). (Figure 5.3)

• Mr. Carter focuses Travis's attention on the *y*-variable, asking him to "think about what the information on the vertical axis told us and how that would help us read the graph." (para. 14)

• Mr. Carter focuses Marsha's attention on what the vertical and horizontal axes represent, since she finds it confusing that the graph looks like hills. (para. 18)

• Mr. Carter asks students to get into groups to discuss "what was the same and what was different about the three graphs." (para. 22)

Providing opportunities for all students to participate in the discussion of the task. Mr. Carter makes the task accessible to all students in two ways: (1) by having students work in groups, and (2) by providing enough background information for all students to be able to participate in the task. The following list identifies some ways in which Mr. Carter provides opportunities for all students to participate in the discussion of the task:

• Mr. Carter explains that the vertical axis tells speed and the horizontal axis tells time. (para. 8)

• Mr. Carter distributes the task to each student and then has students work in groups to answer the questions. (paras. 8 and 22)

• Mr. Carter circulates around the classroom while students work in groups to see if any groups are having difficulties that he may need to address. (paras. 9, 20, and 23)

• Mr. Carter notices that one group does not know what "abrupt" means. He recognizes that this may be a problem for all his students, so he explains to the class what "abrupt" means and gives an example of an "abrupt stop." (para. 9)

• Mr. Carter makes sure the groups include students who understand the concepts and can explain them to students who are struggling. (para. 23)

However, sometimes Mr. Carter chooses to move on even though he has only a vague sense of students' understanding of the important mathematical ideas in the problem. Instances where this occurs are identified in the following list:

• Mr. Carter decides to move on and check in with Tonya later. (para. 11)

• Following James's presentation at the overhead, Mr. Carter decided "not to press further on this" rather than trying to determine what other students in the class thought about what James was saying. (para. 13)

• Even though Travis is still seeing the graph as a picture of Keisha riding down hills, Mr. Carter decided to move on to the next question, "hoping that this issue . . . would come up again." (para. 14)

• In several instances, Mr. Carter gauges student understanding by "glancing around" or "not seeing any visible signs of confusion." (paras. 11 and 18)

Encouraging student-to-student talk. Mr. Carter encourages students who hold different views on particular questions to explain and justify their solutions to one another. The following list provides examples of Mr. Carter encouraging student-to-student talk throughout the lesson in the case:

• Mr. Carter encourages Crystal to respond to Tonya when Tonya thought that an upwards-slanting line meant that Keisha was going up a hill. (para. 11)

- Anthony and Travis exchange views about the meaning of the slanted line going down from left to right. (para. 14)
- Tamika and William discuss the abruptness of the various stops in Keisha's journey. (paras. 16–17)

FACILITATING THE OPENING ACTIVITY

The primary purpose of the Opening Activity is to engage participants with the mathematical ideas that they will encounter when they read "The Case of Robert Carter." The task found in the Opening Activity (Figure 5.1) and the task featured in "The Case of Robert Carter" (Figure 5.3) both incorporate the graph of Keisha's Bicycle Ride but pose different questions about the graph. The questions in the Opening Activity are more open, providing less scaffolding for participants than what Mr. Carter wanted to provide for his students in the case.

In order to complete the Opening Activity successfully, participants must accurately interpret the graph of Keisha's Bicycle Ride, coordinating time and speed. The task is challenging because participants are not given any specific directions on how to interpret the graph, and the graph does not contain any numeric information. In this section, we provide suggestions for using the Opening Activity.

1. Begin by having participants work individually to write the story about Keisha's Bicycle Ride. You may want to provide each small group with a transparency of the graph of Keisha's Bicycle Ride on which they can write one story that they have created, and a piece of chart paper on which they can draw the graph of Keisha's second bicycle ride.

   After participants have completed their individual stories, you may want to have them exchange stories in small groups, determine if the stories produced by the other participants are accurate (and explain why or why not), and select one story to write on the transparency.

2. Assist participants in their work on the task if they appear to be having difficulty. For example:

   - If some participants have difficulty getting started, suggest that they consider what the vertical and horizontal axes represent. This may help participants realize the graph represents speed versus time. You may want to ask questions that allow participants to focus on specific parts of the graph (e.g., What is Keisha doing when the graph slopes up? What is she doing when the graph is flat? What is happening when the graph slopes down? What is Keisha doing when the graph is touching the horizontal axis?).

   - Participants often experience difficulty creating story situations that reflect specific parts of the graph (for Part 1) or creating a graph that meets the given conditions (for Part 2). In order to help participants interpret these events, you might ask them to describe what the graph would look like, given specific story situations (e.g., If Keisha was speeding up very quickly, what would the graph look like? If a dog ran in front of Keisha and she had to slam on her brakes, what would the graph look like?). This may help participants connect the graph to real-world events.

   - Watch for common misconceptions: (1) Participants might see the graph as a picture of Keisha's trip (e.g., participants might see the increase and decrease of speed over time as going up and down a hill, or they might think the first leg of the trip portrayed in the graph shows Keisha going north, then east, then south). You may want to ask participants to describe what information is being represented on the *y*-axis and what this information tells them about a specific phase of Keisha's Bicycle Ride; and (2) Participants might offer incorrect descriptions of Keisha's Bicycle Ride that result from focusing on only one feature of the graph rather than considering the relationship between speed and time (e.g., stating that Keisha came to a more abrupt stop at the end of the first leg because the drop in her speed from its peak to zero was greater at the first stop since the speed was faster than when she started to slow down for the second stop—an idea that does not take into consideration the rate of change in speed). You may want to ask participants to consider how Keisha's speed was changing in each instance.

   - Encourage small groups to discuss the accuracy of the story as it relates to the graph of Keisha's Bicycle Ride and make sure that all the information given in the graph is included in the story. Similarly, it is important to note whether information that is added to the story is consistent with the graph (e.g., if participants add time references to the story, then the amount of time taken to complete each leg of the trip should be considered relative to the total trip—the first leg of the trip could not be completed in 10 minutes if the entire trip took 3 hours).

- Note similarities and differences in the graphs produced by different groups in Part 2 that you will want to highlight during the whole-group discussion.

3. Orchestrate a whole-group discussion to allow participants to share their stories and graphs. During the discussion you may want to:

- Solicit stories that portray ideas or misconceptions that are found in "The Case of Robert Carter." A sample solution and discussion can be found in Appendix D. This may help prepare you for a discussion that addresses all the aspects of the graph. You may want to identify a few stories ahead of time that make salient different components of the graph. You also may want to ask participants to compare and contrast the different stories that are discussed (e.g., Do the stories use the same information? Do the stories omit any information provided by the graph? Do the stories interpret the graph differently?).
- Discuss the different graphs produced by the small groups in Part 2. Have participants discuss the similarities and differences between (1) Keisha's first and second bicycle rides, and (2) the different graphs of Keisha's second bicycle ride. Explain what the differences might mean for a story of this new graph of Keisha's Bicycle Ride. Sample solutions and discussions about the differences between the graphs can be found in Appendix D.
- Discuss whether the relationship between speed and time in Keisha's Bicycle Ride is a functional relationship. A variety of ways of justifying that this relationship is a function are provided in Appendix D. If you have been discussing functions throughout your work in this book, you may want to contrast the nature of the functional relationship in Keisha's Bicycle Ride with that portrayed in other tasks, such as the S-Pattern Task (see the Opening Activity in Chapter 3) or Cal's Dinner Card Deals Task (see the Opening Activity in Chapter 4). You may want to emphasize that the functional relationship in Keisha's Bicycle Ride is different from the other two tasks in three important ways: (1) the

absence of a numeric or formulaic rule relating the two variables; (2) the inability to predict the value of one variable given the value of the other; and (3) the fact that the graph is not linear or quadratic.

FACILITATING THE CASE DISCUSSION

The case discussion is intended to help participants analyze the mathematical and pedagogical ideas in "The Case of Robert Carter." The "Case Analysis" should be of assistance in identifying the key ideas in the case and how each idea plays out in the details of the case. In this section, we provide the case facilitator with suggestions for launching and facilitating the discussion of "The Case of Robert Carter," and for various follow-up activities that might be pursued.

1. If possible, have participants read and reflect on the case before meeting as a group to discuss the case. As participants read the case, we suggest that you ask them to identify decisions that Robert Carter made that appear to influence students' learning of mathematics. (This activity is described in more detail in the section of Chapter 5 entitled "Reading the Case.") This individual activity will help participants think deeply about the pedagogy in "The Case of Robert Carter" and will help them prepare for the small- and large-group discussions. Alternatively, you may want to select one of the questions found in Chapter 5 (in the section entitled "Extending your Analysis of the Case") to guide the reading of the case.
2. Have participants work in groups of three or four to share the decisions made by Robert Carter that they identified as they read the case. Ask each small group to come to a consensus on three decisions that they felt had the most significant influence on students' learning of mathematics. For each decision identified, ask participants to discuss the reasons why Robert Carter might have made each decision at that point in the lesson and to cite specific evidence from the case (e.g., paragraph numbers) to support their claims.
3. Once small groups have completed their work, you should create a master "decisions/rationale" chart that draws on the work of the individual groups. You might begin building this master chart by asking each group to identify one of the three decisions they identified and to justify their

choice by citing evidence from the case. For each decision offered, you should ask the other groups whether or not they identified the same decision. Encourage participants to argue respectfully if they do not agree that an identified decision is the most important. Once each group has contributed a decision to the chart, ask the groups to review their lists and to see if any important decisions have been omitted. Additional decisions can then be discussed and included on the master chart. See Appendix D for a sample chart that was created by a group of teachers who participated in a discussion of "The Case of Robert Carter." You may find this chart helpful in anticipating and making use of responses from participants. In addition, the pedagogical moves discussed in the "Case Analysis" section of this chapter can be used to guide the discussion as needed. For example, if participants do not identify decisions related to encouraging student-to-student talk, you may want to pose a question that raises this issue for discussion or debate (e.g., What do you think about Mr. Carter's decision to have Crystal respond to Tonya?).

You may wish to end the discussion by asking teachers what lessons can be learned from looking at the decisions made by Robert Carter that can be applied to teaching more generally. This may lead to a discussion of how instructional decisions should be based on consideration of students' mathematical understanding. This moves the discussion from the particulars of what Robert Carter did to a more general discussion of the potential impact of the decisions made by a teacher during instruction on students' opportunities to learn and understand mathematics.

4. Following the discussion, you may want to ask participants to consider what Robert Carter gained by assessing his students' work on Tony's Walk and how he might use that information to plan subsequent classes.

EXTENDING THE CASE EXPERIENCE

If you have additional time, you may want to continue to explore the mathematical and pedagogical ideas on which the case is based. The section "Extending Case-Based Experiences" in Chapter 6 suggests three types of activities you might want to assign for these purposes. Specifically, if you are working with participants who currently are teaching, you may want to provide opportunities for teachers to consider their own practice in light of the issues that surfaced in reading and discussing "The Case of Robert Carter." This will help teachers to generalize the issues beyond the specific events of the case.

Appendix A

Sample Responses to The Case of Catherine Evans and David Young

Appendix A contains sample responses for the Opening Activity and for the professional learning task posed in the "Analyzing the Case" section in Chapter 2. Appendix A might be used by those engaging in the activities described in Chapter 2, especially those who are independently reading and studying "The Case of Catherine Evans and David Young," as a way of considering alternative solutions and responses and comparing them with their own. Case facilitators might use Appendix A to gain a sense of the solutions and responses that might be generated by participants during their work on the Opening Activity or during the case discussion.

SAMPLE SOLUTIONS TO THE OPENING ACTIVITY

There are two general approaches that we have seen participants use to solve the Hexagon-Pattern Task: a visual-geometric approach that focuses on the arrangement of hexagons in each figure and an arithmetic-algebraic approach that uses the train number and the perimeter of each train to form the general pattern of growth. Examples of solutions that use each of these approaches are presented in this section.

Visual-Geometric Approaches

Participants often solve this problem by determining a formula (expressed in symbolic notation or as a verbal description) that uses the arrangement of the hexagons to show the functional relationship between the perimeter of a train and the train number.

An example of a visual approach is Kirsten's solution in "The Case of Catherine Evans and David Young" (shown in Figure 2.13). In this approach, each additional hexagon adds only four units to the perimeter of a train since two sides of the hexagon are on the inside and do not contribute to the perimeter. However, the first and last hexagons each contribute one additional unit since their ends are part of the perimeter of the train. This approach can be expressed by the following formulas:

FOR TRAIN FOUR:
$$\text{Perimeter} = (4 \text{ units each}) \times (4 \text{ hexagons}) + (\text{one unit per end})$$

$$P = 4 \times 4 + 2 = 18$$

GENERAL FORMULA:
$$\text{Perimeter} = (4 \text{ units each}) \times (\# \text{ of hexagons}) + (\text{one unit per end})$$

$$P = 4 \times x + 2 = 4x + 2 \text{ (where } x \text{ is the train number)}$$

Another visual solution is presented by Mrs. Evans's student, Devon (paras. 24–25). Devon's approach is similar to Kirsten's in that each middle hexagon is pictured as contributing four units to the perimeter of the train, but his approach differs from Kirsten's by considering the two end hexagons as each contributing five units to the perimeter. Devon's approach can be expressed by the following formulas:

FOR TRAIN FOUR:
$$\text{Perimeter} = (4 \text{ units} \times 2 \text{ middle hexagons}) + (5 \text{ units} \times 2 \text{ end hexagons})$$

$$P = (4 \times 2) + (5 \times 2) = 18$$

GENERAL FORMULA:
$$\text{Perimeter} = (4 \text{ units} \times \# \text{ of middle hexagons}) + (5 \text{ units} \times 2 \text{ end hexagons})$$

$$P = 4 \times (x - 2) + (5 \times 2) = 4(x - 2) + 10$$
$$\text{(where } x \text{ is the train number)}$$

Participants may also use a visual approach, as shown below, in which all six sides of each hexagon are included in calculating the perimeter. Then, for each hexagon, the vertical sides (two per hexagon) are subtracted and the two vertical sides on the ends of the train are added back into the total perimeter. A version of this strategy was used by two of Mr. Young's students, James and Joseph. Although James wanted to add six sides for each hexagon, he did not take into consideration that not all sides of the hexagon would be counted in the perimeter of the train (para. 59). Joseph's solution, however, took into account the sides that would need to be subtracted (para. 62) but, unlike the solution below, Joseph subtracted only the vertical sides that did not contribute to the perimeter.

FOR TRAIN FOUR:
Perimeter = (6 sides × 4 hexagons) – (2 vertical sides × 4 hexagons) + 2 ends

$$P = (6 \times 4) - (2 \times 4) + 2 = 18$$

GENERAL FORMULA:
Perimeter = (6 sides × # of hexagons) – (2 vertical sides × # of hexagons) + 2 ends

$$P = 6x - 2x + 2 \quad \text{(where } x \text{ is the train number)}$$

Another visual-geometric approach to the Hexagon-Pattern Task that does not arise in "The Case of Catherine Evans and David Young" is shown in Figure A.1. In this approach, the hexagon train is thought of as having a bottom and a side, and a top and a side (marked by bold lines). The perimeter of the bottom and a side is the same as the perimeter of the top and a side (i.e., the semi-perimeters are equal), and the number of units along the bottom or the top is equal to two times the train number plus 1 more unit for the vertical side. This approach can be expressed by the following formulas:

FOR TRAIN FOUR:
Perimeter = (semi-perimeter) × 2

$$P = (\# \text{ of units along the top/bottom} + 1 \text{ unit for the side}) \times 2$$

$$P = (2 \text{ units per hexagon} + 1) \times 2$$

$$P = (2 \times 4 + 1) \times 2 = 18$$

GENERAL FORMULA:
$$P = (\text{semi-perimeter}) \times 2$$

$$P = (\# \text{ of units along the top/bottom} + 1 \text{ unit for the side}) \times 2$$

$$P = (2 \text{ units per hexagon} + 1) \times 2 = (2x + 1) \times 2$$

$$P = 2(2x + 1) \quad \text{(where } x \text{ is the train number)}$$

Arithmetic-Algebraic Approaches

Participants also may solve this problem by looking for patterns in numeric data. Participants may use the visual model as the source of numeric data, and then proceed to organize the data in some way (such as in a table) and look for patterns. Solutions A and B that follow illustrate two arithmetic-algebraic approaches.

Solution A. In this strategy, recognizing a recursive pattern, such as Derek's observation of "adding four" (para. 59), requires knowing the perimeter of the previous train in order to find the perimeter of the next train. While recursive patterns are easy to identify, they are difficult to apply to determine the perimeter for large train numbers and they do not lead to a general formula for finding the perimeter of *any* train. However, based on the recursive notion of "adding four," the relationship between repeated addition and multiplication can be used to develop a formula that relates the train number to the perimeter. The general pattern of adding four to find the perimeter of each successive train also can be used to create a table (see Table A.1).

Solution B. From Table A.1, one procedure for creating a linear formula would involve (1) knowing that

FIGURE A.1. An Additional Visual-Geometric Approach to Solving the Hexagon-Pattern Task

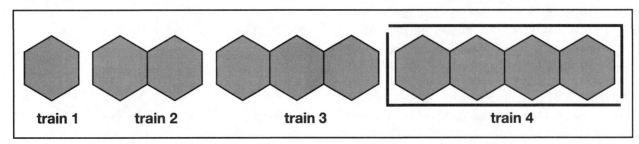

train 1   train 2   train 3   train 4

TABLE A.1. Table of Values Used to Solve the Hexagon-Pattern Task

Train Number	Perimeter
1	6
2	10
3	14
4	18
5	22
6	26
7	30
8	34
9	38
10	42

a constant increase of 4 in the perimeter of successive figures indicates that the pattern is linear (i.e., that the train number, x, could be related to the perimeter, y, by the formula $y = mx + b$); (2) recognizing that the constant increase, 4, replaces the m in the formula $y = mx + b$; (3) using numeric data from the table and the formula Perimeter = $4 \times$ (train number) + b to determine that $b = 2$; and (4) constructing the formula Perimeter = $4 \times$ (train number) + 2.

Another method for creating a formula would involve (1) experimenting with different numbers to find a relationship between the train number and the perimeter; and (2) relating repeated addition to multiplication to obtain Perimeter = $4 \times$ (train number), then comparing these values with the data in the table to determine that 2 more needs to be added to obtain the correct perimeters. The formula (or verbal description) Perimeter = $4 \times$ (train number) + 2 often is tested on several other train numbers and found to always work.

TEACHER-GENERATED SOLUTIONS TO THE "CASE ANALYSIS" ACTIVITY

The list of similarities and differences presented in this section was generated by a group of teachers participating in a professional development experience featuring the "The Case of Catherine Evans and David Young."

Similarities

- Willingness to change (paras. 3, 32, 36, 37, and 41)
- Same task (paras. 10 and 43; 23 and 57)
- Commitment to new program (paras. 3, 30, 32, 33, and 34)
- Same school and same grade level (paras. 5 and 39)
- Both teachers were part of a community (paras. 3, 30, 32, 33, and 34)

Differences

- Focus of instruction—Mrs. Evans focused on doing procedures (paras. 12, 22, and 31); Mr. Young focused on understanding relationships (between number of blocks and perimeter) (paras. 52 and 58).
- Definition of success—Mrs. Evans directed student thinking so students would get the right answer and feel successful (paras. 7, 15, and 20); Mr. Young wanted students to persevere and experience success by figuring out a solution (para. 38).
- Types of questions—Mrs. Evans's had one right answer (paras. 19 and 22); Mr. Young's required explanation (paras. 44, 50, and 54).
- Finding general descriptions—Mrs. Evans's students could apply rules to large numbers but not any number (paras. 19 and 24); Mr. Young's students formed generalizations "approaching symbolic" (paras. 48, 50 and 61).
- Time to think—Mrs. Evans wanted quick answers (paras. 19 and 24); Mr. Young gave students time to think about and explain their solutions (paras. 46, 50, and 57).
- Role of the teacher—Mrs. Evans was a director or teller, conducting whole-group responses (paras. 19, 20, and 31); Mr. Young was a facilitator of learning, having students work in pairs and share their work with the whole class (paras. 47–48 and 59–61).
- What students learn—Mrs. Evans's students learned Angela's way to get an answer (paras. 19 and 31); Mr. Young's students learned there are many ways to solve the problem and that generalizations can be made about the relationship between the figure number, visual diagram, and perimeter (paras. 48, 50, and 51).

Appendix B

Sample Responses to The Case of Ed Taylor

Appendix B contains sample responses for the Opening Activity and for the professional learning task posed in the "Analyzing the Case" section in Chapter 3. Appendix B might be used by those engaging in the activities described in Chapter 3, especially those who are independently reading and studying "The Case of Ed Taylor," as a way of considering alternative solutions and responses and comparing them with their own. Case facilitators might use Appendix B to gain a sense of the solutions and responses that might be generated by participants during their work on the Opening Activity or during the case discussion.

SAMPLE SOLUTIONS TO THE OPENING ACTIVITY

Two general approaches that we have seen participants use to solve the Square- and S-Pattern Tasks are a visual-geometric approach that focuses on the shape of each step in the pattern and an arithmetic-algebraic approach that uses the number of tiles to form the general pattern of growth. Examples of solutions that use each of these approaches are presented in this section.

Visual-Geometric Approaches for Solving the Square-Pattern Task

Participants often view the square pattern in terms of its sides and the relationship between the step number and the number of tiles on each side. Examples of various approaches to viewing the square pattern are described in Solutions A through E.

Solution A. In the approach shown in Figure B.1.a, a relationship between the step number and the arrange-

ment of tiles is identified. Each side of each step has four sets of tiles equal to the step number, plus the four corners. An expression for the number of tiles in any step (n) can be written in one of the following ways: $n + n + n + n + 4$, or $4n + 4$.

Solution B. The approach shown in Figure B.1.b involves looking at the top and bottom sides of each step and noticing that they have two more tiles than the step number, or $2(n + 2)$ tiles. The left and right sides have the same number of tiles as the step number, $n + n$, or $2n$. Therefore, the total number of tiles is $n + 2 + n + 2 + n + n$, or $2(n + 2) + 2n$, which is equivalent to $4n + 4$.

Solution C. In this approach, it is determined that each side of each step has two more than the step number of tiles, or $4(n + 2)$ tiles (as shown in Figure B.1.c). However, this strategy counts each corner twice, so the four "double-counted" corners need to be subtracted. Therefore, the total number of tiles is $4(n + 2) - 4$, which is equivalent to $4n + 4$.

Solution D. The approach shown in Figure B.1.d considers each step to be broken into four equal chunks, each with one more tile than the step number, or $n + 1$. So the total number of tiles for any step is found with the expression $4(n + 1)$, which is equivalent to $4n + 4$.

Solution E. In this approach, each step is viewed as having two squares. As shown in Figure B.1.e, the larger square is enclosed by the dark tiles and the smaller square is composed of the white tiles. So the area of the square enclosed by the dark tiles would be $(n + 2)(n + 2)$, or $n^2 + 4n + 4$ (where n is the step number). The area of the square composed of the white tiles would be $n \times n$, or n^2. To find the total number of tiles for any

FIGURE B.1. Visual-Geometric Approach to Solving the Square Pattern Based on: (a) Sets of Tiles Equal to the Step Number; (b) Grouping the Top, Bottom, and Sides of the Square; (c) Counting All Four Sides and Double-Counting the Corner Tiles; (d) Four Equal Sets, Each with One More Tile than the Step Number; and (e) Viewing as Two Squares

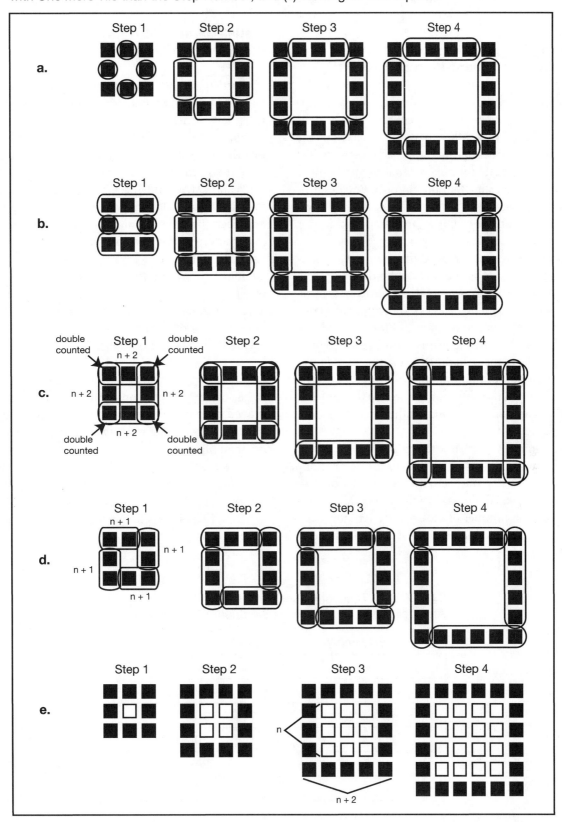

step, the area of the smaller square needs to be subtracted from the area of the bigger square, since these tiles were added to the original arrangement. Therefore, the total number of tiles for any step is determined by the expression $n^2 + 4n + 4 - n^2$, or $4n + 4$.

Arithmetic-Algebraic Approaches for Solving the Square-Pattern Task

Participants also have used arithmetic-algebraic approaches to solve this problem. These approaches focus on the number of tiles rather than on the shape of the step. While arithmetic-algebraic approaches can be used to determine a general formula for finding the number of tiles in any given step, they do not provide a description of what any given figure would look like. Solution F provides an example of this approach.

Solution F. The pattern of adding four to each successive value for number of tiles can be used to create Table B.1. A procedure for creating a linear formula from this table of data involves (1) knowing that a constant increase of 4 in the number of tiles in successive steps indicates that the pattern is linear; (2) recognizing that 4 replaces the m in the formula $y = mx + b$; and (3) determining that the b value in $y = mx + b$ can be found by finding the number of tiles in step 0. This leads to the expression $4x + 4$ for finding the total number of tiles in any step.

Participants not familiar with this method might (1) experiment with different numbers to find a relationship between the step number and the number of tiles; or (2) relate repeated addition to multiplication to obtain the formula number of tiles = $4 \times$ (step number), then compare these values with the data in the table to determine that 4 more needs to be added to obtain the correct number of tiles. The formula number of tiles = $4 \times$ (step number) + 4 often is tested on several other step numbers and found to always work.

Visual-Geometric Approaches for Solving the S-Pattern Task

Participants often view the S-pattern as (1) a rectangle with additional tiles protruding from the upper right and lower left corners, or (2) a square with an extra row on the top and bottom that extends one tile to the right and one tile to the left of the square. These two approaches were modeled in Ed Taylor's class by Ning (see Figure 3.12) and David/Jamal (see Figure 3.13), respectively.

Participants also may use a "rearranging the tiles" approach that involves altering the arrangement of tiles in some way. Charles's solution—making a square by using the bottom row to make a fifth column and then adding on the one tile that is not part of the square (shown in Figure 3.14)—provides an example of this approach. Two additional "rearranging the tiles" approaches that have been produced by teachers are shown in Solutions A (Figure B.2.a) and B (Figure B.2.b).

Solution A. In the approach illustrated in Figure B.2.a, the tile on the top right (marked with an X) is moved so that it is on the top left (shaded and marked with an arrow). The missing tiles (the darker shading) are then filled in so there is a rectangle that has a length that is equal to the step number (n) and a width that is one more than the step number ($n + 1$). [In Step 2 there is a rectangle that is 2×3; in Step 3, a rectangle that is 3×4; in Step 4, a rectangle that is 4×5. Step n would have a rectangle that is $n \times (n + 1)$.]

TABLE B.1. Table of Values Used in an Arithmetic-Algebraic Approach to Solving the Square-Pattern Task

Step Number	Number of Tiles
1	8
2	12
3	16
4	20
5	24
6	28

FIGURE B.2. Visual-Geometric Approaches to Solving the S-Pattern Based on: (a) Filling a Column; (b) Moving the Top Row to Make a New Column; and (c) Filling in Tiles to Form a Square

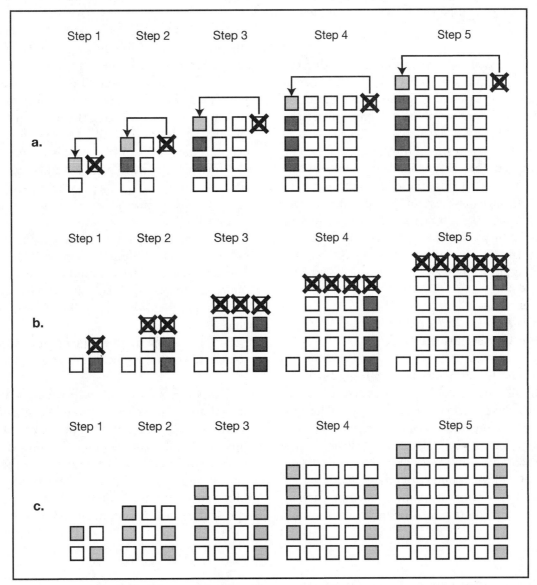

However, the number of darker shaded tiles $(n-1)$ needs to be subtracted since these tiles were added to the original arrangement (e.g., in Step 2, subtract 1; Step 3, subtract 2; Step 4, subtract 3; Step n, subtract $n-1$).

Therefore, the total number of tiles for any step is determined by the expression $n(n+1) - (n-1)$, which simplifies to $n^2 + n - n + 1$ (an equivalent expression to $n^2 + 1$).

Solution B. In the approach illustrated in Figure B.2.b, the top row (marked with Xs) is moved to make a new column (shown in grey shading). This results in a bottom row of $n + 1$ (where n is the step number), and a rectangle that sits on top of it. The rectangle has a width of $n - 1$ and a length of n (e.g., in Step 2 the bottom row is 3, the rectangle on top is 1×2; in Step 3 the bottom row is 4, the rectangle on top is 2×3; in Step 4 the bottom row is 5, the rectangle on top is 3×4; in Step n the bottom row is $n + 1$ and the rectangle on top is $(n-1) \times n$).

Therefore, the number of tiles in any figure can be determined by the expression $(n+1) + n(n-1)$, which simplifies to $n + 1 + n^2 - n$ (an equivalent expression to $n^2 + 1$).

Another visual-geometric approach used by teachers involves building a larger square, as described in Solution C.

Solution C. As shown in Figure B.2.c, in this approach the arrangement of tiles is filled in (the shaded tiles) so that it can be viewed as a large square whose side has a length that is one more than the step number (e.g., Step 2 is 3×3; Step 3 is 4×4; Step 4 is 5×5; Step n is $(n + 1) \times (n + 1)$). So each step in the pattern is $(n + 1)^2$.

For each step, the amount shaded is $2(n)$ and this needs to be subtracted since these tiles were added to the original arrangement (e.g., Step 2 needs to subtract 2×2; Step 3 needs to subtract 2×3; Step 4 needs to subtract 2×4; Step n needs to subtract $2 \times n$).

So the total number of tiles for any step is $(n + 1)^2 - 2n$. (This simplifies to $n^2 + 2n + 1 - 2n$, which is equivalent to $n^2 + 1$.)

Arithmetic-Algebraic Approaches for Solving the S-Pattern Task

Participants also have used arithmetic-algebraic approaches to solve this problem. These approaches focus on the number of tiles rather than on the shape of the step, and hence do not provide descriptions of what any step in the pattern would look like. Dwayne's strategy of making a table of numeric data and looking for a pattern (see Table 3.1) provides an example of this approach.

Another approach that has been used by participants is shown in Solution D. This approach is similar to the one used by Dwayne, but in this case the teacher first identified the recursive pattern in the number of tiles.

Solution D. In this approach, a table similar to the one presented in Table B.2 is generated for the first 5 steps in the pattern. The fact that the number of tiles increases by consecutive odd numbers is determined by an analysis of the growth pattern (e.g., for Step 1 there were 2 tiles, for Step 2 there were 5 tiles $(2 + 3)$, for Step 3 there were 10 tiles $(5 + 5)$, for Step 4 there were 17 tiles $(10 + 7)$). Therefore, the number of tiles for subsequent steps is found by adding on the next odd number (e.g., Step 5 would be $17 + 9$, or 26; Step 6 would be $26 + 11$, or 37; Step 7 would be $37 + 13$, or 50).

A pattern emerges from looking at the step number and the number of tiles: The number of tiles is 1 more than the square of the step number (see Column 3 in Table B.2) (e.g., Step 2 has 5 tiles, which is $2 \times 2 + 1$; Step 3 has 10 tiles, which is $3 \times 3 + 1$; Step 4 has 17 tiles, which is $4 \times 4 + 1$).

So for any step number, the number of tiles will be $n \times n + 1$, which is equivalent to $n^2 + 1$.

Solution E. In this approach, a table of values similar to those presented in Columns 1 and 2 of Table B.2 provides the starting point. The differences between consecutive values of the number of tiles are identified as consecutive odd numbers (shown in the third column of Figure B.3). Because there is not a constant value for the difference, the table of values does not represent a linear function. However, a second differ-

TABLE B.2. Table of Values Used in an Arithmetic-Algebraic Approach to Solving the S-Pattern Task

Step Number	Number of Tiles	Square of Step Number
1	2	1
2	5	4
3	10	9
4	17	16
5	26	25
6	37	36
7	50	49

ence (as shown in the fourth column of Figure B.3) does result in a constant difference of 2. Because there is a constant value for the second difference, the table of values represents a quadratic function. Recognizing that n^2 is part of the formula, leads to looking at the square of the step number (see Column 3 of Table B.2) and the resulting solution of looking at the pattern between the square of the step number and the number of tiles, as described in Solution D.

FIGURE B.3. Arithmetic-Algebraic Approach to Solving the S-Pattern

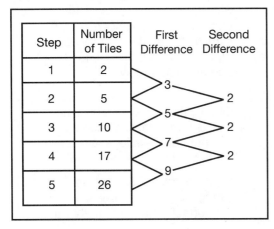

TEACHER-GENERATED SOLUTIONS TO THE "CASE ANALYSIS" ACTIVITY

Table B.3 provides responses generated by teachers who participated in a discussion of "The Case of Ed Taylor" focusing on the following three questions: What are the key pedagogical moves Ed Taylor made that fostered students' learning? Why might Ed Taylor have made those moves? How did the move support students' learning of mathematics?

TABLE B.3. Teacher-Generated Solutions to the "Case Analysis" Activity for "The Case of Ed Taylor"

Key Pedagogical Move	Rationale for Move	Implications of Move
Told students when to use a calculator (para. 21)	Students' lack of computational skills won't hold them back	Students can get computations done and have time to explore the mathematics in the task
Repeated important ideas (paras. 12 and 13)	Gives teacher and students time to think; students can hear it again; provides opportunity to attach an appropriate mathematical label to the student's statement	Signals the importance of the comment; everyone can hear it; clarifies the students' thinking to others; gives students time to think and develop a reply
Made a public list of observations (Figure 3.9)	Students and teacher can refer to it and use during whole-class discussion (e.g., para. 25)	Observations serve as building blocks for the task; students can compare observations; all ideas are accessible to all students
Gave descriptive praise for student contributions (para. 19)	Motivate students by providing positive reinforcement for their thinking	Students know what the teacher expects of them; students are more comfortable sharing their thinking
Asked questions that pressed students to explain their thinking (paras. 24 and 28)	Push students to clarify and justify their thinking	Encourages student discovery and peer help during the whole-class discussion; models the questions students should ask themselves and one another
Provided independent think time, then small-group work, then a whole-class discussion (paras. 8 and 9)	Allow students time to think about the problem themselves so they can contribute to the group's work; give students the opportunity to articulate their mathematical thinking	More ideas are generated and shared; students justify their thinking and evaluate others' thinking
Monitored students working on the task (para. 13)	Assess students' progress	Teacher knows how to direct the lesson (e.g., which students to call on to share their solutions, what difficulties students have had)
Had students explain their solutions at the overhead (para. 10)	Encourage critical thinking and sharing	Students value one another's ideas; they gain a level of comfort with sharing; they see the need to explain their thinking within another representation (language)
Required a written summary (para. 31)	Requires students to reflect on and justify equivalence	Provides teacher with an opportunity to see what individual students understand

Appendix C

Sample Responses to The Case of Edith Hart

Appendix C contains sample responses for the Opening Activity and for the professional learning task posed in the "Analyzing the Case" section in Chapter 4. Appendix C might be used by those engaging in the activities described in Chapter 4, especially those who are independently reading and studying "The Case of Edith Hart," as a way of considering alternative solutions and responses and comparing them with their own. Case facilitators might use Appendix C to gain a sense of the solutions and responses that might be generated by participants during their work on the Opening Activity or during the case discussion.

SAMPLE SOLUTIONS TO THE OPENING ACTIVITY

Teachers who participated in a professional development experience that focused on "The Case of Edith Hart" generated the solutions presented in this section. There are two approaches that were used to find formulas for the cost of each dinner plan: (1) creating a table and identifying patterns, and (2) seeing the graph as a line and identifying the slope and y-intercept. Another approach to the problem is to use the graph and the context of the dinner card deals to identify the initial fee and the increase in cost per meal for each dinner plan, similar to strategies used by students in "The Case of Edith Hart." Examples of strategies for determining the cost of each dinner plan for any number of meals, and for determining which plan is the best, and possible situations that address the third "Consider" question are provided in this section.

Solutions for Determining the Cost of Each Dinner Plan for Any Number of Meals

Solution A. A table can be created from the data points shown on the graph, similar to the one shown in Table C.1. By looking at the difference in cost between consecutive numbers of dinners purchased, a pattern can be found for each dinner plan. For the Regular Price Plan, there is a +10 pattern (the cost increases by $10 between consecutive rows). For Plan A, there is a +8 pattern (the cost increases by $8 between consecutive rows). For Plan B, there is a +6 pattern (the cost increases by $6 between consecutive rows). After identifying this pattern, it is possible, but not necessary, to fill in the costs for 4, 6, and 7 dinners purchased. The constant rates of change found for each plan represent (1) the increase in the cost of each meal plan for each additional meal purchased, (2) the slope of the line formed by connecting the points in the graph of each dinner plan, (3) m, or the coefficient of x in a linear equation of the form $y = mx + b$, or (4) the constant to be multiplied by the number of meals purchased for each dinner plan in a formula (verbal or symbolic). Adding on the initial cost of each plan ($0 for the Regular Price Plan, $4 for Plan A, and $12 for Plan B), the following formulas can be written for the cost of any number of dinners (x) purchased on each plan:

Regular Price Plan: $10x$

Plan A: $8x + 4$

Plan B: $6x + 12$

TABLE C.1. Table Created from the Data Points Shown on the Graph of Cal's Dinner Card Deals

# of Dinners Purchased	Cost for Regular Price Plan	Cost for Plan A	Cost for Plan B
0	0	4	12
1	10	12	18
2	20	20	24
3	30	28	30
4			
5	50	44	42
6			
7			
8	80	68	60
9	90	76	66

Solution B. If the data are treated as continuous rather than discrete, the points on the graph can be connected to form lines for each dinner plan. Then the *y*-intercept (*b*) and slope (*m*) of each line can be identified. Using the slope–intercept form of a linear equation, $y = mx + b$, the formulas presented in Solution A can be written for the cost (*y*) of any number of dinners (*x*) purchased on each plan.

Alternatively, the graph could be used to count out the rate of change between data points for each dinner plan to determine the cost per meal. Participants then would need to make sense of the *y*-intercept as the "cost for 0 meals purchased" or the initial fee of the dinner card. This method of using the graph is similar to strategies used by students in "The Case of Edith Hart."

Solutions to the Question, "Which Plan Is the Best?"

The Regular Price Plan is the best deal if the diner uses the card to purchase only two or fewer dinners ($x \leq 2$). Plan A is the best deal if the diner purchases between two and four dinners ($2 < x < 4$). Plan B is the best deal if the diner purchases four or more dinners ($x \geq 4$).

Answers to the question, "Which plan is the best?" most commonly are determined in several ways: (1) identifying values in the table where dinner plans are equal in cost and where each dinner plan becomes cheaper than the other plans; (2) using the graph to identify points of intersection (which indicate where

dinner plans cost the same for the same number of dinners purchased) and where points on the graph show the lowest costs for the same number of dinners purchased (i.e., the point for one meal plan is below the points for the other two plans for the same number of meals); or (3) solving systems of equations by setting pairs of equations equal to each other, and finding their common solution (i.e., their point of intersection on the graph).

Possible Responses to the Third "Consider" Question

There are two key mathematical characteristics of the dinner card plans situation. The first is the concept of a base price (initial activation fee). The Regular Price Plan has no initial cost for the plan (i.e., nothing is paid unless one actually buys a dinner with the dinner plan), whereas Plans A and B have initial costs for the cards (i.e., Plan A costs $4 and Plan B costs $12 even if a dinner is never bought). The second concept central to the dinner card plans is a constant rate of change (i.e., a linear relationship). For each of the dinner plans, each additional dinner purchased adds the same amount to the total cost (i.e., $10 for each dinner on the Regular Price Plan, $8 for each dinner on Plan A, and $6 for each dinner on Plan B).

The following are examples of other situations that have the same mathematical characteristics as the dinner card plans situation: cellular phone plans or long distance plans that may have a base cost or a monthly fee and then charge a constant rate per minute of use, video rental agreements that may have a base cost for having the rental card and then have constant costs per video rental, and initial entrance fees to a carnival with constant fees per additional ticket purchased to play games or go on rides.

Math Ideas Salient in the Opening Activity
- Collecting and organizing data
- Graphing (reading a scale and coordinate points)
- Making a table and looking for patterns
- Writing a rule or an equation
- Functional relationships
- Identifying variables—independent (number of meals) versus dependent (cost)
- Slope, or rate of change
- y-intercept
- Meaning of the point of intersection
- Discrete versus continuous data

The Function and Limits for the Average Cost per Meal Graphs

For each of the dinner card plans, the average cost per meal is the total cost (for a given number of meals) divided by the number of meals. Hence, the relationship between the graphs in Figure 4.1 and those in Figure 9.1 can be explained as follows: For a point (x, y) on the graph of any of the meal plans in Figure 4.1, the average cost per meal is represented by the point $\left(x, \dfrac{y}{x}\right)$.

on the graphs for the average cost per meal in Figure 9.1. Note that the graphs for Plans A and B approach $8 and $6, respectively, as the initial card fee is spread out over a larger and larger number of meals. As the number of meals increases, the graphs for the average cost per meal in Figure 9.1 become closer and closer to the cost per meal for each of the given meal plans (which also is represented by the slope of the lines in Figure 4.1 and, for Plan A, the constant increase between consecutive entries in Table 4.1). For the Regular Price Plan, the average cost for any number of meals remains constant at $10 since there is no initial card fee. In this way, the context of the meal plans and the relationship between the graphs in Figures 4.1 and 9.1 can illustrate and provide a means of making sense of the notion of "limit" for middle school students. (If you are working with high school mathematics teachers, you may want to share Table C.2, which provides equations for the functions of the graphs of Cal's Dinner Card Deals in Figure 4.1 and for the functions and limits of the graphs of the average cost per meal in Figure 9.1.)

TEACHER-GENERATED SOLUTIONS TO THE "CASE ANALYSIS" ACTIVITY

Table C.3 provides responses generated by teachers to three questions: What did Edith Hart's students learn or were in the process of learning? What did Edith Hart do to facilitate or support her students' learning? What evidence from the case supports your claims?

TABLE C.2. Comparing the Total Cost and the Average Cost per Meal for Cal's Dinner Card Deals

	Functions for the Total Cost	Functions for the Average Cost per Meal	Limits for the Average Cost per Meal
Regular Price Plan	$r(x) = 10x$	$R(x) = \dfrac{10x}{x}$	$\lim R(x) = 10$ as $x \to \infty$
Plan A	$a(x) = 8x + 4$	$A(x) = \dfrac{8x + 4}{x}$	$\lim A(x) = 8$ as $x \to \infty$
Plan B	$b(x) = 6x + 12$	$B(x) = \dfrac{6x + 12}{x}$	$\lim B(x) = 6$ as $x \to \infty$

TABLE C.3. Teacher-Generated Solutions to the "Case Analysis" Activity for "The Case of Edith Hart"

What Ms. Hart's students learned or were in the process of learning	What Ms. Hart did to facilitate or support her students' learning	Evidence from Case (Paragraph Numbers)
Connections between graphs, formulas, and context of a problem	• Used a mathematics task that requires students to use graphs, formulas, and a problem context.	4
	• Asked students questions that require them to make connections between representations.	9–10; 15; 17; 19; 22; 24; 27
Meaning of the point of intersection for two lines in the context of the problem	• Repeated important statements made by students.	8; 10; 11
	• Pressed students to explain their thinking.	10; 19; 24
Slope as the steepness of the line and as the rate of change	• Had students make observations about the graphs, allowing for intuitive notions of slope to surface.	7–8
	• Repeated students' ideas that are important.	8; 24
	• Pressed students to explain their thinking.	12; 19; 24
	• Related back to observations made earlier.	22; 24
	• Asked questions for homework that press students to think more about this issue.	27
Relation of fixed cost in context of problem to the constant in a formula and the y-intercept on a graph	• Asked "what if" questions related to the context of the problem.	14
	• Encouraged student-to-student questions and answers.	18
Discrete versus continuous data	• Asked a homework questions that requires students to think about this issue.	27
Mathematical communication	• Directed student-to-student communication.	18
	• Created a classroom culture where students' thinking must be justified and one another's ideas are questioned.	5
	• Had students take an active role in presenting solutions.	5; 15; 19; 20
	• Used notebooks as a tool for recording ideas that can be referred to later.	5; 7; 8; 11; 22; 23; 24

Appendix D

Sample Responses to The Case of Robert Carter

Appendix D contains sample responses for the Opening Activity and for the professional learning task posed in the "Analyzing the Case" section in Chapter 5. Appendix D might be used by those engaging in the activities described in Chapter 5, especially those who are independently reading and studying "The Case of Robert Carter," as a way of considering alternative solutions and responses and comparing them with their own. Case facilitators might use Appendix D to gain a sense of the solutions and responses that might be generated by participants during their work on the Opening Activity or during the case discussion.

SAMPLE SOLUTIONS TO THE OPENING ACTIVITY

Solve: Part 1

There are many stories that can accurately describe Keisha's Bicycle Ride. However, the most common misconception is to interpret the graph as a picture of Keisha's trip (i.e., seeing it as hills she travels over). For those participants who accurately interpret the graph as depicting speed versus time, there are several aspects of the graph that should be included in their story for it to be complete. The slopes of the graph should be addressed with references to how fast Keisha sped up or how slowly/abruptly she stopped (i.e., considering speed and time simultaneously). The different speeds attained for each leg of the trip, as well as the fact that a constant speed is reached for two of the legs, also should be included. The following story is an example of an accurate and complete solution:

Keisha was really excited about riding her bicycle to school, so she started pedaling really fast. She then rode at a steady speed for a short time, when she needed to slow down and stop at a stop sign. She started riding again when traffic had cleared, but was feeling a little tired, so she couldn't go as fast as she had earlier. She reached a comfortable pace, which she maintained for a while, when a child chasing a ball into the street caused her to slam on her brakes to avoid hitting the child. By the time it was safe to go again, Keisha was feeling very tired, so she reached a constant speed that was much slower than earlier. Finally, she was at school, and she stopped and put her bicycle on the bike rack.

This story addresses each segment of the graph, notes differences between the segments, and considers speed and time together. This particular story does not mention numeric values for time or speed, although some participants may add numeric values into their stories as they relate the real-world experience of riding a bicycle to the graph. You may need to point out that the graph does not give any numeric values. It is also important to make sure that any numeric values for time or speed included by participants are consistent with the graph when considered relative to other times and speeds throughout the entire trip.

Solve: Part 2

In Part 2, participants are asked to sketch a graph showing the time/speed relationship of Keisha's trip that is changed in two ways: (1) this time she slowed down but did not stop at the end of the first leg, and (2) her fastest speed for the entire trip was the constant part of the second leg. Although the graphs may vary slightly, they should dip down, but not touch the horizontal axis at the end of the first leg, and the flat top of the second leg should be higher than that of the other two legs. The solutions produced in the case by Terrance's, Monica's, and Jamal's groups (Figure 5.6) provide examples of graphs that comply with the constraints of the task.

Consider: Part 1

In addition to the differences in the graphs of Keisha's first and second bicycle rides that would be expected (e.g., the graph does not touch the *x*-axis at the end of the first leg; and the horizontal part of the second leg is the highest), some other interesting similarities and differences to discuss when comparing the graphs include: (1) Did each leg of the ride take the same amount of time in both graphs? Did the entire ride take the same amount of time in both graphs? (2) Did each ride cover the same amount of distance? (3) If you included numbers on the graphs, how do they compare? Would you change any of these numbers to reflect the new relative speeds or times? (4) Did the any of the speed changes become more gradual or more abrupt?

When discussing the differences between the graphs produced by participants, several issues may arise: differences in the steepness of the graphs (e.g., the decrease and subsequent increase from the first leg to the second leg of Monica's group's graph is much steeper than that represented in Jamal's group's graph); differences in the highest speed attained during the second leg (e.g., some might suggest Monica's group's graph shows Keisha going much faster than Terrance's group's graph); differences in the length of time Keisha rides her bicycle (e.g., some might suggest that Jamal's group's graph shows Keisha taking a longer trip than depicted by the other graphs); and differences in the relative amount of time or speed in each leg of the graph and in the relative amount of time spent at different speeds. When discussing differences in speed and time it is important to address the issue that there is no scale, units, or numeric information shown on the graphs. Therefore, differences in speed or time are appropriate only if it is assumed that all the graphs use the same scale.

You also might want to discuss what it would mean if (1) a graph had a vertical line versus a very steeply slanted line, (2) there was a space at the end of the second leg before it began to increase again, and (3) the graph had a gap or was disconnected at some point or interval.

Consider: Part 2

The relationship between speed and time in the graphs of Keisha's Bicycle Ride is a functional relationship. This can be justified in two ways.

1. There is only one speed corresponding to any given point in time (e.g., for any *x*, there is only one *y*). In the context of the story, it would be impossible to be going two different speeds at once. Also note that:

   • The function is continuous. In the context of the bicycle ride, there would not be multiple speeds for a given time (no vertical lines), speed might be zero (and the graph would run along the *x*-axis) but it would not be undefined (no gaps in the graph), and even very sudden stops would not be instantaneous (sharply slanting lines rather than "jumps" in speed).

   • The domain is restricted to the values of time portrayed on the graph, since values of time beyond those shown on the graph do not have a corresponding value of speed and do not make sense in the context of the bicycle ride. The range is restricted to values that correspond to possible speeds in bicycle riding.

   • Speed and time are related in the sense that changes in time affect changes in speed. The statement, "At this time, Keisha was going this speed," can be demonstrated and has a unique result for any point in time shown on the graph. Speed depends on time, but not in a numeric or rule-based way. There is no symbolic formula to determine or predict speed for a given value of time.

2. Graphically, the function passes the vertical line test. That is, any vertical line would intersect the graph at only one point. (Failing the vertical line test would indicate that there were two values of speed corresponding to a given time.)

TEACHER-GENERATED SOLUTIONS TO THE "CASE ANALYSIS" ACTIVITY

Table D.1 provides responses generated by teachers who participated in a discussion of "The Case of Robert Carter" that focused on the following two questions: What decisions did Robert Carter make that appeared to influence his students' learning of mathematics? What reasons might Robert Carter have had for making each of these decisions?

TABLE D.1. List of the Decisions Made by Robert Carter

Robert Carter's Decision	*Reason for the Decision*
Circulated around the room while students worked in groups. (paras. 9 and 20)	Mr. Carter wanted to make contact with each group in the early stages of their work.
He explained to the class what "abrupt" meant. (para. 9)	One group did not know what abrupt meant. Mr. Carter thought that this might be a problem for all of his students. Students would need clarification in order to make progress on the task.
He had Crystal respond to Tonya, rather than responding himself. (para. 11)	Tonya was seeing the graph as a picture of hills. Crystal seemed to "get it," and Mr. Carter wanted to encourage more student-to-student talk.
He decided to move on and check in with Tonya later. (para. 11)	He was not sure if Tonya understood, but most students were nodding in agreement with Crystal.
He asked James to explain his idea, even though he wasn't sure where it was going to lead. (para. 13)	Mr. Carter had not previously noticed that the graph did not contain any numbers. He wanted to encourage students to explain their own ideas; to honor students' ways of thinking.
Mr. Carter asked the class if they agreed with Travis's explanation. (para. 14)	Travis described the graph as showing Keisha going down a hill. Since the class had discussed a similar misconception earlier, Mr. Carter wanted to know how other students were interpreting sloping lines.
He asked Travis what he thought of Anthony's explanation. (para. 14)	Anthony provided a correct interpretation of the graph, and Mr. Carter wanted to encourage student-to-student interaction.
He noted that Tamika had an interesting point and asked William what he thought about it. (para. 17)	Tamika was looking only at the change in speed. He wanted to keep the conversation going to see if other students were noticing that the change in speed *and* the amount of time that had passed needed to be considered together.
He asked Jamal, Monica, and Terrance to put their groups' solutions on the board for the class to consider. (para. 20)	All of the new graphs correctly reflected the changes, but there were differences between these graphs that related to the need to consider speed and time together.
He asked students to get into their groups of four to discuss what was the same or different about the graphs. (para. 22)	He wanted to press students to think harder about these graphs, and thought that four heads might be better than two.
He scanned the room to locate Travis and Tonya to see if they were in groups with students who had moved beyond seeing the graph as a picture and made a note to touch base with them tomorrow. (para. 23)	Travis and Tonya previously had interpreted the graph as a picture of hills.
Mr. Carter decided to use Tony's Walk the next day. (para. 25)	It required students to incorporate what they learned from Keisha's Bicycle Ride and was less structured than the previous task.
Mr. Carter decided to ask Tiffany some questions to get a better idea of what she understood. (para. 28)	He felt the need to determine whether she simply wasn't thorough in her written response or whether she needed more opportunities to consider changes in both variables together.
Mr. Carter decided to include more opportunities for students to think about qualitative graphs in other contexts and with other variables. (para. 31)	Students had moved beyond seeing the graph as a picture of hills, but some students needed more experiences in considering changes in both variables together.
Mr. Carter decided to have students look over the responses to Tony's Walk and develop a rubric. (para. 32)	He wanted to raise issues for the students, help them to see the important aspects of the graph and how to integrate both variables in their interpretations.

References

Applebaum, E. B. (1997). Telephones and algebra. *Mathematics Teacher, 90,* 96–100.

Arcidiacano, M., & Maier, E. (1993). *Picturing algebra. Math and the mind's eye, Unit IX.* Salem, OR: The Math Learning Center.

Ball, D. L., & Cohen, D. K. (1999). Developing practice, developing practitioners: Toward a practice-based theory of professional development. In L. Darling-Hammond & G. Sykes (Eds.), *Teaching as the learning profession: Handbook of policy and practice* (pp. 3–32). San Francisco: Jossey-Bass.

Billstein, R., & Williamson, J. (1999a). *Middle grades math thematics: Book 1.* Evanston, IL: McDougal Littell.

Billstein, R., & Williamson, J. (1999b). *Middle grades math thematics: Book 2.* Evanston, IL: McDougal Littell.

Billstein, R., & Williamson, J. (1999c). *Middle grades math thematics: Book 3.* Evanston, IL: McDougal Littell.

Bishop, J. W., Otto, A. D., & Lubinski, C. A. (2001). Promoting algebraic reasoning using students' thinking. *Mathematics Teaching in the Middle School, 6,* 508–514.

Cai, J., & Kenney, P. (2000). Fostering mathematical thinking through multiple solutions. *Mathematics Teaching in the Middle School, 5,* 534–539.

Cai, J., Lane, S., & Jakabcsin, M. S. (1996). The role of open-ended tasks and scoring rubrics in assessing students' mathematical reasoning and communication. In P. C. Elliott (Ed.), *Communication in mathematics: K–12 and beyond, 1996 yearbook* (pp. 137–145). Reston, VA: National Council of Teachers of Mathematics.

Education Development Center, Inc. (1998a). *MathScape: Exploring the unknown: Writing and solving equations* (Student guide). Mountain View, CA: Creative Publications.

Education Development Center, Inc. (1998b). *MathScape: Mathematics of motion: Distance, speed, and time* (Student guide). Mountain View, CA: Creative Publications.

Education Development Center, Inc. (1998c). *MathScape: Patterns in numbers and shapes: Using algebraic thinking* (Student guide). Mountain View, CA: Creative Publications.

Eicholz, R. E., O'Daffer, P. G., Charles, R. I., Young, S. L., Barnettt, C. S., & Fleenor, C. R. (1991). *Addison-Wesley Mathematics: Grade 7.* Menlo Park, CA: Addison-Wesley.

English, L. D., & Warren, E. A. (1998). Introducing the variable through pattern exploration. *Mathematics Teacher, 91,* 166–170.

Even, R. (1989). Prospective secondary mathematics teachers' knowledge and understanding about mathematical functions. Unpublished doctoral dissertation, Michigan State University, East Lansing.

Even, R. (1990). Subject matter knowledge for teaching and the case of functions. *Educational Studies in Mathematics, 21,* 521–544.

Even, R. (1993). Subject-matter knowledge and pedagogical content knowledge: Prospective secondary teachers and the function concept. *Journal for Research in Mathematics Education, 24,* 94–116.

Ferrini-Mundy, J., Lappan, G., & Phillips, E. (1997). Experiences with patterning. *Teaching Children Mathematics, 3,* 282–289.

Foreman, L. C., & Bennett, A. B., Jr. (1995). *Visual mathematics: Course I, Lessons 16–30.* Salem, OR: The Math Learning Center.

Foreman, L. C., & Bennett, A. B., Jr. (1996). *Visual mathematics: Course II, Lessons 1–10.* Salem, OR: The Math Learning Center.

Foreman, L. C., & Bennett, A. B., Jr. (1998). *Math alive! Course III, Lessons 13–17.* Salem, OR: The Math Learning Center.

Friel, S., Rachlin, S., Doyle, D., with Nygard, C., Pugalee, D., & Ellis, M. (2001). *Principles and standards for school mathematics navigations series: Navigating through algebra in grades 6–8.* Reston, VA: National Council of Teachers of Mathematics.

Henningsen, M., & Stein, M. K. (1997). Mathematical tasks and student cognition: Classroom-based factors that support and inhibit high-level mathematical thinking and reasoning. *Journal for Research in Mathematics Education, 29,* 524–549.

Knuth, E. (2000). Understanding connections between equations and graphs. *Mathematics Teacher, 93*, 48–53.

Lambdin, D. V., Lynch, R. K., & McDaniel, H. (2000). Algebra in the middle grades. *Mathematics Teaching in the Middle School, 5–6*, 195–198.

Lappan, G., Fey, J., Fitzgerald, W., Friel, S., & Phillips, E. (1998). *Frogs, fleas, and painted cubes. Connected mathematics*. Menlo Park, CA: Dale Seymour.

Lappan, G., Fey, J., Fitzgerald, W., Friel, S., & Phillips, E. (2002a). *Moving straight ahead: Linear relationships. Connected mathematics*. Glenview, IL: Prentice Hall.

Lappan, G., Fey, J., Fitzgerald, W., Friel, S., & Phillips, E. (2002b). *Say it with symbols: Algebraic reasoning. Connected mathematics*. Glenview, IL: Prentice Hall.

Lappan, G., Fey, J., Fitzgerald, W., Friel, S., & Phillips, E. (2002c). *Thinking with mathematical models: Representing relationships. Connected mathematics*. Glenview, IL: Prentice Hall.

Leinhardt, G., Zaslavsky, O., & Stein, M. K. (1990). Functions, graphs, and graphing: Tasks, learning, and teaching. *Review of Educational Research, 60*, 1–64.

Lesh, R. A., Post, T. R., & Behr, M. J. (1987). Representations and translations among representations in mathematics learning and problem solving. In C. Janvier (Ed.), *Problems of representations in the teaching and learning of mathematics* (pp. 33–40). Hillsdale, NJ: Erlbaum.

The Mathematics in Context Development Team. (1997a). Mathematics in context: Building formulas (Student guide). In National Center for Research in Mathematical Sciences Education & Freudenthal Institute (Eds.), *Mathematics in context*. Chicago: Encyclopaedia Britannica.

The Mathematics in Context Development Team. (1997b). Mathematics in context: Tracking graphs (Student guide). In National Center for Research in Mathematical Sciences Education & Freudenthal Institute (Eds.), *Mathematics in context*. Chicago: Encyclopaedia Britannica.

The Mathematics in Context Development Team. (1997c). Mathematics in context: Ups and downs (Student guide). In National Center for Research in Mathematical Sciences Education & Freudenthal Institute (Eds.), *Mathematics in context*. Chicago: Encyclopaedia Britannica.

The Mathematics in Context Development Team. (1998). Mathematics in context: Patterns and figures (Student guide). In National Center for Research in Mathematical Sciences Education & Freudenthal Institute (Eds.), *Mathematics in context*. Chicago: Encyclopaedia Britannica.

McCoy, L. (1997). Algebra: Real-life investigations in a lab setting. *Teaching Mathematics in the Middle School, 2*, 221–224.

National Council of Teachers of Mathematics. (1989). *Curriculum and evaluation standards for school mathematics*. Reston, VA: Author.

National Council of Teachers of Mathematics. (2000). *Principles and standards for school mathematics*. Reston, VA: Author.

Nickerson, S. D., Nydam, C., & Bowers, J. S. (2000). Linking algebraic concepts and contexts: Every picture tells a story. *Mathematics Teaching in the Middle School, 5–6*, 92–98.

Parke, C. S., & Lane, S. (1996). Learning from performance assessments in math. *Educational Leadership, 54*, 26–29.

Parke, C. S., Lane, S., Silver, E. A., & Mangone, M. E. (2003). *Using assessment to improve middle-grades mathematics teaching and learning*. Reston, VA: National Council of Teachers of Mathematics.

Phillips, E. (1991). *Patterns and functions*. Reston, VA: National Council of Teachers of Mathematics.

Sánchez, V., & Llinares, S. (2003). Four student teachers' pedagogical reasoning on functions. *Journal of Mathematics Teacher Education, 6*, 5–25.

Sand, M. (1996). A function as a mail carrier. *Mathematics Teacher, 89*, 468–469.

Scanlon, D. S. (1996). Algebra is cool: Reflections on a changing pedagogy in an urban setting. In D. Schifter (Ed.), *What's happening in math class? Envisioning new practices through teacher narratives* (pp. 65–77). New York: Teachers College Press.

Schoenfeld, A. H., & Arcavi, A. (1988). On the meaning of variable. *Mathematics Teacher, 81*, 420–427.

Shulman, L. S. (1996). Just in case: Reflections on learning from experiences. In J. Colbert, K. Trimble, & P. Desberg (Eds.), *The case for education: Contemporary approaches for using case methods* (pp. 197–217). Boston: Allyn & Bacon.

Silver, E. A., Alacaci, C., & Stylianou, D. A. (2000). Students' performance on extended constructed-response tasks. In E. A. Silver & P. A. Kenney (Eds.), *Results from the seventh mathematics assessment of the National Assessment of Educational Progress* (pp. 301–341). Reston, VA: National Council of Teachers of Mathematics.

Silver, E. A., Smith, M. S., & Nelson, B. S. (1995). The QUASAR project: Equity concerns meet mathematics education reform in the middle school. In W. G. Secada, E. Fennema, & L. B. Adajian (Eds.), *New directions in equity in mathematics education* (pp. 9–56). New York: Cambridge University Press.

Silver, E. A., & Stein, M. K. (1996). The QUASAR project: The "revolution of the possible" in mathematics instructional reform in urban middle schools. *Urban Education, 30*(4), 476–521.

Smith, M. S. (2000). Reflections on practice: Redefining success in mathematics teaching and learning. *Mathematics Teaching in the Middle School, 5*, 378–382, 386.

Smith, M. S. (2001). *Practice-based professional development for teachers of mathematics*. Reston, VA: National Council of Teachers of Mathematics.

Stein, M. K., Baxter, J., & Leinhardt, G. (1990). Subject matter knowledge for elementary instruction: A case from functions and graphing. *American Educational Research Journal, 27*, 639–663.

Stein, M. K., Grover, B. W., & Henningsen, M. (1996). Building student capacity for mathematical thinking and reasoning: An analysis of mathematical tasks used in reform classrooms. *American Educational Research Journal, 33,* 455–488.

Stein, M. K., & Lane, S. (1996). Instructional tasks and the development of student capacity to think and reason: An analysis of the relationship between teaching and learning in a reform mathematics project. *Educational Research and Evaluation, 2,* 50–80.

Stein, M. K., Smith, M. S., Henningsen, M., & Silver, E. A. (2000). *Implementing standards-based mathematics instruction: A casebook for professional development.* New York: Teachers College Press.

Swan, M., Bell, A., Burkhardt, H., & Janvier, C. (1984). *The language of functions and graphs: An examination module for secondary schools.* Shell Centre for Mathematical Education, University of Nottingham, Nottingham, United Kingdom.

Thompson, C. L., & Zeuli, J. S. (1999). The frame and the tapestry: Standards-based reform and professional development. In L. Darling-Hammond & G. Sykes (Eds.), *Teaching as the learning profession: Handbook of policy and practice* (pp. 341–375). San Francisco: Jossey-Bass.

Thornton, S. (2001). New approaches to algebra: Have we missed the point? *Mathematics Teaching in the Middle School, 6,* 388–392.

Usiskin, Z. (1988). Conceptions of school algebra and uses of variables. In A. F. Coxford & A. P. Shulte (Eds.), *The ideas of algebra, K–12, 1988 yearbook* (pp. 8–19). Reston, VA: National Council of Teachers of Mathematics.

Van de Walle, J. (2004). *Elementary and middle school mathematics: Teaching developmentally.* Boston: Pearson Education/Allyn & Bacon.

Van Dyke, F. (1994). Relating to graphs in introductory algebra. *Mathematics Teacher, 87,* 427–432.

Willoughby, S. (1997). Activities to help in learning about functions. *Mathematics Teaching in the Middle School, 2,* 214–219.

Wilson, M. R. (1994). One preservice secondary teacher's understanding of function: The impact of a course integrating mathematical content and pedagogy. *Journal for Research in Mathematics Education, 25,* 346–370.

About the Authors

Margaret Schwan Smith holds a joint appointment at the University of Pittsburgh as an Associate Professor in the Department of Instruction and Learning in the School of Education and as a Research Scientist at the Learning Research and Development Center. She has a doctorate in mathematics education and has taught mathematics at the junior high, high school, and college levels. She currently works with preserivce elementary, middle, and high school mathematics teachers enrolled in MAT programs at the University of Pittsburgh; with doctoral students in mathematics education who are interested in becoming teacher educators; and with practicing middle and high school mathematics teachers and coaches in urban districts locally and nationally. Dr. Smith is the co-author of *Implementing Standards-Based Mathematics Instruction: A Casebook for Professional Development* (Teachers College Press, 2000) that grew out of the work of the QUASAR Project. In addition, she has authored a book entitled *Practice-Based Professional Development for Teachers of Mathematics* (NCTM, 2001), which explores a particular type of professional development that connects the ongoing professional development of teachers to the actual work of teaching. Finally, she is director of two current NSF-funded projects: ASTEROID—which is studying what teachers learn from COMET cases and other practice-based professional development experiences; and ESP Project—which is focused on enhancing the preparation of secondary mathematics teachers.

Edward A. Silver is Professor of Education and Mathematics at the University of Michigan. Prior to joining the UM faculty in Fall 2000, he held a joint appointment at the University of Pittsburgh as Professor of Cognitive Studies and Mathematics Education in the School of Education and Senior Scientist at the Learning Research and Development Center. He has taught mathematics at the middle school, secondary school, and community college levels in New York, and university undergraduate mathematics and graduate-level mathematics education in Illinois and California. At the University of Michigan, he teaches and advises graduate students in mathematics education, conducts research related to the teaching and learning of mathematics, and engages in a variety of professional service activities. He has published widely in books and journals in several areas, including the study of mathematical thinking, especially mathematical problem-solving and problem-posing; the design and analysis of innovative and equitable mathematics instruction for middle school students, with a special emphasis on encouraging student engagement with challenging tasks that call for mathematical reasoning and problem-solving; effective methods of assessing and reporting mathematics achievement; and the professional development of mathematics teachers. He was director of the QUASAR Project, and he also has led a number of other projects in mathematics education. In addition, he was the leader of the grades 6–8 writing group for the NCTM *Principles and Standards for School Mathematics*, a member of the Mathematical Science Education Board of the National Research Council, and editor of the *Journal for Research in Mathematics Education*.

Mary Kay Stein holds a joint appointment at the University of Pittsburgh as an Associate Professor in the Administrative and Policy Department of the School of Education and Research Scientist at the Learning Research and Development Center. She has a Ph.D. in educational psychology from the University of Pittsburgh and has been studying the processes of educational reform for the past 18 years. Her areas of expertise are the study of classroom teaching and the investigation of ways in which educational policy, school organization, and context influence the learning of both adults and students in educational systems. Dr. Stein directed the classroom documentation effort of the QUASAR Project (1989–1996) and co-directed two follow-up, NSF-funded projects that created professional development materials for teachers (COMET, 1998–2001) and studied the impact of those materials on teacher learning (ASTEROID, 2001–2003). Dr. Stein also studies the processes of large-scale instructional improvement in districts, having directed studies of New York City's Community School District #2 (1996–2001) and the San Diego City Schools (2000–2003). Currently, she is the principal investigator of an NSF-funded multiyear study investigating district-wide implementation of elementary mathematics curriculum (Scaling Up Mathematics: The Interface of Curricula and Human and Social Capital).

Marjorie A. Henningsen is an Assistant Professor of Education at the American University of Beirut, Science and Math Education Center, Beirut, Lebanon. She has a B.A. in mathematics and psychology from Benedictine College, and a masters and doctorate in mathematics education from the University of Pittsburgh. She has been designing and conducting professional development for preservice and inservice elementary and middle school mathematics teachers for over a decade in the United States and throughout the Middle East. She spent over 5 years designing and conducting classroom-based research with the QUASAR Project. Dr. Henningsen is currently the co-director of a nationwide project in Lebanon to study teaching and learning in elementary mathematics classrooms.

Melissa Boston is a research assistant and doctoral student in mathematics education at the University of Pittsburgh. She has taught mathematics in middle school and high school and holds a masters degree in mathematics from the University of Pittsburgh. She also has taught mathematics methods courses for prospective elementary and secondary teachers and has experience working with practicing middle and high school mathematics teachers. She served as a research assistant on the COMET Project and is the project manager for the NSF-funded ESP Project, which is focused on the preparation of secondary mathematics teachers. Her areas of interest include teacher learning from cases and effective case facilitation.

Elizabeth K. Hughes is a graduate student researcher and doctoral student in mathematics education at the University of Pittsburgh. She holds a bachelors degree in mathematics and computer science from Dickinson College and a masters degree in mathematics education from Wake Forest University. She has taught mathematics in middle school and high school as well as for prospective elementary teachers. She has instructed mathematics methods courses for preservice secondary teachers and has supervised their student teaching experiences. She served as a graduate student researcher on the COMET Project and currently works on the ASTEROID Project, which studies teacher learning from cases and other practice-based materials, and the NSF-funded ESP project, which is focused on the preparation of secondary mathematics teachers. Her areas of interest include preservice secondary mathematics teacher education and the use of practice-based materials in developing teachers' understanding of what it means to teach and learn mathematics.

Index